SPEAKING OUT

SPEAKING OUT

Activism and Protest in the 1960s and 1970s

Edited by

HEATHER ANN THOMPSON

Temple University

Prentice Hall

Boston Columbus Indianapolis New York San Francisco
Upper Saddle River Amsterdam Cape Town Dubai London Madrid
Milan Munich Paris Montreal Toronto Delhi Mexico City Sao Paulo
Sydney Hong Kong Seoul Singapore Taipei Tokyo

Publisher: Charlyce Jones Owen
Editorial Assistant: Maureen Diana
Director of Marketing: Brandy Dawson
Senior Managing Editor: Ann Marie McCarthy
Project Manager: Debra Wechsler
Text Research: Kathryn Witty and Samantha Overbay
Senior Operations Supervisor: Mary Ann Gloriande
Operations Specialist: Maura Zaldivar
Creative Director: Jayne Conte
Cover Designer: Bruce Kenselaar
Manager, Visual Research: Beth Brenzel
Manager, Rights and Permissions: Zina Arabia
Manager, Cover Visual Research & Permissions: Karen Sanatar
Cover Art: Getty Images Inc. - Hulton Archive Photos
Full-Service Project Management: Shiny Rajesh
Composition: Integra Software Services, Ltd.
Printer/Binder: R. R. Donnelley & Sons, Inc.
Cover Printer: R. R. Donnelley & Sons, Inc.

This book was set in 10/12 Times.

Credits and acknowledgments borrowed from other sources and reproduced, with permission, in this textbook appear on appropriate page within text.

Library of Congress Cataloging-in-Publication Data

Speaking out : activism and protest in the 1960s and 1970s/[edited by] Heather Ann Thompson.—1st ed.
p. cm.
ISBN-13: 978-0-13-194214-1 (alk. paper)
ISBN-10: 0-13-194214-X (alk. paper)
1. Protest movements—United States—History—20th century. 2. Political activists—United States—History—20th century. 3. United States—Politics and government—1945–1989. 4. Protest movements—United States—History—20th century—Sources. 5. Political activists—United States—History—20th century—Sources. 6. United States—Politics and government—1945–1989—Sources. I. Thompson, Heather Ann, 1963–
E839.5.S64 2010
973.91—dc22

2009002668

10 9 8 7 6 5 4 3 2 1

Prentice Hall
is an imprint of

www.pearsonhighered.com

ISBN 13: 978-0-13-194214-1
ISBN 10: 0-13-194214-X

To my parents, Frank and Ann Thompson,
who believed back then, and still believe, that activism
can indeed build a better world.

CONTENTS

ACKNOWLEDGMENTS

Each of us who wrote for this volume owe a tremendous debt to Kathryn Witty, Samantha Overbay, and Charlyce Jones Owen, who worked tirelessly and for many months to track down the many permissions that we needed to reproduce such a rich assortment of original and historically important documents from the 1960s and 1970s. Thank you all so much for your help.

As the editor of this volume, I am also most grateful to the scholars who took the time to serve as a reader on this project from its earliest stages and who offered many thoughtful comments for making it as comprehensive and interesting as possible. Thank you specifically to Darryl Mace, Cabrini College; John Ibson, California State University, Fullerton; Elwood Watson, East Tennessee State University; Norman Rosenberg, Macalester College; Jerald Podair, Lawrence University; and Arnold. R. Hirsch, University of New Orleans.

And, finally, I would like to say a special thank you to the scholars who wrote a chapter in this volume. You each have rescued and rethought the past in invaluable ways.

HEATHER ANN THOMPSON

SPEAKING OUT

1

Introduction

—Heather Ann Thompson

Americans often assume that their most important rights have always existed and, thus, that these protections are woven securely into the nation's political and cultural fabric. There was a time, however, when millions who called this country home did not enjoy even the most basic rights. Not only did entire segments of the population not have the right to vote for much of American history, but other vital guarantees, ranging from the right to a public education to the right to labor in a safe workplace, did not exist for anyone.

Indeed, since America's earliest days just how many rights the government should extend the people has been the subject of intense debate. At certain times, those who advocated contracting rights and limiting freedoms triumphed while, at other times, those who sought to expand the nation's protections and guarantees won the day. As *Speaking Out* makes clear, this debate got particularly interesting and lively during the decades of the 1960s and 1970s. During this period, Americans who sought greater freedom and more substantial rights came together in new organizations and began to mobilize in new ways. Together these activists brought a host of important changes to laws, customs, public institutions, personal behaviors, and political ideology. Some of these changes remained; others did not. *Speaking Out* offers a most comprehensive look at this moment of great social upheaval and cultural as well as political transformation, and it shines needed new light on its complexity.

There is much about the tumultuous 1960s and 1970s that is already quite familiar to Americans. Mere mention of the phrase "the Sixties" tends immediately to conjure up images of long-haired college students wearing tie-dye, protesting the Vietnam War, and grooving to the music of the Grateful Dead at Woodstock. But as the numerous chapters brought together in *Speaking Out* indicate, such associations can actually obscure more than they reveal about these important decades in our nation's past.

The 1960s as well as the 1970s were about a whole lot more than anti-war marches and acid. They were about girls finally being allowed to play on school and professional sport teams, just like boys. They were about workers making their right to join a union far more meaningful as well as about forcing even public sector employers to the bargaining table. They were about animals being protected from inhumane medical and pharmaceutical testing. They were about citizens having a right not to speak before they had legal counsel when arrested by the police. They were about consumers having some recourse when companies misled them about a product's safety or effectiveness. They were even about certain citizens mobilizing because they felt that the period's quest for greater rights had gone too far. Fundamentally, they were about *all* groups in American society, not simply radical white college students, fighting to redefine what rights would be synonymous with being an American and seeking to shape the future in altogether new ways.

In fact, the 1960s and 1970s spawned the political and cultural changes that they did precisely because virtually every segment of the U.S. population had begun questioning the way that things were and was struggling for a very different future. As the numerous chapters in *Speaking Out* illustrate, a most diverse group of Americans contributed to the political, social, economic, and cultural debates that raged in these decades worked hard to change the country. African Americans from every walk of life and from every part of the country, for example, expended enormous energy fighting the racial and economic injustices that remained almost 100 years after the slavery was abolished and full citizenship had been granted them. Likewise working-class Americans, folks who were nowhere near college campuses and may well have disliked the music of Jimmy Hendrix or had little interest in attending Woodstock, also spent these decades trying to right historic wrongs—in this case those that flourished where they labored each day. Americans with disabilities also came into this period wanting important reforms in the United States, and they worked tirelessly to guarantee equal access to everything from education to public buildings.

For gay and lesbian Americans as well, this was a time to mobilize. Not only did they stand up against numerous and deeply held prejudices against them, but they also struggled mightily to awaken the nation to the human cost of the discrimination that they had so long experienced. By the close of the 1960s and 1970s, Puerto Rican Americans, Native Americans, Chicanos, Asian Americans, the poor, and prisoners had also organized and mobilized with unprecedented energy. Countless girls and women came together in this period as well to demand full equality in a still glaringly unequal nation.

Other Americans saw the 1960s and 1970s as an opportunity to call the country's attention to issues that were less directly about discrimination and more about forcing the government to address a host of additionally serious problems still plaguing the nation—issues that historically it had ignored. These ranged from dangers facing the environment to the risks of nuclear buildup. For these Americans as well, the 1960s and 1970s was a time to join a movement and to agitate for some dramatic reforms.

Ultimately, the 1960s and 1970s were some of the most tumultuous decades of the twentieth century and this was in no small part because Americans did not always embrace the same vision of the future. Although many mobilized for an opening-up of the society and for more expansive rights and freedoms, many others organized at the grassroots level to implement a much more conservative social, economic, and political agenda. This was a segment of the population that became very politically active in the 1960s and 1970s because they felt that the successful activism of movements on the Left was directly impinging upon *their* personal rights. In response to African American activists successfully getting laws passed to prohibit housing segregation, for example, certain groups of white homeowners came together to defend what they believed was their "right" to keep their neighborhoods racially homogeneous.

Conservative Americans took to the streets in record numbers in the 1960s and 1970s not only because they felt that passing laws to ameliorate income, gender, or racial inequalities in the nation had gone too far and, as a result, were eliminating privileges that they had long enjoyed and held dear, but also because many of them thought that such laws were utterly unnecessary to begin with. In their view, American society was sufficiently egalitarian and, by passing laws and making rules that were not needed, citizens were giving the government too much power over the people. This, conservatives believed, was a dangerous road to travel.

The 1960s and 1970s, therefore, were most complex. While the social and political movements of these decades often fought for different, and at times, even incompatible, changes to the society, they also learned a great deal from one another, and the successes of some groups clearly inspired others to greater activism. Notably, for example, almost every one of the activist groups who sought to expand rights or fight injustices in this period, ranging from Native Americans to workers to environmentalists to the disabled, were greatly inspired by the African American civil rights movement that had been making its mark since well before World War II. Because the African American struggle for greater rights and recognition in particular had such a profound influence on so many other social and political movements of this era, those on the Left as well as the Right, *Speaking Out* introduces readers to the contours of African American activism not only in the South, but also in the West, Midwest, and urban North during this period.

In addition to taking inspiration from, or being motivated to act because of, the African American activism that came of age across the country in the 1950s and 1960s, the plethora of activist groups that came together in the 1960s and 1970s also drew heavily from the protest traditions of earlier decades. Gay and lesbian Americans, consumers, those seeking greater protections for animals, women's groups, and other activists were often as inspired by the struggles of activists in the teens, twenties, and the 1930s as they were by the civil rights movement successes of the 1950s. Some groups, such as those formed by Puerto Rican Americans, Chicanos, and Asian Americans, were influenced deeply by the activism of grassroots organizations in other countries altogether.

Indeed, contrary to much popular opinion, the activism of the 1960s and 1970s was not simply a "generational" phenomenon in which America's youth became alienated from all things "establishment." Nor can it fully be understood, as some scholars have suggested, as the product of postwar affluence or but one expression of a more general backlash against Cold War ideology and policy. As the various essays in this volume make clear, this period of social and political tumult, and each of the specific movements that came to define it, had a history that usually pre-dated the Cold War era and involved many Americans who were well past 30-years-old. And, of course, there were many activists in this period who saw "the establishment" as something to preserve rather than to overthrow. What made the period of the 1960s and 1970s unique was that Americans, who for years and even decades had been seeking social and political change or seeking to preserve the status quo, consciously began to take notice of each other's successful tactics and chose to build off of each other's victories in immediate and concrete ways. As a result, many Americans were able to change the course of history profoundly.

In order to illustrate the full complexity of the activism of the 1960s and 1970s, and thus highlight the broad-based way in which it impacted the evolution of American history, *Speaking Out* includes chapters on 21 different activist movements that came of age in this period. These chapters are written by recognized scholars who have studied these movements in depth and have written about them in their other works. The chapters in *Speaking Out* not only offer a comprehensive overview of the most important social and political activist groups of the 1960s and 1970s, but they also locate each group's origins as well as its strengths, weaknesses, and legacy. As these authors make clear, ultimately the activist groups of this period each had their share of successes, and each made their share of mistakes and miscalculations. Thus, together, they left a most complicated legacy for future generations.

Underscoring this point, each chapter in *Speaking Out* is followed by a series of primary source documents. These documents are authored by a diverse group of activists—Americans who often heralded from very different walks of life but who nevertheless found themselves wanting to reform or revolutionize the country in the very same ways. In addition to including a number of "classic" documents from the movements of this period, *Speaking Out* also introduces readers to numerous lesser known movement texts, as well as to the many unsung activists who really made the struggles of this period matter historically. Drawing from as many grassroots as leadership voices not only illustrates the depth and breadth of this activist moment in the nation's past, but it also shows clearly the extent to which seemingly disparate political and social movements in fact shared a great deal in terms of ideology, strategy, strengths and weaknesses.

In *Speaking Out,* readers have an opportunity to learn more not only about why Americans came to enjoy the many rights and protections that they did over the course of their history, but also about why these "guarantees" are in fact so very fragile. In this volume, they will see as well just how important *all* residents of the United States have been to the ongoing process of ensuring that the United States does not just promise freedom and equality to its people, but that it delivers them both.

2

African American Activism in the Midwest

—James Ralph

African Americans in the Midwest have a long history of fighting for racial equality. They opposed the Black Codes that were so prevalent in the region before the Civil War. They sought to realize the full promise of democracy during the Reconstruction era. They challenged the discriminatory treatment that accompanied the rising white supremacy of the late nineteenth and early twentieth centuries. And they rallied behind the National Association for the Advancement of Colored People (NAACP), founded in 1909 and the most significant protest organization of the twentieth century.

World War II was decisive in shaping the subsequent contours of African American activism in the Midwest. A huge wave of Southern black migrants flowed northward during the war and for the next 20 years. Fleeing racial proscriptions in the South and seeking greater freedom and economic opportunities in the North, many of these migrants headed for the largest cities of the Midwest, but some streamed into more modestly sized communities.

Emboldened by higher wages and energized by the wartime rhetoric of freedom, Midwestern blacks assailed racial barriers, supporting A. Philip Randolph's March on Washington Movement and joining progressive labor unions. The Gandhian approach to ending racial proscriptions first took root in Chicago in 1942 as black and white, male and female, pacifists formed the Congress of Racial Equality (CORE). Over the next few years, CORE chapters emerged across the North, but their most significant concentration was in the Midwest.

The strident anti-communism of the late 1940s and early 1950s cooled (but did not eliminate) African American activism in the region. Most white Midwesterners viewed advocates of fundamental social change and aggressive demonstrations suspiciously. Much of the work to improve race relations and the position of African Americans fell to mainline organizations like Urban League affiliates or human relations commissions.

The dissatisfaction of Midwestern blacks with the slow pace of change bubbled over in an eruption of demonstrations in the late 1950s. A group of black women, for instance, led the picketing of segregated lunch counters in Kansas City, Missouri. And in 1958 and 1959, members of the NAACP Youth Councils in Wichita, Kansas, Oklahoma City, Oklahoma, and St. Louis, Missouri, turned to direct action to assail discrimination in local restaurants and other public accommodations. These protests, which pre-dated the more famous sit-ins in Greensboro, North Carolina, in 1960, foreshadowed the rising militancy in the region.

The exploding Southern civil rights protest in the first half of the 1960s energized Midwestern activism. The spreading Southern sit-in movement in 1960 prompted sympathy demonstrations across the Midwest. In 1963, many Midwestern communities sent delegations to the March on Washington, ensuring a national mobilization. Two years later, African Americans and progressive whites expressed their solidarity with the drive for voting rights in Alabama.

Midwestern blacks were not, however, focused exclusively on erasing Jim Crow policies in the South. Their activism was rooted in their own experiences in their localities. Demographic trends, the shifting nature of the region's economy, and the impact of government policies in the postwar era had intensified racial segregation in the Midwest. During the 1960s, African Americans rallied against a range of racial inequities, especially in public accommodations, employment, education, and housing. In some Midwestern communities, for example, in St. Louis, re-energized CORE chapters led the charge. In other cities, it was NAACP branches that took the lead. In Peoria, Illinois, for instance, John Gwynn, a postal worker and president of the local NAACP, inspired hundreds of blacks (and some whites) to join nonviolent protests in 1963 and 1964 for fair housing and particularly for greater employment opportunities. The Peoria NAACP annually mounted demonstrations until the early 1970s.

In some places, African Americans were most upset by racial disparities in the experience of black and white students in public schools. In Chicago, overcrowding in predominantly black schools triggered sit-in demonstrations led by Alma Coggs and other distressed parents and students. This unrest led to legal action, supported by the Chicago Committee for Equal Education, and ultimately coalesced into the strongest citywide movement in the Midwest, directed by the Coordinating Council of Community Organizations (CCCO), which included some predominantly white groups. (Similar coalitions of activist organizations developed in Cleveland, Ohio, and other Midwestern cities.)

The CCCO did everything it could to pressure Chicago officials to take corrective action. In late 1963 and early 1964, it staged two massive school boycotts which 400,000 African American youth joined. In the summer of 1965, led by a former school teacher, Al Raby, it organized daily marches on the Board of Education and City Hall.

As had happened in the 1950s, the failure of civil rights groups to deliver substantial gains for Midwestern blacks in the 1960s led to mounting frustration. Despite the notable prosperity of this decade, African Americans were too often still relegated to the social, political, and economic margins of Midwestern cities. Their frustration was the backdrop to inner-city eruptions in the middle of the 1960s. Often, confrontations with police, who were viewed less as public servants than oppressors by inner-city residents, sparked aggressive street action that resulted in damage to property and injury and loss of life. The National Guard was called to restore order in Cleveland and Chicago in 1966. The next year, Detroit endured one of the deadliest uprisings of the twentieth century, and a wave of violent unrest struck more than 40 Midwestern communities including major incidents in Cincinnati, Ohio, Milwaukee, Wisconsin, and Jackson, Michigan.

In a remarkable twist, the leading agents of the Southern civil rights movement, Martin Luther King, Jr., and his organization, the Southern Christian Leadership Conference (SCLC), decided to head North in order to demonstrate that nonviolence could address racial inequalities outside of the South. In the fall of 1965, King and SCLC accepted CCCO's invitation to come to Chicago and form the Chicago Freedom Movement. This alliance stated that its mission was to "end slums." After months of grassroots mobilizing, King, Raby, and the Chicago Freedom Movement leadership decided to focus on combating rampant housing discrimination throughout metropolitan Chicago.

The open-housing demonstrations in Chicago in July and August 1966 highlighted the extent of racial division in the Midwest. Angry whites pelted peaceful marchers, black and white, despite police protection. On one demonstration, King was struck in the head by a rock. The open-housing marches forced Chicago's political, civic, business, and religious leaders to gather to resolve the mounting crisis. The resulting Summit Agreement, which brought an end to the open-housing demonstrations, was not insubstantial, but it did not meet the expectations of even some in the Chicago movement's rank and file.

The Chicago Freedom Movement never became the inspiring model for broadly based civil rights action in other Northern cities as King had hoped. A white Catholic priest, Father James Groppi, of the Milwaukee NAACP Youth Council led energetic protests against housing segregation in 1967. This interracial effort, powered by African Americans with an inclusive Black Power perspective, stood out, however, as quite distinctive in the region.

Though the phrase Black Power shot out of Mississippi in the summer of 1966, black nationalist influences had long been prominent in the Midwest. The birthplace of the Nation of Islam was in Detroit and its headquarters became Chicago. Even interracial activist groups in the mid-1960s, like ACTION in St. Louis, were self-consciously focused on building a stronger black community. By the late 1960s, a growing number of African Americans embraced black solidarity, called for black empowerment, celebrated African American culture, and identified with liberation movements across the world.

Older civil rights coalitions like CCCO with substantial white participation generally collapsed in the era of the growing influence of Black Power and the mounting dissent over the Vietnam War. The Black Power impulse led to a proliferation of new organizations throughout the Midwest. Some focused on developing a stronger black presence and black studies programs on college campuses in Madison, Wisconsin, Bloomington, Indiana, and elsewhere. Others were grounded in organized labor such as the Dodge Revolutionary Union Movement (DRUM), founded in 1968. Frustrated by the institutionalized discrimination in the auto industry, black autoworkers at Detroit's Dodge Main plant called for affirmative action appointments throughout the plant and attacked the United Auto Workers union as unresponsive to their interests. Still others were concerned about a continuing lack of input into public education. In 1969, 25 black community groups in Detroit, for instance, formed Parents and Students for Community Control (PASCC). No Black Power group, however, gained more notoriety than the Black Panther Party which had chapters throughout the region. In the late 1960s, the Illinois state chapter was one of the most active, until its director, Fred Hampton, and an associate were murdered in a police raid in Chicago in 1969.

The Black Power impulse was felt in smaller communities too. In the late 1960s and early 1970s, the Reverend Charles Koen led a United Front that vigorously confronted white supremacists in Cairo, Illinois, a small city on the far southern tip of the state. Black Cairoites and a few white allies sustained for years a boycott against downtown businesses that would not hire African Americans.

The heyday of the mobilization of Midwestern blacks, whether of an integrationist or Black Power hue, was well over by the mid-1970s. Activist fatigue and internal controversies, along with official repression from municipal, state, and federal authorities, help to account for the decline of insurgency. During the 1970s, African American activism was, on the whole, more diffuse and less prominent than during the 1960s. It manifested itself in a myriad of struggles, which garnered little publicity such as the efforts of public housing residents to gain a voice in decision making in their projects, the involvement of black parents and youths in local controversies over busing and school desegregation, or the determination of black residents to address environmental racism. As in the 1960s, black women were especially active in these struggles.

The activism of the 1960s had, moreover, stimulated black political empowerment in the region. Blacks had long been active participants in politics, and their political influence increased with their growing population across the twentieth century. In 1967, black voters, in the wake of years of civil rights activism, rallied behind the candidacies of Richard Hatcher in Gary, Indiana, and Carl Stokes in Cleveland, Ohio, and thus elected the first African American mayors of major cities in the country. Black political success soon followed in other cities, especially when the black share of the population was substantial. In 1973, Coleman Young, a veteran union organizer, was elected the mayor of Detroit, the second largest city in the Midwest. A decade later, Harold Washington would become the first black elected mayor of Chicago, the region's largest city. Black elected officials in this era in the Midwest were generally Democrats and their politics left of center.

The most important African American activist in the Midwest in the 1970s was Jesse Jackson. During the Chicago Freedom Movement, he headed up the Chicago chapter of Operation Breadbasket, which focused on selective buying campaigns to boost black employment. After the open-housing marches, Operation Breadbasket became the center of African American activism in the city. In 1969, Jackson was one of the leaders in the Coalition of United Community Action which turned to militant protests to crack the lily-white building trades in the city. These demonstrations, along with others during the 1960s in Cleveland, Columbus, and St. Louis, revealed the grassroots support in black communities for affirmative action programs. By 1971, Jackson was so well known nationally and his chapter of Operation Breadbasket so robust that he broke with the SCLC to form his own organization with a national vision, Operation

PUSH. During the rest of the decade, Jackson, supported by a talented team including the Reverend Willie Barrow, sought to open up opportunities for minorities in the American economy. On the basis of this work, Jackson would embrace electoral politics and make his historic runs for the presidency in 1984 and 1988.

Overall, one of the defining qualities of African American activism in the Midwest during the 1960s and 1970s was its local orientation. And its success was such that by 1980, no community with a sizeable black population could so blithely ignore the concerns of African Americans as it had 20 years earlier. But a dearth of coordinating leaders and organizations meant that Midwestern activism never became as potent as the Southern civil rights movement at its height in the 1960s.

CHICAGO COMMITTEE FOR EQUAL EDUCATION, *Equal Education for All!* (1962)

In January 1962, the Chicago Committee for Equal Education, whose ranks included Alma Coggs, one of the leaders of the first school sit-ins, issued this pamphlet.

Here in the City of Chicago in January, 1962, there are over twenty thousand children who DO NOT GO TO SCHOOL FOR A FULL DAY, in a fully equipped classroom, even though there are rooms and equipment available.

Over ninety percent of those children who are subjected to the inequalities of the double shift, overcrowded buildings, and poorly equipped classrooms, are Negro students, confined to their inadequate quarters by the school district containment policy of the Chicago Board of Education, under the direction of General Superintendent of Schools, Dr. Benjamin C. Willis.

Over ninety percent of the rooms and equipment sufficient to correct these conditions is located in EXISTED FACILITIES in school districts limited to white students, and the remainder of the vacant space is in areas where only a handful of Negro students attend until segregated facilities can be built.

Although he is paid a salary of $48,500.00 per year, FROM TAX MONEY, Dr. Willis has steadfastly refused to change his policies which have led to segregated schools for the Negro children in the City of Chicago. He has also refused to provide a detailed report on the number of EXISTING rooms and the EXACT use of each room, EVEN THOUGH THE BOARD OF EDUCATION HAS REQUESTED THESE FACTS!!

The refusal of Dr. Willis to supply this, or any other pertinent data on school utilization, and his refusal to develop a policy which would provide equal educational opportunities for all children, led to the filing of a lawsuit in Federal District Court to test the constitutionality of Dr. Willis' policies.

Source: Church Federation of Chicago Papers, Chicago Public Schools Folder, Chicago Historical Society.

The Chicago Committee for Equal Education is composed of many of those individuals and civic organizations which had tried for many years to reason with Dr. Willis to eliminate his unyielding policy of segregating Negro pupils. The Committee is supporting this lawsuit in every way possible. . . .

The Chicago Committee for Equal Education
Chicago, Illinois
January, 1962

Board of Directors

Chairman	Rev. James R. Webb, Jr.
First Vice Chairman	Mr. William L. Williams
Secretary	Mrs. Laurance Johnson
Treasurer	Mrs. Louis Coggs

CHICAGO FREEDOM MOVEMENT, *Program of the Chicago Freedom Movement* (1966)

In July 1966, the Chicago Freedom Movement issued a lengthy program of its vision and its goals, including this critical section.

An Open and Just City

To wipe out slums, ghettoes, and racism we must create an *open* city with equal opportunities and equal results. To this end we have drawn up program proposals for employment and income, housing and metropolitan planning, education, financial services, police and legal protection. We only sketch the major ideas of the full program here as that document shall be released shortly.

Two different approaches are necessary to do the job. The first approach involves gigantic development programs for the slum ghettoes similar to those for underdeveloped nations. The second involves proposals for the various institutions of the whole metropolitan area.

We propose three major redevelopment program areas for three slum areas. The redevelopment projects will constitute a concrete application of the domestic Marshall Plan idea. A redevelopment authority, with majority control by persons and institutions in the area, will shape a unified plan for housing, employment, educational, social, and cultural development. Massive expenditures would create a climate for further public and private spending. The objective would be to make what are now the slum ghettoes as good places to live as any in Chicago.

Source: Personal Collection, also available on www.cfm40.org.

In education our program is based on proposals that all schools should have at least the same expenditures as the best suburban public schools. Racial separation should be broken down by such new ideas as educational parks and city-suburban educational cooperation.

In employment our program proposals call for fair employment by the elimination of all forms of job bias and of all measures which screen out minority groups. The proposals call for full employment at decent wages by the creation of tens of thousands of new jobs in rebuilding our city and in new sub-professional positions in health, education, and welfare. We call for effective job training and retraining with the provision of a job at the successful completion of the program.

In housing our program calls for an open city in which no man is discriminated against. We call for adequate financing and programs for the redevelopment of slum and deteriorating housing and for the elimination of exploitation by slum lords. We call for humanization of the present public housing projects. We propose the development of a vastly increased supply of decent low and middle cost housing throughout the Chicago area. . . .

In politics and government we call for increased representation of Negroes, Latin Americans, and other exploited minorities. . . .

The task of wiping out racism, slums, and ghettoes in order to make Chicago an "open city" is large, but necessary. We recognize that many of the proposals in our full program are long-range ones—some of which will take a number of years before they are in full operation—and Chicago is receiving its total benefits. However, a good number of our proposals can be implemented this summer by the action of government and private executives; therefore, it is these proposals that constitute the demands for the summer campaign of the Chicago Freedom Movement.

Since people and organizations resist change, the Freedom Movement shall have to demonstrate by the tools of non-violent direct action that our summer demands can be implemented. We shall prove that the Chicago metropolitan area can be an open city. For this purpose we have chosen a small number of specific target demands, around which we shall organize non-violent direct action campaigns. With the creative help and pressure of the Freedom Movement, government and private organizations will find that the target demands can be met. Then they will be able to meet the other immediate summer demands.

DODGE REVOLUTIONARY UNION MOVEMENT, *DRUM Demands* (1968)

The Dodge Revolutionary Union Movement, a group of African American autoworkers in Detroit, Michigan, who sought to rid the Chrysler Corporation as well as the United Auto Workers union of its discriminatory practices,

Source: DRUM Newsletter, Vol. 1, No. 9. Series I. From the DRUM Collection, 1968–1972, Box 1, The Walter Reuther Library of Labor and Urban Affairs.

wrote this set of demands. Their intention was to initiate a spontaneous "wildcat" strike at the Dodge Main plant to get these demands met.

1. DRUM demands 50 Black foremen.
2. DRUM demands 10 Black general foremen immediately.
3. DRUM demands 3 Black superintendents.
4. DRUM demands a Black plant manager.
5. DRUM demands that the majority of the employment office personnel be Black.
6. DRUM demands all Black doctors and 50% Black nurses in the medical centers at this plant.
7. DRUM demands that the medical policy at this plant be changed entirely.
8. DRUM demands that 50% of all plant protection guards be Black, and that every time a Black worker is removed from plant premises that he be led by a Black brother.
9. DRUM demands that all Black workers immediately stop paying union dues.
10. DRUM demands that two hours pay that goes into union dues be levied to the Black community to aid in self-determination for Black people.
11. DRUM demands that the double standard be eliminated and that a committee of the Black rank and file be set up to investigate all grievances against the corp., to find out what type of discipline is to be taken against Chrysler Corp. employees.
12. DRUM demands that all Black workers who have been fired on trumped up racist charges be brought back with all lost pay.
13. DRUM demands that our fellow Black brothers in South Africa working for Chrysler Corp. and its subsidiaries be paid at an equal scale as white racist co-workers.
14. DRUM also demands that a Black brother be appointed as head of the board of directors of Chrysler Corp.

United Front of Cairo, Illinois, *Where We Stand* (1969)

The United Front of Cairo, Illinois, issued this pamphlet on August 29, 1969.

It has been five months since the United Front has been in operation. At this time we should review the accomplishments of the United Front and assess what needs to be done.

Source: Illinois Conference of Churches Papers, Box 19, Abraham Lincoln Presidential Library, Springfield, Ill.

Through the efforts of the United Front the following has been accomplished for the Black People of Cairo:

1) 100 low income jobs have been given to the poor of Cairo through the Department of Labor. . . .

However, lest it seem that black and concerned people can stop working and supporting the United Front, it might be brought to mind that much work still needs to be done. The following are objectives of the United Front which still need to be fulfilled.

1) An equal black-white ratio in all city jobs be achieved. At present there are no blacks in the Cairo Fire Dept., the Cairo Water Company, Cairo Public Utilities, and less than one third of the Cairo Police Dept. is black in a city with a black population of over 50%. . . .

For a hundred years black people in Cairo have lived in slavery. But now black people have stood up to their oppressors and said, "White Hats will go because blacks are keeping their dough." And the White Hats did go! The blacks have said to Governor Ogilvie, "Pharoah, let my people go." And the Governor will have to let God's people go. The black man is standing up against the injustices of the racist whites in Cairo and they will stop their oppression.

Much has been done in the past five months, but much has yet to be done. Remember freedom is not free; the price must be paid. But the price is less when blacks work together and victory is not unrealistic. *Support the United Front and the victory will be won.*

RICHARD HATCHER, *Inaugural Address* (1968)

Richard Hatcher delivered this message at his inauguration as mayor of Gary, Indiana, on January 1, 1968.

My fellow Americans. Today we are witnessing a rebirth of Gary's determination to take its rightful place among the great cities of our nation. With a resolute mind we embark upon a four-year journey, to change the face of our city and unite the hearts of our citizens; to tear down slums and build healthy bodies; to destroy crime and create beauty; to expand industry and restrict pollution.

Gary, Indiana, is a warm city—it has welcomed in large numbers into its midst emigrants from southern Europe, black people from the Deep South and those who come from South of the border. In diversity, we have found strength; however, today is a new day. Let it be known that as of this moment, there are some who are no longer welcome in Gary, Indiana. Those who have made a profession of violating our laws—are no longer welcome. . . .

Source: Alex Poinsett, *Black Power Gary Style: The Making of Mayor Richard Hatcher,* Chicago: Johnson Publishing Company, 1970, pp. 98–103.

A special word to my brothers and sisters who because of circumstances beyond your control, find yourselves locked into miserable slums, without enough food to eat, inadequate clothing for your children and no hope for tomorrow. It is a primary goal of this administration to make your life better. To give you a decent place to live. To help create job opportunities for you and to assist you in every way in breaking the vicious chain of poverty. To give you your rightful share of the good life. . . .

And finally, to all of our citizens, whether you live in Glen Park, in Midtown or in Miller, I make a special appeal. We cannot solve our problems, we cannot save our city if we are all divided. The great promise of our city will not be realized until we treat each other as equals without respect to race or religion. To quote our president, "Until justice is blind to color, until education is unaware of race, until opportunity is unconcerned with the color of men's skins, emancipation will be a proclamation and not a fact. The Negro today asks justice. We do not answer him when we reply by asking patience." We have talked long enough in this city about equality. The time is here to live it. If we really want good government, peace and unity, now's the time to practice what we preach. Good government comes in assorted colors and nationalities. . . .

PEOPLE UNITED TO SERVE HUMANITY, *Operation P.U.S.H. Platform* (1971)

This document articulates the goals of Jesse Jackson's new organization in 1971. It would soon call itself People United to Serve Humanity.

We, the People United to Save Humanity, believe that humanity will be saved and served only when justice is done for all people. We believe that we must challenge the economic, political, and social forces that make us subservient to others; and that we must assume the power (of being) given us by the Power of God. We believe that our worth as humane people is expressed in our united efforts to secure justice for all persons. We, therefore, state our declaration of goals.

1. PUSH for a comprehensive economic plan for the development of Black and poor people. This plan will include status as underdeveloped enclaves entitled to consideration by the World Bank and the International Monetary Fund.
2. PUSH for humane alternatives to the welfare system.
3. PUSH for the revival of the labor movement to protect organized workers and to organize unorganized workers.
4. PUSH for a survival Bill of Rights for all children up to the age of 18 guaranteeing their food, clothing, shelter, medical care and education.

Source: Papers of the NAACP, Part 30, General Office Files, 1966–1972, Series A: Subject Files, Reel 10, Frame 00698 (microfilm).

5. PUSH for a survival Bill of Rights for the aging, guaranteeing adequate food, clothing, shelter, medical care and meaningful programs.
6. PUSH for full political participation including an automatic voter registration as a right of citizenship.
7. PUSH to elect to local, state and federal offices persons committed to humane economic and social programs.
8. PUSH for humane conditions in prisons and sound rehabilitation programs.
9. PUSH for a Bill of Rights for veterans whose needs are ignored.
10. PUSH for adequate health care for all people based upon need.
11. PUSH for quality education regardless of race, religion or creed.
12. PUSH for economic and social relationships with the nations of Africa in order to build African/Afro-American unity.
13. PUSH for national unity among all organizations working for the humane economic, political and social development of people.
14. PUSH for a relevant theology geared to regenerating depressed and oppressed peoples.
15. PUSH for Black excellence.

We are dedicated to reaching our goals through the research, education, development and execution of direct action programs that provide for economic, political and cultural independence.

3

African American Activism in the North

—WENDELL E. PRITCHETT

Protest in Northern cities during the 1960s and 1970s was diverse, varied, and built on a long history of community organization. African American activism in Northern cities, from the efforts of Richard Allen in colonial Philadelphia to those of Frederick Douglass in post-revolutionary New York (and elsewhere), was as old as the black communities in the United States. At the beginning of the twentieth century, black migration to the North increased dramatically, resulting in the establishment of two crucial organizations, the NAACP and the Urban League. These "integrationist" groups, whose leaders believed that black progress was best secured through cooperation with whites competed with "nationalist" approaches such as those of Marcus Garvey, who argued that blacks should form their own economic and social institutions to produce a multitude of opinions about the proper course to racial equality. By the Great Depression, African Americans had established numerous organizations dedicated to protesting job and housing discrimination, fighting against policy brutality, and advocating equal rights in both the public and private sphere across the urban North. Such activism only increased during World War II and thereafter.

During the early 1960s, while national attention increasingly focused on the civil rights struggle in the South, African Americans and their white allies in the North were equally determined to, among other things, integrate schools, more fairly allocate government resources, end racially based housing restrictions, and eliminate discrimination in employment. In Philadelphia, activists demanded that business serving black communities hire and promote black workers and that the local government deny funding to contractors who discriminated. Although such efforts often put civil rights leaders at odds with labor unions, in New York City they also achieved gains within organized labor. In 1963, the black and Latino members of Local 1199, which represented hospital workers, successfully struck for collective bargaining rights in the city's large nonprofit hospital sector. At the same time that advocates demanded equal treatment in the workplace, black leaders such as Rev. Leon Sullivan promoted economic development within the black community. Through the Opportunities Industrialization Centers and investment funds he created, Sullivan attempted to put economic capital under the control of African Americans.

Government institutions were a particularly important battleground in the struggle for civil rights. In New York City in 1964, black parents removed their children from the city's public schools for several weeks to protest the Board of Education's continued obstruction of efforts to promote racial integration. At the same time, activists in cities across the country mobilized against the dislocation of African Americans for the construction of high ways and the implementation of urban renewal (dubbed "Negro removal") programs. They also demanded the lifting of barriers to access for housing in cities and the suburbs that surrounded them.

The increasing role of the federal government in the urban North, especially through President Lyndon Johnson's War on Poverty, provided additional resources to support local activism. In many cities, particularly Oakland, New York City, Philadelphia, and Cleveland, funding from the federal Community Action Program enabled activists to establish professional community organizations that provided education, job training, health care, social services, and it also provided a rallying point for neighborhood protest. In Brooklyn, for example, the program supported the aspirations of activists like Major Owens, who established the Brownsville Community Council (BCC), an organization that grew between 1964 and 1966 from a volunteer agency to an institution with a $2 million annual budget. Like many community action groups across the country, the BCC was a coalition of blacks and Latinos, recognizing the fact that both of these groups suffered from housing and job discrimination as well as social exclusion.

As they had for decades, African American activists in Northern cities collaborated constantly with civil rights protestors in the South. In making their claims for equal treatment, Northern activists frequently pointed out that there was little difference between the de jure (by law) discrimination of the South and the de facto (in fact) discrimination perpetrated by Northern institutions. During the 1960s, activists moved easily and frequently between the regions in pursuit of racial equality. The Chicago Freedom Movement (CFM) represented one of the most well-publicized collaborative efforts. Although "racism in the large Northern cities has not featured lynchings," activists argued, "racism in Chicago has been a stark reality." With the assistance of Dr. Martin Luther King, Jr., and the Southern Christian Leadership Conference (SCLC), Chicago activists, including Al Raby and Rev. Jesse Jackson, organized a major campaign to protest housing discrimination, job exclusion, and political neglect in the windy city.

In July of 1966, Dr. King went to Chicago City Hall and placed on the door a list of demands, insisting the city put its financial and moral weight behind the goal of racial integration by refusing to support business and community institutions that discriminated. Activists also demanded an increase in the minimum wage and the construction of affordable housing in racially integrated areas. Beginning in 1966, the CFM staged several marches through white neighborhoods that excluded black homeseekers. Whites in many neighborhoods responded violently, assaulting marchers with rocks and setting their cars on fire. In the halls of government also, activists met with opposition to most of their demands.

Although activists continued to demand racial integration in neighborhoods and schools, like their Southern counterparts they endured much hostility from white citizens and the institutions they controlled. Eventually, such intense opposition led many African Americans to focus more heavily on improving conditions within their own communities. In 1967, black and Latino activists in Brooklyn secured foundation funding for an experimental effort to improve local schools. Soon thereafter, they succeeded in winning from the New York City Board of Education increased authority over, and autonomy for, a small number of elementary and junior high schools. Activists hoped to use these schools to focus greater attention and resources on the special needs of the children in their community. They argued that "community control" of the schools would promote greater involvement of parents and other neighborhood residents and would produce better educational outcomes. Supporters called the idea "one of the most hopeful beginnings in the search for quality education for the children of the ghetto." Community-based management, however, was opposed by union officials representing New York City public school teachers. During the fall of 1968, this conflict erupted into a citywide battle, during which time the teachers walked out of the schools and forced the Board of Education to dramatically scale back the program.

Community control remained a crucial focal point for activists during the 1970s. The Black Panther Party explicitly rejected racial integration and argued that blacks should focus their attention on developing black-led social, economic, and political institutions. In their "Ten Point Plan," the leaders of the group insisted upon the "power to determine the destiny of our Black community" through a "plebiscite" in which all African Americans (and only they) would participate. Based largely in Oakland, California, with significant chapters in many other cities such as Detroit, Philadelphia, Chicago, the Panthers focused their efforts on self-help and armed defense of community. They organized programs to provide food, clothing, and housing to the poor and to demand control over resources within the black community. In Philadelphia, for example, the Panthers protested job discrimination and police brutality and battled for control over public schools.

Although battles with police resulted in a dramatic decline of the Black Panthers in many cities during the early 1970s, other grassroots organizations emerged to take their place. A leader among these groups was the National Welfare Rights Organization (NWRO). The goal of the NWRO was to secure the transfer of money to poor communities through both private and public means. To help the poor to obtain the material goods available to other Americans, activists campaigned for access to credit, demanding, for example, that the Sears Company end its policy of denying credit cards to current or recent recipients of welfare. NWRO activists promoted consumer cooperatives and protested economic discrimination in local communities as well as among national chains, and they demanded that major companies distribute their wealth to poor Americans. At the same time, however, activists did not abandon the fight to get greater resources from federal, state, and local governments. Leaders like Roxanne Jones of Philadelphia led protests insisting the governments expand the provision of public assistance and eliminate regulations that discriminated against the poor. Thanks to the dedicated African American activists in the NWRO, this organization not only addressed the economic needs of poor and working-class women, but it also took the issue of racial equality very seriously thus connecting the Northern feminist and civil rights movements in vitally important ways.

The fact that African American activists in the North committed themselves to a number of grassroots and working class–based causes often considered outside the realm of traditional civil rights activism ultimately helped the urban poor to achieve more gains on the community level than they ever had before. In Brooklyn, for example, the BCC founded schools, health-care facilities, job training programs, and other services that became neighborhood institutions. These initiatives gave employment and professional training for thousands of African Americans as well as Latinos, and they also provided social stability to the city's poorest communities. As a result of these organizations, the amount of resources—from federal, state, and local governments—directed at poor communities increased dramatically.

Importantly, Northern African Americans' commitment to grassroots activism and locally based institutions helped promote the rise of a new class of black and Latino politicians. Showing the tremendous strides made by activists in New York, for example, in the city of Brooklyn the leader of the BCC, Major Owens, was elected to the New York State Assembly and then to the U.S. Congress, where he served from 1981 to 2007. Across the nation, African Americans gained political power, and several major cities elected black mayors, among them Coleman Young of Detroit, Carl Stokes of Cleveland, and Kenneth Gibson in Newark.

Ironically, the major weaknesses in African American activism in Northern cities during this period were intimately connected to its strengths. Because most of the activists' attention lay in specific communities, their efforts never evolved into a national "movement" for social change. Unlike other efforts that focused specifically on changes in national laws and policy and resulted in the passage of the Civil Rights Act of 1964 and the Voting Rights Act of 1965, most initiatives in Northern cities had little impact on national policy. One exception to this was the National Committee Against Discrimination in Housing, which, while devoting most of its efforts to fighting housing discrimination in individual communities, also worked to secure the passage of laws banning housing bias, most importantly the Fair Housing Act of 1968. In general, however, activists pursued a variety of strategies and never agreed upon a national program.

The rise of black political power was also problematic. Though African Americans won seats in city councils and mayor's offices across the country, these victories came as cities tottered on the brink of financial ruin. In most cities, the rise to power was accompanied by the departure of middle-class and working-class white residents. They moved to the suburbs and took with them much of the economic base of the city. Because of declining tax bases and increasing service cost, African American mayors faced gigantic budget deficits that prevented them from implementing their programs.

The reliance on government resources to promote equality also had significant limitations. During the 1960s, with the rapid growth of the American economy, governments had the ability to increase their budgets and to distribute these resources to poor communities. However, as inflation increased, the economy turned sour, and during the 1970s governments at all levels dramatically scaled back social programs. The demands by activists in the Black Panthers, NWRO, and other organizations during the 1970s led to a political and social "backlash," as whites elected conservative politicians who promised to scale back the "welfare state," and racial equality receded in importance as a national issue.

Despite its weaknesses, however, African American activism in the North paved the way for important urban institutions such as the thousands of Community Development Corporations (CDC) that have been actively rebuilding urban areas for the past three decades. These organizations have played a major role in the slow rebirth of many cities by building hundreds of thousands of units of housing, promoting economic development, and providing social cohesion to their communities. Activists also left a legacy of political empowerment that continues to this day, as blacks and Latinos hold important offices across the country. At the same time, while most people celebrate the achievements of CDCs and acknowledge the importance of black political power, there are those for whom African American activism during the 1960s and 1970s, and its legacy, remains a highly contentious topic. Indeed, opponents of government programs commonly maintain that such activism was excessive and blame the social problems that continue to trouble the nation on the alleged "excesses" of that period.

MARTIN LUTHER KING, JR., *Demands Placed on the Door of Chicago City Hall* (1966)

During the summer of 1966, Chicago activists organized a series of events to protest discrimination in the city. They were joined by the Southern Christian Leadership Conference and its leader, Dr. Martin Luther King, in their efforts to force the Chicago government to ban racial discrimination in housing, employment, and other areas.

REAL ESTATE BOARDS AND BROKERS

1. Public statements that all listings will be available on a nondiscriminatory basis.

BANKS AND SAVINGS INSTITUTIONS

1. Public statements of a nondiscriminatory mortgage policy so that loans will be available to any qualified borrower without regard to the racial composition of the area.

Source: Chicago Freedom Movement 40 Web site: http://cfm40.middlebury.edu/node/21.

THE MAYOR AND CITY COUNCIL

1. Publication of headcounts of whites, Negroes and Latin Americans for all city departments and for all firms from which city purchases are made.
2. Revocation of contracts with firms that do not have a full scale fair employment practice.
3. Creation of a citizens review board for grievances against police brutality and false arrests or stops and seizures.
4. Ordinance giving ready access to the names of owners and investors for all slum properties.
5. A saturation program of increased garbage collection, street cleaning, and building inspection services in the slum properties.

POLITICAL PARTIES

1. The requirement that precinct captains be residents of their precincts.

CHICAGO HOUSING AUTHORITY AND THE CHICAGO DWELLING ASSOCIATION

1. Program to rehabilitate present public housing including such items as locked lobbies, restrooms in recreation areas, increased police protection and child care centers on every third floor.
2. Program to increase vastly the supply of low-cost housing on a scattered basis for both low and middle income families.

BUSINESS

1. Basic headcounts, including white, Negro and Latin American, by job classification and income level, made public.
2. Racial steps to upgrade and to integrate all departments, all levels of employment.

UNIONS

1. Headcounts in unions for apprentices, journeymen and union staff and officials by job classification. A crash program to remedy any inequities discovered by the headcount.
2. Indenture of at least 400 Negro and Latin American apprentices in the craft unions.

GOVERNOR

1. Prepare legislative proposals for a $2.00 state minimum wage law and for credit reform, including the abolition of garnishment and wage assignment.

ILLINOIS PUBLIC AID COMMISSION AND THE COOK COUNTY DEPARTMENT OF PUBLIC AID

1. Encouragement of grievance procedures for the welfare recipients so that recipients know that they can be members of and represented by a welfare union or a community organization.
2. Institution of a declaration of income system to replace the degrading investigation and means test for welfare eligibility.

FEDERAL GOVERNMENT

1. Executive enforcement of Title I of the 1964 Civil Rights Act regarding the complaint against the Chicago Board of Education.
2. An executive order for Federal supervision of the nondiscriminatory granting of loans by banks and savings institutions that are members of the Federal Deposit Insurance Corporation or by the Federal Deposit Insurance Corporation.
3. Passage of the 1966 Civil Rights Act without any deletions or crippling amendments.
4. Direct funding of Chicago community organizations by the Office of Economic Opportunity.

PEOPLE

1. Financial support of the Freedom Movement.
2. Selective buying campaigns against businesses that boycott the products of Negro-owned companies.
3. Participation in the Freedom Movement target campaigns for this summer, including volunteer services and membership in one of the Freedom Movement Organizations.

EMERGENCY CITIZENS' COMMITTEE, *Statement to Save School Decentralization and Community Control* (1968)

In the fall of 1968, New York City teachers went on strike to protest an experimental effort to allow "community boards," made up of parents and local residents, to influence the management of local schools. "Community Control" became the rallying cry for African American activists across the city and in other school districts.

Whereas, it has come to our attention that a concerted campaign is now underway to abolish the Ocean Hill-Brownsville experiment in school decentralization and community control, and

Source: Papers of the American Jewish Committee, New York, New York.

Whereas, it is our conviction that the Ocean Hill-Brownsville experiment—with all its difficulties—is one of the most hopeful beginnings in the search for quality education for the children of the ghetto, and

Whereas, community control—essential for the development of quality education for all areas of the city—is at stake in the Ocean Hill-Brownsville experiment, and

Whereas, quality education for the entire city of New York depends on *the* provision of quality education for children of deprived areas, and

Whereas, the betrayal of Ocean Hill Brownsville experiment would destroy constructive ghetto leadership and encourage extremism and violence throughout the city, therefore,

We resolve, to place our total support behind the Ocean Hill-Brownsville experiment, in the full understanding that all positive social *change* interrupts the status quo and will inevitably bring some measure of confusion, but in the complete conviction that the alternative is the betrayal of effective education for the city as a *whole and* a betrayal of the rights of minority groups to play a vigorous role in the education of their own children. The city cannot afford to allow entrenched private interest groups to deny the public-interest. Social chaos will be the result.

We pledge that we will do all in our power to fight the efforts to abolish Ocean Hill-Brownsville, and that our future support for political and educational leadership of this city and state will depend on the clarity and courage of its response to the current crisis;

We pledge, further, that in the event of the destruction of Ocean Hill-Brownsville Governing Board or the shut-down of its district *schools with* the transfer of the children out of their community, we will take the leadership in organizing and funding an alternative school system for the 8500 children who are now victims of a power struggle and whose future—and, therefore, our own future—is at stake in Ocean Hill-Brownsville today.

Co-chairman, Rev. Donald Harrington
Community Church
Dr. Mamie Phipps Clark
Executive Director
Northside Center for Child Development

BLACK PANTHER PARTY, *What We Want, What We Believe* (1966)

In the fall of 1966, activists from several cities joined together to create the Black Panther Party. They presented their 10-point plan as an alternative approach to black equality at a time when many people were frustrated with the mainstream civil rights movement.

Source: Clayborne Carson, ed., "The Eyes on the Prize": The Civil Rights Reader, New York: Viking, 1991, p. 220.

We want freedom. We want power to determine the destiny of our Black Community.

We want full employment for our people.

We want an end to the robbery by the capitalists of our Black Community.

We want decent housing fit for shelter of human beings.

We want education for our people that exposes the true nature of this decadent American society.

We want education that teaches us our true history and our role in present-day society.

We want all Black men to be exempt from military service.

We want an immediate end to POLICE BRUTALITY and MURDER of Black people.

We want freedom for all Black men held in federal, state, county and city prisons and jails.

We want all Black people when brought to trial to be tried in court by a jury of their peer group or people from their Black communities, as defined by the Constitution of the United States.

We want land, bread, housing, education, clothing justice, and peace. And as our major political objective, a United Nations-supervised plebiscite to be held throughout the Black colony in which only Black colonial subjects will be allowed to participate, for the purpose of determining the will of Black people as to their national destiny.

JOHNNIE TILLMON, *Welfare Is a Women's Issue* (1972)

Ms. Johnnie Tillmon was a welfare mother who formed a community group on behalf of poor women in Los Angeles in 1963 and went on to lead the National Welfare Rights Organization in Washington, DC, as its Associate Director in 1971 and its Executive Director in 1972. In 1972, she wrote this explanation of the NWRO which argued that the efforts to fight sexism, racism, and poverty were intimately connected.

I'm a woman. I'm a black woman. I'm a poor woman. I'm a fat woman. I'm a middle-aged woman. And I'm on welfare.

In this country, if you're any one of those things you count less as a human being. If you're all those things, you don't count at all. Except as a statistic.

Source: Ms. Magazine, Spring, 1972: 111–116.

I am 45 years old. I have raised six children. There are millions of statistics like me. Some on welfare. Some not. And some, really poor, who don't even know they're entitled to welfare. Not all of them are black. Not at all. In fact, the majority—about two-thirds—of all the poor families in the country are white.

Welfare's like a traffic accident. It can happen to anybody, but especially it happens to women.

And that's why welfare is a women's issue. For a lot of middle-class women in this country, Women's Liberation is a matter of concern. For women on welfare it's a matter of survival.

Survival. That's why we had to go on welfare. And that's why we can't get off welfare now. Not us women. Not until we do something about liberating poor women in this country.

Because up until now we've been raised to expect to work, all our lives, for nothing. Because we are the worst educated, the least-skilled, and the lowest-paid people there are. Because we have to be almost totally responsible for our children. Because we are regarded by everybody as dependents. That's why we are on welfare. And that's why we stay on it.

Welfare is the most prejudiced institution in this country, even more than marriage, which it tries to imitate. Let me explain that a little. Ninety-nine percent of welfare families are headed by women. There is no man around. In half the states there can't be men around because A.F.D.C. (Aid to Families With Dependent Children) says if there is an "able-bodied" man around, then you can't be on welfare. If the kids are going to eat, and the man can't get a job, then he's got to go.

Welfare is like a super-sexist marriage. You trade in a man for the man. But you can't divorce him if he treats you bad. He can divorce you, of course, cut you off anytime he wants. But in that case, he keeps the kids, not you. The man runs everything. In ordinary marriage, sex is supposed to be for your husband. On A.F.D.C., you're not supposed to have any sex at all. You give up control of your own body. It's a condition of aid. You may even have to agree to get your tubes tied so you can never have more children just to avoid being cut off welfare.

The man, the welfare system, controls your money. He tells you what to buy, what not to buy, where to buy it, and how much things cost. If things—rent, for instance—really cost more than he says they do, it's just too bad for you. He's always right.

That's why Governor [Ronald] Reagan can get away with slandering welfare recipients, calling them "lazy parasites," "pigs at the trough," and such. We've been trained to believe that the only reason people are on welfare is because there's something wrong with their character. If people have "motivation," if people only want to work, they can, and they will be able to support themselves and their kids in decency.

The truth is a job doesn't necessarily mean an adequate income. There are some ten million jobs that now pay less than the minimum wage, and if you're a woman, you've got the best chance of getting one. Why would a 45-year-old woman work all day in a laundry ironing shirts at 90-some cents an hour? Because she knows there's some place lower she could be. She could be on welfare. Society needs women on welfare as "examples" to let every woman, factory workers and housewife workers alike, know what will happen if she lets up, if she's laid off, if she tries to go it alone without a man. So these ladies stay on their feet or on their knees all their lives instead of asking why they're only getting 90-some cents an hour, instead of daring to fight and complain.

Maybe we poor welfare women will really liberate women in this country. We've already started on our own welfare plan. Along with other welfare recipients, we have organized so we can have some voice. Our group is called the National Welfare Rights Organization (N.W.R.O.). We put together our own welfare plan, called Guaranteed Adequate Income (G.A.I.), which would eliminate sexism from welfare. There would be no "categories"—men, women, children, single, married, kids, no kids—just poor people who need aid. You'd get paid according to need and family size only and that would be upped as the cost of living goes up.

As far as I'm concerned, the ladies of N.W.R.O. are the front-line troops of women's freedom. Both because we have so few illusions and because our issues are so important to all women—the right to a living wage for women's work, the right to life itself.

MAYOR COLEMAN YOUNG, *Inaugural Address* (1974)

Coleman Alexander Young became the first African American mayor of Detroit, Michigan, after a bitterly contested election in 1973. When Young took office, he gave an inaugural address that reflected the African American's commitment to reforming the discriminatory police department and improving treatment of minorities generally. White suburbanites, many of whom lived north of "Eight Mile Road," took offense at this speech. Many whites who lived in Detroit moved to the suburbs as soon as an African American became the mayor.

. . . The first problem that we must face as citizens of this great city, the first fact that we must look squarely in the eye is that this city has too long been polarized.

We can no longer afford the luxury of hatred and racial division. What is good for the black people of this city is good for the white people of this city. What is good for the rich people of this city is good for the poor people of this city. What is good for those who live in the suburbs is good for those of us who live in the central city.

It is clear that we have a commonality of interests. The suburbs cannot live without the city. The white population of this city cannot live while its black people suffer discrimination and poverty.

And so I dedicate myself—with the help of Common Council, and more basically with your help—toward beginning now to attack the economic deterioration of our city . . . I recognize the economic problem as a basic one, but there is a problem

Source: Detroit News, January 1, 1974.

of crime, which is not unrelated to poverty and unemployment, and so I say we must attack both of these problems vigorously at the same time.

The police department alone cannot rid this city of crime. The police must have the respect and cooperation of our citizens. But they must earn that respect by extending to our citizens cooperation and respect.

We must build a new people-oriented Police Department, and then you and they can help us drive the criminals from our streets.

I issue as forward warning now to all those pushers, to all ripoff artists, to all muggers: It's time to leave Detroit; hit Eight Mile Road. And I don't give a damn if they are black or white, or if they wear Superfly suits or blue uniforms with silver badges: Hit the road.

4

African American Activism in the South

—JANE DAILEY

When and what was the civil rights movement, and who made it move? It is important to note at the beginning that the civil rights movement did not originate with the student sit-ins in 1960, and it did not end with the assassination of Rev. Martin Luther King, Jr., in 1968. Many narratives of the movement begin with the 1954 *Brown* decision, which outlawed segregation in public schools, and proceed quickly through the Montgomery bus boycott (1955), which brought King to center stage; the Little Rock high school integration crisis (1957), which forced President Eisenhower to use federal power to uphold the law; and the inauguration of the sit-in movement in January 1960. Attention then focuses on the student movement and its monuments—the Freedom Rides of 1961; the integration of the University of Mississippi in 1962; the Birmingham campaign in 1963; 1964's Freedom Summer; the Selma-to-Montgomery March of 1965—and culminate with the passage of landmark legislation in 1964 and 1965 protecting civil rights and the right to vote.

The trouble with this chronology lies not in the dates or the events, but in the aura of spontaneity that surrounds them. The triumphs of the civil rights movement of the 1950s and 1960s were rooted in decades of patient legal challenges to the law of segregation and episodic local activism by inspired community leaders. For example, although Martin Luther King, Jr., emerged from the Montgomery Bus Boycott a national spokesman for civil rights, the 26-year-old Baptist minister was a newcomer to Montgomery and by no means the most significant leader in the local black community. That title was held by E. D. Nixon, a fifty-something Pullman porter with a sixth-grade education, who had given Montgomery nearly three decades of outspoken activist leadership through the Brotherhood of Sleeping

Car Porters and the National Association for the Advancement of Colored Persons (NAACP).

Forty-three-year-old seamstress Rosa Parks, whose refusal to surrender her seat on a municipal bus triggered the boycott, also had deep roots in the protest tradition. Well before Parks held onto the seat on that bus in Montgomery, she was running voter-registration campaigns (she had passed the registration hurdle in 1943). She was also the secretary of the Montgomery branch of the NAACP. Although it remains fashionable to explain Parks' actions on the bus as the product of fatigue, she was more organized than tired.

That organization underlay the civil rights activism that seemed to burst from the South as the 1960s began. What differentiates a movement from a moment is the sense of momentum that propels activists forward and that inspires others to join the campaign. For that reason, it is fair to date the civil rights *movement*, as opposed to struggle, from 1960. In January of that year, when four students from North Carolina Agricultural and Technical State University asked to be served at the whites-only counter of Woolworth's department store in Greensboro, it became clear that the decades-long black freedom struggle had entered a new phase.

The black and also white men and women who spent the 1960s working to achieve equal citizenship for all were motivated by many different impulses. Some, particularly older people who had served in or lived through World War II, were repulsed by the distance between the conditions of life in the South and America's professed democratic values. Others believed deeply in the human right of self-determination and brought lessons learned observing national liberation movements in colonial Africa and Asia to the American crusade. Still others were drawn to the movement by a sense of social justice that was anchored in a profound commitment to the basic tenets of Christianity. All were convinced of the utility of direct action protests, as opposed to simply legal action, to challenge Jim Crow and his keepers.

There was great debate, however, about what constituted "direct action." Whereas a deep commitment to nonviolent activism animated a large group of civil rights leaders, others, such as North Carolina NAACP leader Robert F. Williams, argued the merits of what he referred to as "armed self-defense." Civil rights activists faced white violence on a daily basis and were often watched over by fellow activists keeping the peace with, as one Alabamian, put it, "my non-violent .38 police special." These divergent attitudes toward coercion were reflected in the leading civil rights organizations' tactics. The Southern Christian Leadership Conference (SCLC), founded in 1956 as a result of the Montgomery bus boycott, was committed to nonviolent protest and negotiation, but a second important organization, the Congress of Racial Equality (CORE), founded in the middle of World War II, was willing to force confrontations with the segregation system in order to initiate change. The Student Non-Violent Coordinating Committee (SNCC, pronounced "snick"), which grew out of the Greensboro sit-in in 1960, represented the younger, more militant, less patient post-*Brown* generation of civil rights activists who on occasion actively courted white violence in order to draw attention to their cause. The Black Power movement of the late 1960s was not afraid of either rhetorical or defensive force.

Whether encouraged by activists or simply endured, violent confrontation with segregationists began to bear fruit in the 1960s. In 1961, an integrated group of CORE workers embarked on a "freedom ride" through the South designed to draw a reluctant federal government into the civil rights struggle by exposing Southern noncompliance with federal law and by provoking the Justice Department into enforcing a recent Supreme Court decision that barred segregation in facilities involved in interstate transit. The violent assaults on riders in Alabama and arrests in Mississippi drew Attorney General Robert Kennedy into the civil rights fray and eventually succeeded in shaming the Interstate Commerce Commission into enforcing the law of the land. After the Freedom Rides, even those most dedicated to nonviolent direct action understood the power of television images of howling white mobs assaulting straight-laced young black people integrating a skating rink or trying to register to vote. Influenced by television coverage of the Ole Miss riot in September 1962, the House of Representatives began to draft new federal civil rights legislation. Building on this momentum, King led a group to Birmingham, Alabama, to force a showdown against segregation in one of the most violently racist cities in America. The images of police chief "Bull" Connor's officers attacking young black men and women with batons, snarling police dogs, and high-pressure fire hoses shocked the world and embarrassed the United States. Criticized for pushing his agenda beyond the social breaking point, King's "Letter from Birmingham Jail," composed while serving a sentence for violating a state ban on protest marches, blasted the complacency of "whites of goodwill" and capitalized on the violence in the Deep South by declaring that the only alternative to civil disobedience was revolution.

This message was heard clearly in Washington, where both Kennedy brothers were increasingly involved in negotiating the civil rights struggle. While Bobby Kennedy worked behind the scenes with Birmingham businessmen to defuse the crisis and initiate a process of gradual desegregation, John Kennedy tried to convince Alabama governor George C. Wallace to allow the peaceful integration of the University of Alabama. When Wallace refused, and furthermore declared his undying commitment to upholding segregation now and forever, Kennedy came down finally and decisively on the side of the movement. The following week, Kennedy called on Congress to draft laws in support of voting rights, to help school districts trying to desegregate, to ban segregation in public facilities, and to empower the attorney general to initiate legal proceedings against school districts that failed to comply with federal law. Building on growing national disgust with the defense of Jim Crow and support for the goals of the civil rights protestors, SCLC announced a massive march on Washington for August 1963. The August 28 civil rights demonstration at the Lincoln Memorial, which drew some 250,000 people, remains a symbolic landmark in the struggle for equal citizenship rights.

The assassination of John F. Kennedy in Texas on November 22, 1963 spurred passage of the slain president's proposed civil rights act. Lyndon B. Johnson propelled the 1964 Civil Rights Act through Congress, and then, understanding that black economic inequality was as severe as black political inequality, Johnson launched the social welfare programs he called the "Great Society." Voting rights still remained at the top of civil rights organizations' agenda, however, and for good reason: in 1964 only two million of the South's five million blacks of voting age were registered to vote. That summer, a coalition of civil rights organizations, led by SNCC's Bob Moses, launched a massive voter registration drive in Mississippi staffed by local blacks and white college students from across the nation. The interracial Freedom Summer group was greeted by an unprecedented campaign of violence, including 35 bombings, numerous beatings, and the kidnapping and murder of James Chaney, Andrew Goodman, and Michael Schwerner. An African American, Chaney was a local Mississippian, but Goodman and Schwerner were white student volunteers, and news of their deaths, broadcast by a riveted media, clarified for white Americans outside the region the degree of violent resistance to black equality in the South.

The extent of that resistance was demonstrated once again in Selma, Alabama, where King and SCLC chose to mount their own voter registration campaign in 1965. Aiming to provoke Selma's sheriff Jim Clark into a newsworthy confrontation, waves of Selma blacks were arrested while trying to register. In February, police attacked a night march in a small town near Selma and fatally shot 26-year-old Jimmie Lee Jackson, who was shielding his mother and grandmother from the police. Jackson's death prompted black leaders to organize a 54-mile march from Selma to the governor's mansion in Montgomery to demand protection for those registering to vote. Defying an order forbidding the march, on March 7 more than 600 protestors followed SCLC and SNCC leader John Lewis onto the Edmund Pettus Bridge. There they were attacked by bullwhip-wielding mounted state troopers, whose gas masks protected them from the noxious fumes unleashed on the demonstrators.

Vowing to continue the march, the Alabama protestors were joined by Americans from all over the country. Especially prominent were clergymen of all faiths, whose appearance at the side of King and other ministers added credence to civil rights activists' longtime claim that God was on their side. White supremacists could grumble about the presence of "outside agitators," but their presence, and the nationwide rallies organized in support of the Selma marchers, demonstrated conclusively that civil rights was a national issue. On Capitol Hill, President Johnson declared that "it is not just Negroes, but really all of us who must overcome the crippling legacy of bigotry and injustice," and asked Congress to craft a powerful new voting bill, the Voting Rights Act of 1965.

The legacies of the civil rights movement in the South are legion. The legal triumphs of the NAACP, even when unevenly implemented, inspired other champions of minority rights in America. The Lambda Legal Defense and Education Fund, founded in 1973 to fight for gay rights in the courts, for example, was modeled directly on the NAACP's Legal Defense and Education Fund. The National Indian Youth Council, organized in 1961, applied direct action techniques to their own agenda; in 1963, for instance, Northwest Indians mounted "fish-ins" to enforce longstanding treaty rights. Thanks to the last-minute prohibition of discrimination by sex in the 1964 Civil Rights Act, the greatest group beneficiary of civil rights legislation in America has turned out to be women. Black cultural nationalism, which rejected assimilation to white norms and encouraged pride in difference, strongly influenced other freedom movements, including the Chicano mural movement and the gay rights movement. Gay activists echoed African American insistence that "Black is Beautiful" when they adopted the slogan "Gay is Good" in 1968. The Southern civil rights movement stimulated legal battles to establish full civil equality for other subgroups of Americans, encouraged ethnic minorities such as Jews and Italians to embrace, rather than conceal or downplay, their cultural difference from the nation's white Protestant majority, and firmly established civic equality for all as a fundamental American ideal.

STETSON KENNEDY, *Jim Crow Guide to the U.S.A.* (1959)

In this spoof of the standard tourist guide, self-proclaimed white southern "dissident-at-large" Stetson Kennedy uses mockery, irony, exposure, and humor to promote human rights and attack Jim Crow.

. . . in 29 states of the U.S.A. it is against the law for persons of a different race to make love, marry, or have children. Should you enter into a forbidden interracial marriage in any of these states, your marriage would automatically be void; your children by any previous legal marriage might be taken from you by the state; your children by the interracial marriage would be branded illegitimate and might also be denied their rights of inheritance; and you and your spouse would be charged with lewd and lascivious conduct, a misdemeanor, a felony, or an infamous crime (depending upon the state), and fined and/or imprisoned for as long as ten years in some states. A number of states say that parties to such marriages must be sent to jail.

The Constitution of the U.S.A. says that "full faith and credit shall be given in each state to the public acts, records, and judicial proceedings of every other state." However, a Federal court has ruled that this "full faith and credit" clause does not require any state to recognize marriages which are contrary to the local idea of morality—such as an interracial marriage in one of the states which forbid such marriages. . . .

If you become party to an interracial marriage in some foreign country, it will not be recognized as legal in these 27 American states, even if you are a diplomatic representative not subject to certain other U.S. laws. If you are a resident of North Carolina, Delaware, Maryland, Mississippi, Montana, Tennessee, Texas, or Virginia and go to some other state and enter into an interracial marriage where it is legal to do so, and then return to your home state, your marriage will be void herein and you may be prosecuted. If your home is in Mississippi, Oklahoma, Tennessee, Texas, or Virginia, you will also be banished from ever again living within the boundaries of your home state, either with or without your illegal spouse. . . .

Source: Stetson Kennedy, *Jim Crow Guide to the U.S.A.*, London: Lawrence & Wishart, 1959.

JULIAN MAYFIELD, *Challenge to Negro Leadership: The Case of Robert Williams* (1961)

Civil rights activists strongly disagreed about how to respond to white violence, especially after the 1961 Freedom Riders were assaulted in Alabama. North Carolina NAACP leader Robert Williams' challenge to the NAACP, and his stand on armed self-reliance, occurred in this highly charged atmosphere of competition for leadership in the movement and disputation over how and when to meet white violence. From The Single Issue, a pamphlet distributed at the NAACP national convention in New York, July 1959.

For some time now it has been apparent that the traditional leadership of the American Negro community—a leadership which has been largely middle class in origin and orientation—is in danger of losing its claim to speak for the masses of Negroes. This group is being challenged by the pressure of events to produce more substantial and immediate results in the field of civil rights or renounce the position it has long held. . . .

But the challenge to middle-class Negro leaders—including the newer type like Martin Luther King—remains. It is inherent in the rapid growth of the militant, white-hating Muslim movement among working-class Negroes. It can be heard in the conversations of black intellectuals and students from the South who regard the efforts of the NAACP, the Urban League, and most religious and civic leaders with either disdain or despair, in the belief that they are doing too little, too timidly and too late.

Probably nothing more clearly illustrates this challenge, however, than the case of *Wilkins vs. Williams*. Robert F. Williams is the president of the Union County, North Carolina branch of the NAACP. Wilkins vs. Williams was a hearing before the board of directors of the NAACP in New York City, which grew out of three criminal cases that were disposed of in one day by the Superior Court in Monroe, the seat of Union County.

Before this court on May 5, 1959, stood James Mobley, B. F. Shaw, and Louis Medlin. Mobley, a mentally retarded colored man was charged with assault with intent to commit rape on a white woman. (He admitted he had caught her wrist during an argument.) Shaw, a white man, was charged with assault on a Negro chambermaid who claimed he had kicked her down a flight of stairs in the hotel where she worked. The case of the other white defendant, Medlin, was the most inflammatory he was accused of having entered the home of a Negro woman, eight months pregnant, of attempting to rape her, and, when she resisted and tried to flee across a field, of brutally

Source: Commentary, April 1961.

assaulting her and her six-year-old son. A white woman neighbor had witnessed the assault and summoned the police. . . .

After Medlin was arrested their first impulse was to mount an assault against the Monroe jail, seize the prisoner, and kill him. It was Robert Williams who restrained them. He pointed out that murdering Medlin would place them in the position of the white men who, shortly before, had dragged Mack Charles Parker from a jail in Poplarville, Mississippi, and lynched him. Besides, Williams argued, so much national and international attention was focused on Monroe that the judge and juries would be forced to punish the white men.

But Williams was wrong. Impervious to world opinion the court freed both Shaw and Medlin, and committed the mentally retarded Negro to prison for two years. (Only the last minute discovery by his attorney of a technicality, which reduced the charge from rape to assault, prevented the judge from handing down a thirty-year sentence.) On the steps of the courthouse, Williams issued an angry statement to a UPI reporter:

> We cannot take these people who do us injustice to the court and it becomes necessary to punish them ourselves. In the future we are going to have to try and convict them on the spot. We cannot rely on the law. We can get no justice under the present system. If we feel that injustice is done, we must right then and there; on the spot be prepared to inflict punishment on the people. Since the federal government will not bring a halt to lynching in the South, and since the so-called courts lynch our people legally, if it's necessary to stop lynching with lynching, then we must be willing to resort to that method.

Roy Wilkins, executive secretary of the NAACP, called Williams from New York to ask about the statement. Williams confirmed it as his and said he intended to repeat it that afternoon for several radio and television stations eager to interview him. He would make it clear, he assured Wilkins that he was not speaking for the NAACP but for himself, though he would stress that his views represented the prevailing feeling of the colored people in Union County. . . .

Thus the stage was set for a contest between a highly respected leader of a distinguished national organization and a relatively unknown young Southerner capable of issuing rash statements on the steps of a courthouse. *Wilkins vs. Williams* aroused heated discussions in nearly every Negro community in the country, but it was obvious from the beginning that Williams was bound to lose. . . . The committee upheld the action of its executive secretary and suspended Williams for six months. A few weeks later, the delegates to the Association's fiftieth annual convention voted 764 to 14 against Williams and in favor of suspension. . . .

. . . But Washington will act only under strong pressure, and this the Negro people must create by a more militant assertion of their rights—including "meeting violence with violence."

ELLA J. BAKER, *The Southern Patriot* (1960)

Responding to the sit-in movement, longtime civil rights activist Ella Baker organized a student conference at Shaw University in North Carolina in April 1961. Critical of the SCLC's hierarchy and misogyny, Baker advised the students to develop group-centered leadership and avoid anointing a single leader—advice the new Student Non-Violent Coordinating Committee (SNCC) took.

The Student Leadership Conference made it crystal clear that current sit-ins and other demonstrations are concerned with something much bigger than a hamburger or even a giant-sized Coke. Whatever may be the difference in approach to their goal, the Negro and white students, North and South, are seeking to rid America of the scourge of racial segregation and discrimination—not only at lunch counters, but in every aspect of life. . . .

By and large, this feeling that they have a destined date with freedom, was not limited to a drive for personal freedom, or even freedom for the Negro in the South. Repeatedly it was emphasized that the movement was concerned with the moral implications of racial discrimination for the "whole world" and the "Human Race."

This universality of approach was linked with a perceptive recognition that "it is important to keep the movement democratic and to avoid struggles for personal leadership." It was further evident that desire for supportive cooperation from adult leaders and the adult community was also tempered by apprehension that adults might try to "capture" the student movement. The students showed willingness to be met on the basis of equality, but were intolerant of anything that smacked of manipulation or domination. . . . .

SALLY BELFRAGE, *Freedom Summer* (1964)

In this excerpt from her 1965 book *Freedom Summer*, Sally Belfrage comments on the difficulties of interracial cooperation in Mississippi and the impact of the 1964 Civil Rights Act on SNCC and on the local people SNCC claimed to lead and internal debates over tactics.

In describing the then Chairman of SNCC, with whom he was sharing a Mississippi jail cell, Bob Moses wrote in 1961 that "McDew . . . has taken on the deep hates and deep loves which America, and the world, reserve for those who dare

---

Source: Ella J. Baker, *The Southern Patriot*, June 1960.
Source: The Eyes on the Prize Reader, pp. 180–186.

to stand in a strong sun and cast a sharp shadow." This could as well describe many SNCC Negroes, whose deep hates and loves were often translated into simple whites and blacks. They were automatically suspicious of us, the white volunteers; throughout the summer they put us to the test, and few, if any, could pass. Implicit in all the songs, tears, speeches, work, laughter, was the knowledge secure in both them and us that ultimately we could return to a white refuge.

But we didn't have to come, did we? We could have stayed at home and gone to the beach, or earned the money we so badly needed for next semester at old Northern White. And here we are: We Came. Among all the millions who could have realized their responsibility to this revolution, we alone came. Few Northern Negroes even came. We came. Don't we earn some recognition, if not praise? I want to be your friend, you black idiot, was the contradiction evident everywhere. . . .

MARTIN LUTHER KING, JR., *Our God Is Marching On!* (1965)

Martin Luther King delivered this speech from the steps of the Alabama state capitol before an estimated 25,000 people at the conclusion of the weeklong march from Selma to Montgomery, which captured the imagination of America and the world and speeded passage of the 1965 Voting Rights Act.

. . . They told us we wouldn't get here. And there were those who said that we would get here only over their dead bodies, (*Well. Yes, sir. Talk*) but all the world today knows that we are here and we are standing before the forces of power in the state of Alabama saying, "We ain't goin' let nobody turn us around." (*Yes, sir. Speak*) [*Applause*] . . . Today I want to tell the city of Selma, (*Tell them, Doctor*) today I want to say to the state of Alabama, (*Yes, sir*) today I want to say to the people of America and the nations of the world, that we are not about to turn around. (*Yes, sir*) We are on the move now. (*Yes, sir*)

Yes, we are on the move and no wave of racism can stop us. (*Yes, sir*) We are on the move now. The burning of our churches will not deter us. (*Yes, sir*) The bombing of our homes will not dissuade us. (*Yes, sir*) We are on the move now. (*Yes, sir*) The beating and killing of our clergymen and young people will not divert us. We are on the move now. (*Yes, sir*) The wanton release of their known murderers would not discourage us. . . . .

Let us march on poverty (*Let us march*) until no American parent has to skip a meal so that their children may eat. (*Yes, sir*) March on poverty (*Let us march*) until no starved man walks the streets of our cities and towns (*Yes, sir*) in search of jobs that do not exist. (*Yes, sir*) Let us march on poverty (*Let us march*) until wrinkled stomachs in Mississippi are filled (*That's right*) and the idle industries of

---

Source: Speech at the conclusion of the Selma-to-Montgomery march on March 25, 1965.

Appalachia are realized and revitalized, and broken lives in sweltering ghettos are mended and remolded.

. . . . Let us march on ballot boxes (*Let us march*) until the Wallaces of our nation tremble away in silence. . . . Let us march on ballot boxes (*Let us march. March*) until brotherhood becomes more than a meaningless word in an opening prayer, but the order of the day on every legislative agenda. Let us march on ballot boxes (*Yes*) until all over Alabama God's children will be able to walk the earth in decency and honor.

HOWELL RAINES, *Interview with Bayard Rustin* (1977)

When the Fellowship of Reconciliation (FOR) in New York learned in December 1955 that African Americans in Montgomery were staging a boycott of municipal transportation, longtime civil rights workers Stanley Levison, Ella Baker, and Bayard Rustin were sent to lend a hand. While Baker organized the SCLC, Rustin, a pacifist and tireless organizer, drafted speeches for King, raised money, and otherwise helped the young minister find his activist feet.

Well, my meeting with Dr. King came about because I at that time worked for an organization called the Fellowship of Reconciliation. It was a pacifist organization. . . .

Now, quite contrary to what many people think, Dr. King was not a confirmed believer in nonviolence, totally, at the time that the boycott began. On my second visit there the house was still being protected by armed guards. In fact, when I went in, I went in with a chap whose name was Bill Worthy, who became famous because he went to China contrary to the government's desire and they took his passport. He'd been a Nieman fellow at Harvard and was well known. As Bill went to sit down in the King living room, I said, "Hey, Bill, wait!" I said, "There's a gun in that chair." And he might have sat on it. But it was gradually over several weeks that Dr. King continuously deepened his commitment to nonviolence, and within six weeks, he had demanded that there be no armed guards and no effort at associating himself in any form with violence. . . . I take no credit for Dr. King 's development, but I think the fact that Dr. King had someone around recommending certain readings and discussing these things with him was helpful to bring up in him what was already obviously there. That's how we met.

. . . .What Dr. King delivered to blacks there, far more important than whether they got to ride on the bus, was the absence of fear, the ability to be men in the same way that the Jews in the Warsaw ghetto knew that they couldn't win, but, knowing they were going to die, they said, "Let us go down expressing our manhood, which is to fight back." So Dr. King had this tremendous facility for giving people the feeling

Source: Howell Raines, *My Soul is Rested*, New York: Putnam Press, 1977, pp. 52–57.

that they could be bigger and stronger and more courageous and more loving than they thought they could be. . . . .

In this connection Martin did not need to be a strategist or a tactician. His Southern victories were made in part because Southern reaction provided a great dynamism. All right, they used fire hoses. This draws people in. [With broad gestures, a dramatic voice] They bombed churches. This draws people in. They murdered some kids in Mississippi. This draws people in. If the Southerners had been smart and just let Martin alone . . . but Martin had a facility for putting to good use the mistakes of his adversaries. And this is a King ability.

STOKELY CARMICHAEL, *What We Want* (1966)

Described by Martin Luther King as "a psychological call to manhood," the slogan "Black Power" meant different things to different people. In a long essay in the *New York Review of Books* directed at liberal white supporters of civil rights, SNCC leader Stokely Carmichael—who had popularized the term in the first place—defines it and addresses its potential consequences.

One of the tragedies of the struggle against racism is that up to now there has been no national organization which could speak to the growing militancy of young black people in the urban ghetto. There has been only a civil rights movement, whose tone of voice was adapted to an audience of liberal whites. It served as a sort of buffer zone between them and angry young blacks. None of its so-called leaders could go into a rioting community and be listened to.

In a sense, I blame ourselves—together with the mass media—for what has happened in Watts, Harlem, Chicago, Cleveland, Omaha. Each time the people in those cities saw Martin Luther King get slapped, they became angry; when they saw four little black girls bombed to death, they were angrier; and when nothing happened, they were steaming. We had nothing to offer that they could see, except to go out and be beaten again. We helped to build their frustration. . . .

We cannot be expected any longer to march and have our heads broken in order to say to whites: come on, you're nice guys. For you are not nice guys. We have found you out . . . This is the significance of black power as a slogan. For once, black people are going to use the words they want to use—not just the words whites want to hear. And they will do this no matter how often the press tries to stop the use of the slogan by equating it with racism or separatism. . . .

For racism to die, a totally different America must be born. This is what the white society does not wish to face; this is why that society prefers to talk about integration. But integration speaks not at all to the problem of poverty, only to the problem of blackness. . . .

Source: Stokely Carmichael, "What We Want," *New York Review of Books*, September 22, 1966.

Integration, moreover, speaks to the problem of blackness in a despicable way. As a goal, it has been based on complete acceptance of the fact that *in order to have a* decent house or education, blacks must move into a white neighborhood or send their children to a white school. This reinforces, among both black and white, the idea that "white" is automatically better and "black" is by definition inferior. This is why integration is a subterfuge for the maintenance of white supremacy. . . .

. . . . But it takes time to become free of the lies and their shaming effect on black minds. It takes time to reject the most important lie: that black people inherently can't do the same things white people can do, unless white people help them. . . . This does not mean we don't welcome help, or friends. But we want the right to decide whether anyone is, in fact, our friend. . . . We cannot have the oppressors telling the oppressed how to rid themselves of the oppressor.

I have said that most liberal whites react to "black power" with the question, What about me? . . . One of the most disturbing things about almost all white supporters of the movement has been that they are afraid to go into their own communities—which is where the racism exists—and work to get rid of it. They want to run from Berkeley to tell us what to do in Mississippi; let them look instead at Berkeley. They admonish blacks to be nonviolent; let them preach non-violence in the white community . . . There is a vital job to be done among poor whites. We hope to see, eventually, a coalition between poor blacks and poor whites . . .

5

African American Activism in the West

—William L. Van Deburg

On May 6, 1969, the legendary African American trade union organizer A. Philip Randolph was honored at a black-tie dinner held in the Grand Ballroom of New York's Waldorf Astoria hotel. After listening to numerous praise-filled tributes, the 80-year-old civil rights activist offered his own perspective on more than a half-century of struggle. Calling the gala event a "rededication," Randolph revisited a theme he had explored many times in the past—most memorably in his 1937 keynote address to the Second National Negro Congress. "Salvation for the Negro masses must come from within," he declared. "Freedom is never granted; it is won. Justice is never given; it is exacted." Certainly, the message was timeless. Taking his words to heart, Randolph's Depression-era audience had returned to their hometowns, newly inspired. They formed tenants' unions, organized domestic workers, and demanded enactment of anti-lynching legislation and the elimination of poll taxes. Eventually, 50 branch councils of the NNC were established in 19 states—and as far West as Seattle and Oakland.

In later years, from the Pacific Northwest to the Border Southwest, post–World War II black Americans also banded together to defend their communities and to advance race-specific agendas. Minority group residents of Houston's Fourth Ward, Dallas' Deep Ellum, the Central District in Seattle, and Las Vegas' West Side made their discontent known by protesting restrictive housing covenants, segregated schools, and job market discrimination. In 1958, members of the local NAACP Youth Council launched a series of "sitdowns" at segregated Oklahoma City lunch counters, soda fountains, and cafeterias. Two years later, activists in Reno and Las Vegas mounted a spirited challenge to the exclusionary practices of resort and casino owners. In 1963, some 900 Texans marched on the state capitol in Austin to evidence their displeasure over the slow pace of pending civil rights legislation.

Mirroring protest activity in other regions during the late 1950s and early 1960s, members of California's NAACP, CORE, and Urban League chapters mounted nonviolent direct action campaigns against *de facto* school segregation, "sharecropper wages," police misconduct, and the intimidation of blacks who attempted to rent or purchase homes in all-white neighborhoods. Along with less well-known groups they also lobbied for better job-training programs, served as advocates for black residents displaced by urban renewal projects, and called for the creation of community police review boards. Throughout the era, boycotts and picketing were used to draw media attention to racial injustice. For example, in 1960 the NAACP won concessions from the management of San Francisco's Jack Tar Hotel by threatening to hold a picket line outside the new facility. Soon thereafter, CORE members from San Francisco and the East Bay demonstrated outside area Woolworth's and Kress stores to show their support for the sit-ins that were occurring throughout the South.

Unfortunately, hard-won victories at both the local and national levels brought little more than incremental change and frustration grew. Nowhere was this more apparent than in the Watts section of Los Angeles. Between 1940 and 1960, wave after wave of unskilled job-seekers from Southern states had permanently altered the racial balance of this 2.5 square-mile district. Once-dominant Anglos fled to the suburbs and Mexican Americans relocated in East L.A. By 1965, 87 percent of Watts residents were African Americans, population density was the highest in the county, and joblessness topped 13 percent. Major grievances included overcrowded, understaffed public schools; lack of reliable public transportation to industrial plants with high-salary union jobs; exploitative shopkeepers; uncaring, absentee landlords; and unequal enforcement of the law by a police force that was 96 percent nonblack.

Sparked by a dispute over the arrest of motorist Marquette Frye for drunk driving, the civil disturbances which engulfed Watts during mid-August 1965 can be traced to these unaddressed concerns. Described as a "mindless orgy" by the mainstream press and public officials but considered a "rebellion" or "police riot" by black residents, the five-day conflagration necessitated the deployment of 13,900 National Guard troops, 934 police, and 719 sheriff's deputies. By one count, rioters numbered between 31,000 and 35,000 while another 64,000 to 72,000 were involved as "close spectators." Thirty-four people died and 1,032 were injured seriously enough to require medical treatment. Total property damage exceeded $40 million. After Watts, both the nature of Black America's discontent and the precariousness of societal equilibrium should have been obvious to all. Increasingly, black Californians—especially young people who had been politicized by the civil disturbances—searched for solutions to the problems of a racialized civic order in the Black Power movement.

During the period 1965–1975, California-based activists created numerous Black Power organizations of various sizes, with different and often conflicting ideological perspectives. Some led community control initiatives, challenging entrenched bureaucracies and absentee entrepreneurs for "ownership" of their neighborhood schools and businesses. Others sought to expand the base of electoral participation and erect new political structures that would enable average citizens to influence public policy. Still others led demonstrations on college campuses in support of Black Studies programs and joined their white classmates in protesting university ties with the military–industrial complex and conscription for the war in Vietnam.

In attempting to form power blocs within mainstream institutions, such activists considered themselves to be pro-black, not anti-white. Rooted in the pluralistic tradition, they understood that U.S. society functions through the interaction of competing interest groups. If granted equal access to power and continually strengthened through their unique cultural roots, the various ethnic constituencies would be capable of forming a multicultural society in which each component supported and enriched all others. To be sure, a major goal was to win increased autonomy. But, alteration of existing power relationships was thought to be long overdue. They sought no more than the opportunities, privileges, and respect accorded to other groups. Black Californians had to increase their decision-making power if they were to gain an equitable share of the state's resources.

Compared to those whose activism was most fully grounded in pluralism, Black Power-era nationalists were skeptics. Suspicious of claims that radically divergent groups can live in peace and on a basis of equality while participating in the same social institutions, they believed it inevitable that one component of the social matrix would come to dominate and oppress the others. The result would be assimilation and the eradication of important subgroup mores. To avert this tragedy, black nationalists sought to close ranks and move toward a position of group strength.

Chief among cultural nationalist groups operating in California during these years was the Los Angeles-based US Organization. Founded in 1965 by Maulana Karenga (a.k.a. Ron Everett), a UCLA political science graduate student who was active in the civil rights movement and had helped organize rallies against nuclear proliferation and capital punishment in the years before Watts, US (meaning "black people" as opposed to "them," the white oppressors) championed the notion that true liberation was impossible without breaking the white culture's domination of black minds. African Americans had to "overturn" themselves, reject the values of the larger society, and reshape reality in their own image. In this formulation, the cultural revolution preceded, facilitated, and ultimately would secure the gains of a future political revolution.

US members embraced every aspect of the era's cultural renaissance—leading the West Coast "back to black" movement in clothing and hairstyle; championing the teaching of Swahili as a language of self-determination; and inaugurating the celebration of black holidays such as *Uhuru* Day (August 11, commemorating the Watts rebellion) and *Kwanzaa* (a year's end observance of seven key values—the *Nguzo Saba*—by which blacks seeking liberation were to order their lives). Politically, this culturally attuned cohort sought to operate as an elite vanguard force. Although he spoke often of achieving unity without uniformity, Karenga's commitment to "cultural reconversion" as a precondition for political revolution made most of these alliances short-lived.

By the end of the decade, followers of the revolutionary nationalist Black Panther Party for Self-Defense had become Karenga's most voluble critics. Up and down the West Coast, on street corners and university campuses, spokespersons for the two groups competed for primacy in the black public sphere. Founded in Oakland in 1966 with a core membership of less than a hundred, the Panthers' community service ethic—as well as their youthful bravado and penchant for the dramatic—soon carried their image and influence far beyond the Bay Area. As of 1970, the Party was operational in more than 30 cities nationwide. All chapters were governed through a Central Committee headed by Chairman Bobby Seale, Minister of Defense Huey P. Newton, and Information Minister Eldridge Cleaver. They also adopted a ten-point program calling for full employment, decent housing, exemption from military service, an end to police brutality, and freedom for imprisoned black "colonial subjects." In California, the Party leadership established ad hoc alliances with both the Brown Berets (Chicana/o) and the Red Guard, a Chinese American revolutionary group from the Bay Area. Various Panther units also collaborated with members of Students for a Democratic Society and invited supporters of the gay and women's liberation movements to their conferences and rallies.

Best remembered for their 1967 protest in Sacramento against the Mulford (gun control) Bill, the Panthers also initiated armed citizens' patrols that "policed the police" in black neighborhoods. This was accomplished by monitoring the officers' conduct, advising detained suspects of their legal rights, and reporting incidents of harassment. Other "survival" programs attempted to organize and sustain poor black folk until the anticipated revolution could be launched. In order to "meet the needs of the people," grassroots Panther activists provided breakfasts for children, free shoes and clothing, legal assistance, and screening for sickle cell anemia. They also counseled welfare recipients, protested the eviction of black tenants, and organized periodic grocery giveaways. Liberation schools, adult education classes, and an Intercommunal Youth Institute provided low income and working-class residents with alternatives to prevailing pedagogical practices and political ideologies. The Party's ongoing efforts to establish a "people's city" in Oakland through a radical reordering of municipal priorities contributed importantly to the election of Alameda County Superior Court Judge Lionel Wilson as the city's first African American mayor in 1977.

Rivalry between the Black Panthers and US reached a peak early in 1969 when members of the two nationalist groups engaged in a deadly shoot-out on the UCLA campus. By the mid-1970s, tactical errors, counterintelligence intrigues, bad press, and the death, exile, imprisonment, or defection of key figures had destroyed any hope of achieving unity within the movement as a whole. To many, Black Power was scarcely more than a short-lived and relatively inconsequential fringe enthusiasm.

Today, however, historians believe that the black freedom movement of these years had tangible political and psychological effects and left a distinctive cachet upon the cultural landscape. Most significantly, it motivated long-marginalized and discouraged black Americans to redefine themselves as members of a beautiful, capable, highly cultured race, to become entrepreneurs, and to run for public office.

To be sure, historians haven't overlooked the mistakes of the youthful activist cadres. African Americans who continued to be guided by the nonviolent philosophy of Martin Luther King, Jr., had found the nationalists' rhetoric unnecessarily divisive; their separatist agenda an escapist fantasy. Many potential nonwhite allies considered the black pluralists' speeches to be just as incendiary. Black women on the verge of initiating their own liberation movement resented the male militants' chauvinism and their monopoly on decision making. Throughout the era, ideological sectarianism and intragroup rivalries hindered the ability of even the most charismatic leaders to gain the trust of more than a limited constituency.

Nevertheless, this idealistic, confrontational generation's work on behalf of minority group liberation was not in vain. Its legacy is secure. During the final decades of the century, both the positive and negative experiences of Black Power militants informed the organizational efforts of other ethnic- and gender-based rights advocates throughout California and across the nation. Internationally, their group empowerment model was utilized by South Africans working to create a Black Consciousness movement that would speed the demise of apartheid. It was also employed to mobilize support for a Black Power movement in Trinidad and a Black Soul movement in Brazil.

Hoping to take the freedom struggle to its next stage, New Millennial inheritors of the protest tradition have taken prominent roles in efforts to win federal reparations payments for the descendants of slaves, to free black "political prisoners," and to abolish the death penalty. Others wage less widely reported local crusades against economic and social injustice, organize festive Kwanzaa celebrations at year's end, or infuse their hip-hop lyrics with "nation-conscious" messages.

ARTICLE. *17 Chain Stores Picketed by Sympathizers of Negro Sit-downs* (1960)

In 1960, picketing by West Coast supporters of nonviolent direct action initiatives in the South received much newspaper coverage.

Seventeen Los Angeles Woolworth and Kress stores were picketed yesterday by local sympathizers with the lunch counter sitdown demonstrations by southern Negro students. The Los Angeles pickets included white and Negro students, both men and women, from UCLA, SC, Los Angeles City College and Los Angeles State College. They marched up and down in front of the stores carrying signs reading "Kress—Stop Supporting Segregation," "We Protest Woolworth's Southern Policy," "Did They Die in Vain at Gettysburg?" and "Woolworth's—Let My People Eat." Few persons paid any attention to the lines. Most of the stores were crowded with shoppers. . . .

Picketing at four stores—Kress at 621 S Broadway and Woolworth's at 719 S Broadway, 656 S Alvarado St. and 7124 Sunset Blvd.—was done by men and women who identified themselves as members of the Independent Student Union. . . . [Picket captain Danny Benson said] it is made up of students who "want to express their opinions through action" and that "we are going to keep the picketing up until we get some reaction from the board (of directors of Kress) in New York." He said the student group is endorsed by the National Association for the Advancement of Colored People, the Congress of Racial Equality and the Jewish Labor Committee. . . .

The pickets handed out circulars reading in part: "Kress and Woolworth are two of the large chain stores which practice discrimination in the South. Our refusal to patronize these stores in areas outside the South will serve to impress upon owners of the stores the fact that this practice must end."

Source: Los Angeles Times, March 27, 1960.

In connection with the picketing, the Jewish Labor Committee, 590 N Vermont Ave., issued a statement saying, "The JLC will provide manpower for the swelling sympathy protest movement in Los Angeles, and other forms of support."

EDITORIAL. *Wrong Tactic for Los Angeles* (1960)

In this editorial, one of California's largest newspapers reacted strongly to the idea that the West Coast also needed civil rights change.

California has the third largest Negro population among states outside of the South and Los Angeles has the third largest Negro population among all the cities in the United States, North and South. The Negroes constitute 12% of the population within the Los Angeles city limits.

But Los Angeles has not had a serious Negro "problem." There have been no polling place difficulties, no commercial discriminations great enough to attract public notice, and certainly no school controversies. Negroes' civil rights are not challenged here and their economic condition improves through their own efforts. . . .

This being the historical case, one wonders why the National Assn. for the Advancement of Colored People should attempt to change the trend. . . . To [demonstrate] in the South takes courage. But to demonstrate in the Los Angeles metropolitan area for a cause that does not exist here is not courageous, it is simply foolish. Tactically it is very bad. It is improbable that such demonstrations will stir up angry racial animosities here; Los Angeles is too sophisticated, too cosmopolitan and too prosperous for them.

But the tactic can injure goodwill and corrode tolerance. It can inject racial consciousness into situations where it does not exist. . . .

LETTERS TO THE EDITOR. *Student Picketing Debated* (1960)

Los Angeles residents had mixed reactions to west coast student's support of southern civil rights activism.

. . . . It is not hard to begin to believe that a movement is afoot to drive a wedge between the white and colored residents of this area. The professional agitators who are pushing the demonstrations in this area are doing a disservice to the minority groups in this area and they insult the hard-working people of all races who are trying to promote peace and harmony for all.

N. A. ROBERTS, La Canada.

It is evident that the editors of your newspaper have never felt the pangs of discrimination or segregation or else they wouldn't be so apt to take issue with any group (National Assn. for the Advancement of Colored People) that attempts to champion

Source: Los Angeles Times, March 26, 1960.
Source: Los Angeles Times, March 30, 1960.

the cause of minorities. When there is no longer segregation or discrimination in any form, not only in Los Angeles but all over the United States, then I, too, will think like the editors and take issue with the NAACP.

JAMES DOBBINS, Los Angeles.

ALISTAIR COOKE, *Causes Sought as Watts Smoulders* (1965)

BBC commentator Alistair Cooke's account of the 1965 Watts rebellion reveals the difficulty "outsiders" had in fathoming the nature and extent of black discontent.

Today Watts, one of the eighty or hundred small towns that interlock across the beach meadows, the mountains, and inland valleys of Southern California to form the weird urban complex known as Los Angeles, was said to be becalmed or cowed or smouldering, according to the colour and temperament of one's informant. . . .

In the sooty pall of uncounted fires and the rubble of a thousand looted stores, the Californians are, in their energetic fashion, calling in their heads of police, their Governor and his cabinet, their State senate, their sociologists (in a city whose university school of sociology is especially distinguished) to find out how it happened and why.

It is very early to isolate first causes or assign blame, but there has been no foot-dragging among resident Civil Rights spokesmen; institutional psychiatrists and liberals, who overnight have put together these "reasons" for the explosion of a routine drunken driving charge into the most mindless orgy of race-rioting that has happened in this country since the second world war, or in California since the anti-Chinese riots of the last century.

Watts has the lowest per capita income of any part of Los Angeles except its downtown "Skid Row" section for chronic drunks. Its population is 90 per cent Negro. Its crime rate is the highest of the Los Angeles' suburbs: it had a record of close to 200 murders, rapes and felonious assaults, and 800 other crimes in the last three months. Unemployment is if anything, worse tha[n] the usual Negro rate. The school drop-outs are about normal for a Negro community. These statistics are, however, hardly explanations. They are parallel or chronic facts about an undiagnosed disease which, in the past four days, flared into an acute attack . . .

Sometime around eight o'clock in the evening a highway policeman saw a car wobbling and weaving along a Watts boulevard. He waved it down and gave the driver a sobriety test while twenty or thirty people looked on. The first essential fact is that the policeman was white and the drunk was a Negro. (Four of the seven looting orgies of 1964's "long hot summer" started with this unfortunate fact, for wherever a white policeman arrests a Negro in the United States with coloured people looking on, the chance of a shambles are acute.)

Source: Guardian, August 15, 1965.

There was no trouble until the mother of the 21-year-old driver came on the scene, upbraided him and goaded him not into shame but into rage, which he then turned on the cop. A bigger crowd was gathering now and the cop asked, or radioed, for help. He meanwhile drew his gun.

The young Negro let off a howl of defiance, the mother jumped the policeman, and there was a scuffle of onlookers. Many of whom—a Negro resident remarked later—were from out of town. The policeman got his help, and the mother and son were taken to the station house.

At what is usually a welcome moment, when the tension sags and the crowd breaks up grumbling or cackling, the crowd was excited by rumours of "police brutality" and suddenly consolidated into an army carrying stones and bottles and some guns. Its original protagonists had gone, so the first targets of its rage were the city buses and the shop windows of stores both white and coloured, and protesters of any colour. Eighty policemen were sent in to try and confine the uproar to the few blocks where it had all started. . . .

. . . it is a bitter, and perhaps hopeless, irony of the Watts episode that it should have happened at the end of a decade which did more for the American Negro tha[n] the three hundred years that went before, and at the end of one year that did more for him than that after that decade, and only a few days after the President signed the historic Federal Voting Rights Act of 1965.

It is a great and liberating law, but it can only liberate the next generation . . .

M. RON KARENGA, *Kwanzaa: Concepts and Functions* (1979)

In this 1979 article written for a college-student audience, US Organization founder Maulana Karenga explains the origin and purpose of the Kwanzaa holiday; its chief symbols and underlying value system.

. . . As a holiday, Kwanzaa grew out of the general context of the Afro-American people's turn toward Africa for roots and revitalization during the 60's and out of the specific context of US Organization, a social change organization which was a fountainhead and vanguard of the cultural nationalist movement at that time. Thus, it was part of the "Back to Black" movement, the movement back toward our African selves which included the Natural, African dress, names and marriage ceremonies and Black or African Studies—Continental and Diasporan.

As founder and national chairman of US, I argued then and continue to argue that the key crisis in Black life is the crisis of ideology and values, the crisis of culture—i.e., the critical lack of a coherent system of views and values that would give us, as a people, a moral, material and meaningful interpretation to life, as well

---

Source: Black Collegian, December–January 1979–1980.

as demand an allegiance and practice which would insure our liberation and a higher level of human life. . . . Until the oppressor's monopoly on our minds is broken and we acquire new values and new views of self, society and the world, liberation is impossible, and by definition, unthinkable. . . .

The idea of Kwanzaa comes from the harvest celebrations in traditional African societies, but the symbols and concepts come from our needs, conditions and development as Afro-American people. . . . The seven basic symbols are:

1. mazao (crops) symbolic of the traditional harvest celebrations and of the rewards of productive and collective labor;
2. mkeka (mat) symbolic of our tradition and history and thus, the foundation on which we build;
3. kinara (candleholder) symbolic of our roots, our parent people, i.e., Continental Africans;
4. vibunzi (ears of corn) symbolic of our children and thus, our future which they embody;
5. zawadi (gifts) symbolic of the labor and love of parents and the commitments made and kept by the children;
6. kikombe cha umoja (unity cup) symbolic of the foundational principle and practice of unity which makes all else possible; and
7. mishumaa saba (the seven candles) symbolic of the Nguzo Saba (The Seven Principles), the matrix and minimum set of values by which Black people must live in order to rescue and reconstruct their lives in their own image, and according to their own needs.

The two supplementary symbols are: 1) the bendera (flag), the Black, Red and Green colors Marcus Garvey gave us as national colors—Black for our people, Red for struggle and Green for our hopes and youth who are our hope; and 2) a copy of the Nguzo Saba (The Seven Principles). The Nguzo Saba are: 1) Umoja (Unity); 2) Kujichagulia (Self-determination); (3) Ujima (Collective Work and Responsibility); 4) Ujamaa (Cooperative Economics); 5) Nia (Purposes); 6) Kuumba (Creativity); and 7) Imani (Faith).

The Nguzo Saba are posed here as the necessary core and moral minimum of any value system constructed to rescue and reconstruct our lives in our own image and interests. . . .

Kwanzaa serves five basic socio-political functions.

First, it is a practical expression of Black consciousness and commitment to themselves, their history and future . . .

Secondly, Kwanzaa is an annual formal reaffirmation of Black people's commitment to self-determination . . . a statement to ourselves, society and the world that we will define and speak for ourselves, instead of being defined and spoken for by others. . . .

Thirdly, Kwanzaa is a means of introducing core values which reinforce and reflect the bonds between us . . .

Fourthly, Kwanzaa is a model of self-determination and creativity which other Blacks can and should emulate. . . .

Finally, Kwanzaa is a life-experience, not just a seven-day observance.

Therefore, during Kwanzaa, we remember our past, reassess our thought and practice and recommit ourselves to values and practice which will insure our liberation and a high level of human life.

ELDRIDGE CLEAVER, *On Meeting the Needs of the People* (1969)

Written from exile in Algiers—where he had fled rather than be imprisoned on charges stemming from a 1968 shoot-out with Oakland police—Eldridge Cleaver's essay highlights the Black Panther Party's anti-capitalist and community-centered service orientation.

Back during the days when I was still running around in Babylon talking crazy about the pigs, if anyone had told me that someday I'd find myself in this exile situation trying to send a message back about the Black Panther Party's Breakfast for Children program and the white radicals of Berkeley with their People's Park, I probably would have taken it as a put-down. But it's all for real, and what is more I find myself very enthusiastic about these developments.

Both of these actions expose the contradiction between the pretenses of the system and the needs of the people. They stand as an assertion that the pigs of the power structure are not fulfilling their duties and that the people are moving, directly, to fill their own needs and redress their grievances. . . .

Breakfast for Children and the People's Park are qualitatively different types of actions from anything we have been into in the past. They represent a move from theory to practice and implementation. . . . We recognize that the Breakfast for Children program and the People's Park are authentic and accurate responses to the situations of black people and white people in Babylon.

Breakfast for Children pulls people out of the system and organizes them into an alternative. . . . The Panther program liberates [black children], frees them from that aspect of their poverty. This is liberation in practice. In the white mother country where class struggle is the appropriate tactic and expropriation of the expropriators the proper means to revolution, the act of seizing that land and establishing a People's Park could not have been more to the point. . . .

Many people think of revolution only as overt violence—as guns shooting and conflagrations, as flames leaping into the air, bodies in the streets and the uprising masses storming city hall. This is only one phase of the revolutionary process, and the violence is not an end in itself but only the means through which the necessary power is seized so that the rearrangements in the system can be carried out. It is the

Source: Ramparts, September 1969.

means for expropriating the land, the natural resources, the machines, all the means of production, the institutions of society—for taking them out of the control, out of the hands of those who now have them and who have abused them, who have perverted these things and have converted them into instruments with which to pursue their own private gain at the expense of the wider public good. . . .

. . . There will be a new day in Babylon, there will be a housecleaning in Babylon, and we can halt the machinery of oppression, purge our institutions of racism, and put the oppressors up against the wall—or maybe more appropriately, up against the fence that they have built around the People's Park.

POWER TO THE PEOPLE!

6

Animal Rights Activism

—Susan J. Pearson

Twenty-first century scholars and activists do not agree about when the "animal rights" movement began. As with so much else, the answer depends on how you define the terms. Like participants in other social movements, animal advocates are divided by philosophy, goals, and tactics. Many scholars of the movement, and many animal rights activists themselves, claim that animal advocacy before the 1960s and 1970s was characterized by a welfare-based rather than a rights-based philosophy. The distinction between welfare and rights is the difference between reform and abolition. Animal welfare advocates want to insure that animals' lives are as free of pain and suffering as possible; they want to reform the ways that humans use and interact with animals. Animal rights advocates, on the other hand, question the very assumptions and institutions that foster humans' instrumental use of animals and want to abolish, rather than reform, those practices. And while advocacy on behalf of animals did not begin in the 1960s and 1970s, these decades did witness the emergence of an explicit animal rights philosophy, new organizations dedicated to pursuing abolitionist goals, and a more direct and confrontational style of activism.

Organized animal protection in the United States began in the nineteenth century just after the end of the Civil War. Inspired by the activities of British men and women who had founded the Royal Society for the Prevention of Cruelty to Animals (SPCA) in 1824, a wealthy New Yorker named Henry Bergh founded the American SPCA (ASPCA) in 1866. The movement quickly took hold in the traditional centers of reform in the Northeast and eventually spread to all regions of the country. By 1908, over 350 SPCAs and Humane Societies had been formed across the nation. In 1877, the American Humane Association, a confederate body of state and local SPCAs, was created to coordinate anti-cruelty activity across state lines.

Like its British predecessor, the first American SPCAs defined cruelty as behavior that caused "unnecessary suffering" in animals and their tactics included securing new legislation, prosecuting individuals for cruel behavior, and conducting public education to increase humane sentiment. From their beginning in 1866 through the end of World War II, most American SPCAs and the AHA pursued a wide-ranging agenda. They tried to mitigate labor conditions for the nation's working animals, to restrict the use of feathers and fur in fashion through legislation and consumer boycotts, to regulate the interstate transportation of livestock, and to convince meatpackers to slaughter food animals painlessly. Anti-cruelty reformers also undertook positive initiatives: the creation of ambulances and clinics for animals, humane education for children, and the establishment of the nation's first animal shelters. In general, these early efforts sought to make human's instrumental use of animals less painful. Though these reformers sometimes claimed that animals had rights, they did not generally challenge the assumption that humans were superior to animals and therefore entitled to use nonhumans instrumentally for a variety of purposes.

Though SPCA and Humane Society reformers before World War II agreed on most of this broad agenda, as early as the late nineteenth century, the issue of vivisection—experimentation on live animals—began to divide them. Where the largest and oldest SPCAs and the AHA wanted vivisection regulated to insure that it was performed by professionals on anesthetized animals, more radical activists began to argue that the practice should be abolished altogether. Disenchanted with what they saw as the conservatism of the mainstream animal protection organizations, anti-vivisectionists began to form single-issue splinter groups. The American Anti-Vivisection Society was founded in 1883 by Philadelphian Caroline Earle White, a woman already highly active and influential in Pennsylvania's animal protection circles, and in 1895, a group of Bostonians founded the New England Anti-Vivisection Society. These groups more aggressively campaigned on the local, state, and national level for legislation to both regulate and restrict animal experimentation.

Though most of the anti-vivisectionist's legislative campaigns went down to defeat, the early movement is important both because it aroused significant, organized opposition among the medical and scientific community and because it presaged some of the philosophical and tactical characteristics that would crystallize in the postwar animal rights movement. For it was the issue of animal experimentation that provided one of the catalysts for the formation of more outspoken splinter groups in the years following World War II. Distraught over the mainstream animal protection movement's accommodation with scientific and corporate interests, and in particular its apparent unwillingness to directly combat cruelty in experimentation and slaughter, dissident groups began to emerge in the 1950s. In 1951, Christine Stevens formed the Animal Welfare Institute (AWI) and in 1954 disillusioned staff members left the AHA to form the Humane Society of the United States (HSUS). Other defectors from the old-line organizations formed Friends of Animals and the International Society for Animal Rights, both in 1957. And while most of these new groups did not expound what would today be called an "animal rights" philosophy, their emergence represented the beginning of a less quiescent era in animal advocacy.

Frustration with the conservatism of the traditional SPCAs and AHA was compounded by the more intensive instrumental use of animals. Supported by a one-hundred-fold increase in federal grant monies between 1944 and 1963, scientific research blossomed following World War II, and the demand for animals to supply laboratories proceeded apace. At the same time, the centralization of farming operations led not only to increased meat production, but also to modern "factory farming" in which animals' lives and mobility were severely restricted. Eager to confront the entrenched and institutionalized abuse of animals, these new organizations, led by the AWI and HSUS, quickly pursued national legislation to regulate animal slaughter and vivisection. In 1958, they successfully shepherded the Humane Slaughter Act through Congress. For the first time, national legislation now required that all animals (except those butchered using kosher methods) be rendered insensible, either through anesthesia or mechanical stunning, before slaughter.

Regulation of animal experimentation was next on the agenda. Since the nineteenth century, anti-vivisectionists had fought against the seizure of impounded animals by laboratories, but by the 1950s, the ASPCA was funneling unwanted pound animals to researchers. Distraught that animal shelters might be forced to supply homeless animals to researchers, anti-vivisectionists had long held out the specter of the lost family dog or cat, impounded and unclaimed, subjected to a slow and painful death at the hands of a scientist. In 1966, AWI, the HSUS, and their allies were successful in convincing Congress to enact the Laboratory Animal Welfare Act (AWA), which regulated the sale, transport, and housing of animals used in experiments. The bill was the result not only of hard-fought lobbying, but also of national media spectacles. In 1965, the Lakavage family of Pennsylvania lost their family dog, a Dalmatian named Pepper, only to discover that she had been obtained by a dealer who sold animals to research labs and had died after being experimented on in the laboratory of a New York hospital. In 1966, activists from AWI convinced *Life* magazine to do a photo essay on the trade in animals for research. Titled, "Concentration Camps for Dogs," the essay was a gruesome look behind the scenes that helped mobilize public opinion in favor of the pending legislation. For the first time in over 50 years, the medical and scientific community was on the defensive.

Though it had roots in the 1950s, the emergence of a more vocal and more confrontational brand of animal welfare organization dovetailed with the protest activities and countercultural milieu of the late 1960s and 1970s. Many of the values promoted by civil rights, anti-war, feminist, and environmental activists also supported the growth of a more coherent animal rights philosophy. As many protesters situated their activism within a more general critique of mainstream American values, they articulated concerns that echoed with animal advocacy. Feminists and civil rights activists challenged traditional social hierarchies, exposing the roots of inequality as conventional rather than natural and couching their claims for equality in the language of liberation and rights. Anti-war activists and environmentalists questioned the dominance of a capitalist, technocratic, and consumerist ethos that valued efficiency, profit, and fleeting self-satisfaction above all else. Civil rights protestors and environmental groups like Greenpeace also crafted a style of activism centered not only on traditional methods of public education and legislative change, but also on dramatic, public confrontations, civil disobedience, and other forms of direct action. In this climate, animal advocates began to explicitly challenge the assumption of human superiority, the use of animals as raw material, and they began to refine their language and tactics.

The burgeoning American animal rights movement was also profoundly influenced by organizations and philosophies from across the Atlantic. In 1963, radical British activists formed the Hunt Saboteurs, and in 1972, the Animal Liberation Front (ALF). Both groups spoke explicitly of defending animal rights, and both were dedicated to spectacular displays of direct action. In 1971, British psychologist Richard Ryder coined the term "speciesism" to describe prejudice against animals as similar to that against women and minorities. The term was made famous, however, by another philosopher, Peter Singer, who would become a highly influential figure in the new animal rights movement. In a widely read essay in the 1973 *New York Review of Books*, and then in his landmark 1975 book, *Animal Liberation*, the Australian-born and British-educated Singer introduced the wider public to the concept of "speciesism" and to an argument for treating animals with equal ethical consideration. Singer explicitly drew parallels between the treatment of animals and the treatment of women and African Americans. Like racism and sexism, Singer claimed that speciesism was a form of irrational prejudice that blinded humans to both the true nature of animals and the proper grounding of ethics. Singer argued that sentience, or the ability to feel pain, was the basis of moral consideration and that because sentience clearly crossed the species barrier, so too should ethical consideration. Reflecting the concerns and activities of dissident animal advocates since the 1950s, Singer's brief against human treatment of animals centered on factory farming and vivisection. *Animal Liberation* thus connected animal rights to contemporary human, liberation movements, provided a philosophical argument for a more radical form of animal activism, and it graphically detailed the inhumane treatment of animals in ways that moved many to action.

Though the splinter groups of the 1950s and the changing consciousness of the 1960s made modern animal rights possible, the movement's ranks did not begin to swell until the 1970s and 1980s. Inspired by the arguments of *Animal Liberation* and the tactics of direct action, New York activist Henry Spira helped to launch a new generation of American animal rights activists. Formerly involved in labor and civil rights organizing, Spira founded Animal Rights International (ARI) in 1974 and in 1976, he organized a campaign to target federally funded experiments conducted on cats at New York City's Museum of National History. Spira published accounts of the experiments in the local press and organized pickets outside the Museum for 18 months. Eventually, the campaign was successful: the Museum stopped its experiments and shut down its laboratory altogether. During the 1980s, Spira and ARI went on to coordinate a number of successful campaigns against the use of animals to test cosmetic safety.

Just as the 1970s was a period of growing militancy among anti-war, feminist, and anti-racisist activists, so too the decade witnessed the birth of more brash, direct, and radical forms of American animal rights activism. During the late 1970s, an American branch of the radical ALF also conducted its first direct actions: they freed two porpoises from a research center in Hawaii and released five animals from a New York University laboratory. Throughout the 1980s, American ALF activists continued to conduct high-profile raids of laboratories in which they both freed animals and videotaped the often-squalid conditions in which such animals had been held. Though ALF represents an extreme, and highly controversial, faction of the animal rights movement that many animal advocates are quick to disavow, their actions illustrate how a new generation of activists asked not simply that animals be used painlessly, but that instrumentalism be abolished altogether. It is difficult to assess the legacy of this more militant form of activism and the animal rights philosophy behind it. The number of animals used in laboratory testing, for example, has gone down dramatically since its height in the 1970s. On the one hand, much of this is probably attributable to the work of the more mainstream "welfare" organizations, which continued to lobby for amendments to the AWA and to seek congressional funding for alternatives to animal experimentation. On the other hand, it is also likely that many researchers and institutions themselves sought to develop such alternatives precisely because of the negative publicity, not to say danger, that the use of animals in laboratory experiments might bring.

Though ARI still exists and ALF continues to perform occasional direct actions, it is People for the Ethical Treatment of Animals (PETA), founded in 1980, that has come to represent the face of the modern animal rights movement. HSUS, meanwhile, has become the largest animal protection organization in the country and though it is active in the areas of animal experimentation and factory farming, unlike PETA and other rights-based groups, it seeks the reform rather than the abolition of these practices. And while the distinction between "welfare" and "rights" based animal advocacy is important both philosophically and historically, there are important continuities between the two. Historically, the animal rights movement grew out of and built upon a 100-year legacy of animal protection activity that had helped to make compassion toward, if not rights for, animals into a commonplace sentiment. And many of the issues that first attracted the attention of nineteenth-century animal protectionists—animal experimentation, the care and handling of food animals in life and death, and the management of stray animals—continue to top the agenda of all animal advocates.

CAROL OPPENHEIM, *Cat Lovers Pounce on Lab Research* (1977)

Beginning in the mid-1970s, New York activist Henry Spira helped to launch a new generation of American animal rights activists. Formerly involved in labor and civil rights organizing, in 1976 he organized a campaign to target federally funded experiments conducted on cats at New York City's Museum of National History. Like the earlier activists who helped insure the passage of the AWA, Spira and his allies similarly focused public attention on animal suffering; but unlike earlier activists, they asked for an end to, rather than a regulation of, experimentation on animals.

Source: Chicago Tribune Press Service, May 15, 1977.

NEW YORK-Twenty alley cats, appearing healthy and well fed, clambered about their cages or, extended paws in bids for affection, just like in a pet shop. Or maybe an animal shelter. But they tire in a laboratory for a federally funded research project on the sexual behavior cats. And they're the subject of a raging controversy between animal welfare advocates and the American Museum of Natural History.

The cat lovers charge that the museum is "surgically mutilating" the animals and subjecting them to "useless, nonproductive, repetitive torture that gives science a bad name and adds nothing whatever of value to the sum of human knowledge." Museum officials say the charges are "grossly misleading or groundless" and that the research project "conforms to every required standard of animal care and welfare of relevance and significance."

THE RESEARCH PROJECT has been going on for 16 years, but animal lovers found out about it only 18 months ago. Since then, the museum has been the target of weekly picketing by groups ranging from 20 to 600 and scathing newspaper ads casting as much as $9,600.

One of the protest leaders is Henry Spira, a high school English teacher who has foresworn meat and leather and keeps two cats in his tiny apartment five blocks from the museum.

Using the Freedom of Information Act, Spira last year got copies of the museum's applications for funds from the National Institute of Child Health and Human Development. These proposals, which persuaded NICHD to provide $100,000, graphically described how the experiments would be conducted.

Specifically, the researchers proposed to blind the cats; deafen them; destroy their sense of smell; damage their brains: sever nerves in their penises; cut off their testicles; and eliminate skin sensation in the chest, stomach, and pelvic areas.

The NICHD has renewed the grant three times based on progress reports, the latest of which showed that brain damage caused cats to choose improper sexual partners such as rabbits and dogs.

Dr. Lester R. Aronson, director of the project, has published numerous scientific papers on his cats' sex lives. The Science Information Exchange, the definitive research index, cites less than half of them as worthy of reading.

ARONSON REFUSED to be interviewed. Robert Stolberg, a scientific assistant in the museum's department of animal behavior who is responsible for the cats' care, said, "We have never touched an animal's eyes or ears. We have no horror chamber and no sound-proof room to mask their supposed scream. . . . We do introduce an electrode into the cat's brain which forms a puncture wound, and we do alter the central nervous system to mediate sexual response."

Stolberg permitted a reporter to inspect the cats used in the experiment and all appeared to hear and see. The protesters, none of whom have been in the lab, admit they have no evidence cats were blinded and deafened.

Yet, despite the museum's contention the animals are anestheticized during, surgery and given careful postoperative care, the protestors believe the cats suffer.

"CATS CAN'T DO math or fill out income tax forms, but they have the same emotions and the same nervous system as humans," Spira said.

Pegeen Fitzgerald, a local radio personality with a reputation for championing vegetarian and animal welfare causes, reported she purchased a duplicate of the device the museum uses to hold the cats' heads while surgery is performed.

"There is absolutely no way of putting a cat on that device without breaking his eardrums which, of course, deafens him," she said.

The museum refused to allow an inspection of its restraining device, but Stolberg said it does not cause injury. He said a photo of a cat imprisoned in a device, used in the protesters' newspaper ads, is "completely unlike" the museum's.

Mrs. Fitzgerald, who signed the ad, said the photo came from a sales catalog, "When you read the descriptions of these devices, it's hair-raising. It's just cruel to hang a cat up that way."

When the researchers first began submitting applications for federal funds, they described the significance of their research as "a new approach to the study of factors influencing the decline of sexual behavior after castration."

The researchers later said the experiments "should contribute in major ways to the eventual solution" of the "urgent clinical problems" of hypersexuality and hyposexuality.

THE CATS ARE observed while mating and later are terminated or sacrificed—two euphemisms for killed—so that surgically induced brain lesions can be studied for clues to their behavior. The protestors estimate at least 350 cats have undergone autopsies.

Museum officials, in separate statements, seem at odds as to whether this research will benefit humans.

Dr. Thomas D. Nicholson, museum director, said the project will provide basic knowledge for such human problems as sexual disorders, impotence, frigidity, infertility, and overpopulation.

Carol Patterson, the museum's spokes-woman, at one point said the studies will aid research into rape, but at another point denied this same statement. She finally said the project is "basic research to find knowledge rather than applied research which is goal-oriented."

Mrs. Fitzgerald questioned how scientists can make a valid comparison between human behavior and cats "who spent their lives in cramped cages in an artificial environment of—alternating boredom and terror."

NEW YORK TIMES, *Your Money Is Paying for Torture at the American Museum of Natural History* (1976)

Kittens and cats, like these, are blinded and maimed and then studied for sexual performance at the American Museum of Natural History. YOUR PROTEST, ON OCT. 2nd, CAN STOP IT. . . .

Source: New York Times, September 30, 1976.

Without our knowledge or consent, Congress has been paying for cat sex mutilations during the past 20 years. . . . The cat experiments, once secret, have gained national media attention . . . Dr. William Sadler, chief of the National Institutes of Health office responsible for the Museum's experiments, admitted that protests and inquiries had brought his office to a standstill. New York's senators are receiving more Museum protest mail than on any issue since Watergate. And Congressman Mario Biaggi has called for a congressional hearing.

The Museum's cat sex experiment is becoming a test case focusing on the multibillion dollar medieval research establishment. This is a double ripoff. Congress wasting our dollars on absurd make work projects. And, creating, against our moral convictions, a living hell for animals. We need effective clinical research projects using modern technology. We favor science, not cruelty; innovation, not barbarism.

PETER SINGER, *Equality for Animals?* (1979)

Peter Singer's Animal Liberation (1975) was a manifesto for the new generation of animal rights activists. Building on contemporary interest in women's and civil rights, Singer argued that speciesism—prejudice against animals—was no more defensible than racism or sexism. The capacity to suffer, which crosses species lines, Singer claimed, should be the basis for moral consideration.

I shall suggest that, having accepted the principle of equality as a sound moral basis for relations with others of our own species, we are also committed to accepting it as a sound moral basis for relations with those outside our own species—the nonhuman animals.

This suggestion may at first seem bizarre. We are used to regarding the oppression of blacks and women as among the most important moral and political issues facing the world today. These are serious matters, worthy of the time and energy of any concerned person. But animals? Surely the welfare of animals is in a different category altogether, a matter for old ladies in tennis shoes to worry about. How can anyone waste their time on equality for animals when so many humans are denied real equality?

This attitude reflects a popular prejudice against taking the interests of animals seriously—a prejudice no better founded than the prejudice of white slaveowners against taking the interests of blacks seriously. It is easy for us to criticize the prejudices of our grandfathers, from which our fathers freed themselves . . . What is needed now is a willingness to follow the arguments where they lead, without a prior assumption that the issue is not worth attending to. . . .

. . . If a being suffers, there can be no moral justification for refusing to take that suffering into consideration. No matter what the nature of the being, the principle of

---

Source: Chapter excerpted from *Practical Ethics*, Cambridge, 1979, http://www.utilitarian.net/singer/by/1979—.htm.

equality requires that its suffering be counted equally with the like suffering—in so far as rough comparisons can be made—of any other being. . . . A simpler case may help to make this clear.

If I give a horse a hard slap across its rump with my open hand, the horse may start, but it presumably feels little pain. Its skin is thick enough to protect it against a mere slap. If I slap a baby in the same way, however, the baby will cry and presumably does feel pain, for its skin is more sensitive. So it is worse to slap a baby than a horse, if both slaps are administered with equal force. But there must be some kind of blow—I don't know exactly what it would be, but perhaps a blow with a heavy stick—that would cause the horse as much pain as we cause a baby by slapping it with our hand. That is what I mean by 'the same amount of pain' and if we consider it wrong to inflict that much pain on a baby for no good reason then we must, unless we are speciesists, consider it equally wrong to inflict the same amount of pain on a horse for no good reason.

There are other differences between humans and animals that cause other complications. Normal adult human beings have mental capacities which will, in certain circumstances, lead them to suffer more than animals would in the same circumstances. If, for instance, we decided to perform extremely painful or lethal scientific experiments on normal adult humans, kidnapped at random from public parks for this purpose, adults who entered parks would become fearful that they would be kidnapped. The resultant terror would be a form of suffering additional to the pain of the experiment. The same experiments performed on nonhuman animals would cause less suffering since the animals would not have the anticipatory dread of being kidnapped and experimented upon. This does not mean, of course, that it would be right to perform the experiment on animals, but only that there is a reason, which is not speciesist, for preferring to use animals rather than normal adult humans, if the experiment is to be done at all. It should be noted, however, that this same argument gives us a reason for preferring to use human infants—orphans perhaps—or retarded humans for experiments, rather than adults, since infants and retarded humans would also have no idea of what was going to happen to them. . . . if we use this argument to justify experiments on nonhuman animals we have to ask ourselves whether we are also prepared to allow experiments on human infants and retarded adults.

U.S. SENATE, EIGHTY-NINTH CONGRESS, *Animal Dealer Regulation Hearings Before Committee on Commerce* (1966)

In 1966, Congress passed the Laboratory Animal Welfare Act (AWA) to regulate the sale and conditions of animals used in federally funded research labs. The legislation was the result of a hard-fought campaign by members of the HSUS and allied organizations. In newspaper reports,

---

Source: U.S. Senate, Committee on Commerce. *Animal Dealer Regulation Hearings.* Government Printing Office: Washington, DC, 1966.

magazine articles, and in testimony before congress, activists brought the issue of animal suffering and animal testing before the public eye, where it would remain for several decades.

Statement of Declan Hogan, Special Agent, The Humane Society of the United States:

My name is Declan Hogan, and for the past 6 months I have been working as an undercover agent with the Humane Society of the United States, with the specific purpose of gathering information on a nationwide basis of the supplying of dogs, cats, and other animals to research institutions.

In the past I have owned and operated several fashionable night clubs here in Georgetown. I have never been a humanitarian or will I ever dedicate my life to humane work. But after what I have seen after posing as a dog dealer I fully understand why dedicated humanitarians exist.

I spent a week studying reports of HSUS investigations of dog dealers. I couldn't visualize anything like the treatment of animals I was reading about and was pretty well convinced some of these emotional people were surely painting a grim picture.

I was given a 1954 Chevy pickup truck made over in the kind of unassuming manner dog dealers use in buying dogs. In subsequent months, I traveled more than 32,000 miles covering some 15 States. I saw all kinds of dealer operations, with animals bound for research suffering under the most appalling conditions. I was particularly shocked at the scope and magnitude of the business, and the unscrupulous methods of procuring and handling that are commonplace.

Senator, I could talk for an hour and a half on cruelty I've seen which is thoroughly unanimous with all dog dealers. . . . During the six month period that I worked as an undercover agent for the dealer, that at least half of the animals sent to research institutions are stolen [and] I saw thousands of animals suffering cruelly throughout the chain of supply to research institutions. At every level of operation—from the small, grassroots dealer handling just a few dogs to the big supplier of huge quantities of all species—I observed conditions hideous enough to stagger the imagination. I saw starving dogs fight bloodily over a little bread thrown among them. I saw cats infected with enteritis lying unheeded in their own feces. I saw piles of dead animals on dog farms, some of the bodies decomposing while surviving dogs scavengered for food among-them. . . . I witnessed cannibalism among animals and dogs rooting for water in scum-coated containers that were long neglected. I saw dogs and cats transported, jammed tightly in makeshift panel trucks with no food, water, or rest throughout trips lasting as long as 48 hours.

I found this cruelty and abuse at practically every laboratory *animal* supplier I investigated and I learned, from talking with dealers, that such conditions are commonplace across the country. . . . Many dealers know they are buying stolen pets but do so because of the great demand and because these animals bring higher prices. . . . Dealers can buy dogs for $2 to $4 and resell them to laboratories for $15 to $30. Individual animals are seldom held over a week and the dealer thus has constant demand for more and more animals.

Statement of Helen Jones, President, The National Catholic Society for Animal Welfare, Washington, DC:

Photographs and word pictures cannot begin to describe the suffering of the animals in the auctions. One must be there to see and to hear. There is thirst, aggravated by fear, and hunger—and the absence of food and water—as terrified animals are carried or dragged into the auction place. . . . There is the transfer of animals from crate to crate by means of a choke collar attached to a pole. There is the chant of the auctioneer as he asks what he is offered for a crate of puppies, rabbits, cats, dogs, kittens, guinea pigs, pigeons, some being sold by the crate, others by body weight, as crate after crate is hoisted or tossed onto the conveyor line. Dogs, some aged, are weaving and drooling from motion sickness from the long trip to the auction. The dealers examine their teeth to determine whether they are too old to be worth bidding on or to survive the trip to the dealers' place and then to the laboratories. . . . And although it is the nature of animals to suffer terror or pain silently, now and then there are the cries of animals that never stop crying out in utter misery and terror.

. . . In commerce in animals, the smallest, the weakest and those that represent the least economic investment fare the worst. That is the case in the sale of animals at auction or by weight to dealers for resale to laboratories. There are those who say that the auction sales of animals for research can be regulated. But misery on such a scale cannot be regulated or made acceptable. It is an affront to public decency.

7

Anti-Nuclear Activism

—LAWRENCE S. WITTNER

The anti-nuclear activism of the 1960s and 1970s had deep roots in the events of the preceding decades. The atomic bombing of Hiroshima and Nagasaki in August 1945 stirred up a furor in the United States and around the world. The public uproar had an ethical dimension, for this mass murder of civilians deeply distressed people with strong moral convictions. In addition, even larger numbers of people believed that the world was heading toward nuclear annihilation. The new *Bulletin of the Atomic Scientists*, with its "doomsday clock" set only minutes before midnight, typified this assumption. As a result, in the late 1940s, a nuclear disarmament movement emerged that brought together pacifists, scientists, and world government advocates. Although this first wave of anti-nuclear activism faded with the advance of the Cold War, it did sensitize the general public to the looming dangers of the nuclear era. In addition, it led the Truman administration to back away from further use of nuclear weapons and to propose plans for nuclear disarmament.

Another wave of anti-nuclear activism began in the mid-1950s, in response to U.S. and Soviet testing of the H-bomb—a weapon a thousand times as powerful as the bomb that had destroyed Hiroshima. Such tests not only highlighted great power preparations for a nuclear war, but created vast clouds of nuclear fallout that irradiated people around the globe. In these circumstances, older groups returned to the anti-nuclear struggle and prominent intellectuals such as Albert Einstein, Bertrand Russell, Albert Schweitzer, and Linus Pauling condemned the nuclear arms race. In 1957, Norman Cousins, a well-known magazine editor, founded the National Committee for a Sane Nuclear Policy (SANE), which quickly grew into the largest and best-known of the disarmament organizations, with some 25,000 members. Although SANE's original aim was to end nuclear testing, it gradually expanded its goals to include nuclear disarmament. Another group founded in 1957, the Committee for Nonviolent Action, brought nonviolent civil disobedience into the anti-nuclear campaign, while the Student Peace Union (SPU), organized in 1959, began rallying college students against the nuclear arms race.

Although the Eisenhower administration came to office committed to the development and use of nuclear weapons, it felt hard-pressed by anti-nuclear activism and the growing public concern about nuclear war. As a result, the administration scuttled nuclear war-fighting plans and, in 1958, reluctantly joined the Soviet and British governments in halting nuclear testing and negotiating for a nuclear test ban treaty.

Thus, by the early 1960s, the anti-nuclear movement was becoming an increasingly visible, influential force in U.S. life. In New York City, young mothers organized a Civil Defense Protest Committee that galvanized such widespread opposition to participation in compulsory civil defense drills that the city (and soon the nation) abandoned them. SANE, though, continued as the movement's flagship. In the spring of 1960, it held an overflow rally of 20,000 people at New York City's Madison Square Garden, where they were addressed by Cousins, Eleanor Roosevelt, and United Auto Workers president Walter Reuther. Drawing widespread public attention through its newspaper ads, SANE produced the best known of them in April 1962. Headlined "Dr. Spock is Worried," it featured a picture of the famed pediatrician looking with grave concern upon a young child.

The Soviet Union's resumption of nuclear testing in the fall of 1961 heightened the popular sense that the nuclear arms race was spiraling out of control. On November 1, a new organization, Women Strike for Peace (WSP), staged women's anti-nuclear protests in 60 American cities with some 50,000 participants. Its signs proclaimed: "End the Arms Race—Not the Human Race." Headed by Dagmar Wilson, a children's book illustrator, WSP played upon its image as a group of simple, middle-class "housewives." In fact, however, its membership—which it claimed numbered 100,000—was well educated and politically sophisticated. Meanwhile, in another effort to block the resumption of U.S. nuclear testing, thousands of students turned out in January 1962 to picket the White House. As the movement escalated, WSP joined SANE and the SPU in staging demonstrations that demanded a nuclear test ban treaty and an end to the nuclear arms race—measures that polls showed had strong support in the broader society.

During the late 1950s and early 1960s, many comparable movements developed abroad, particularly in Western Europe and Asia. These included the Campaign for Nuclear Disarmament (CND) in Britain, Australia, New Zealand, and Canada; the Movement Against Atomic Armaments in France; the Struggle Against Atomic Death in West Germany; and the Japan Council Against Atomic and Hydrogen Bombs. An anti-nuclear emblem, developed in 1958 for the first of British CND's massive Aldermaston marches, quickly spread around the world as a symbol of disarmament and world peace.

This flowering of anti-nuclear activism in the United States and abroad had a significant impact upon the administration of John F. Kennedy. When the Soviet Union resumed nuclear testing in the fall of 1961, Kennedy—angered by the action—wanted to resume U.S. atmospheric nuclear testing. But he hesitated to give the order for it, as he feared a popular backlash. Although Kennedy ultimately did order U.S. atmospheric nuclear testing to resume, he delayed such action until April 1962 and proclaimed, at the same time, his determination to secure a test ban treaty.

Symptomatically, the U.S. President commissioned Norman Cousins to serve as his test ban emissary to Soviet Premier Nikita Khrushchev. Shuttling between the two Cold War leaders, Cousins convinced Khrushchev that Kennedy sincerely wanted a treaty and Kennedy that he would have to signal a break with the long record of Soviet–American confrontation. Kennedy provided the signal through his American University address of June 1963, a call for peace partially written by Cousins. The following month, the two nations signed the Partial Test Ban Treaty, the first nuclear arms control agreement in world history.

After Senate ratification of the treaty in the fall of 1963, the anti-nuclear movement dwindled. Although its leaders sought to maintain a high level of popular mobilization, this proved difficult in the face of further government-sponsored nuclear arms control and disarmament measures (including the Nuclear Non-Proliferation Treaty of 1968). Furthermore, anti-nuclear activists were part of the nation's peace constituency, which—particularly after early 1965—became caught up in the struggle against the escalating Vietnam War. SANE, WSP, and other U.S. peace groups threw themselves into the growing anti-war movement and gradually discarded their anti-nuclear focus. Other avant-garde causes of the time—women's liberation, racial equality, anti-imperialism, and ecology—also diverted the attention of activists from the nuclear weapons issue.

Of course, given the ongoing nuclear danger, there were exceptions. In the late 1960s and early 1970s, members of the Federation of American Scientists and the new Union of Concerned Scientists lobbied against the construction of U.S. anti-ballistic missile systems, charging that they would lead to the building of more nuclear missiles by other nations. In 1971, to protest against underground nuclear testing, a small group of American expatriates in Canada founded Greenpeace. The new group spread to the United States and other nations, where it melded environmentalist and nuclear disarmament concerns.

Nevertheless, in the late 1960s and early 1970s the anti-nuclear campaign was largely somnolent. In the United States, nuclear disarmament groups shrank to a fraction of their former selves or disappeared entirely. Much the same phenomenon occurred abroad.

Starting in the mid-1970s, however, a number of factors sparked the movement's revival. The construction and operation of nuclear power plants stirred concerns about their safety; and this, in turn, renewed public fears of nuclear weapons and nuclear war. Furthermore, the end of the Vietnam War freed peace activists to return to their earlier focus upon nuclear weapons. In addition, the Cold War rumbled on. The Soviet government intervened in a number of Third World nations and began the deployment of a new generation of nuclear missiles, the SS-20s. For its part, the U.S. government came forward with plans for emplacement of new nuclear weapons of its own: neutron bombs and cruise and Pershing II missiles. In the midst of these developments, the United Nations—troubled by the continuing nuclear arms race—convened a Special Session on Disarmament, which helped concentrate attention on the nuclear problem.

Against this backdrop, a powerful anti-nuclear campaign again began taking shape. In May 1977, the Clamshell Alliance mobilized thousands of youthful demonstrators to shut down the construction site of the nuclear power plant at

Seabrook, New Hampshire, where 1,400 of them were arrested for staging a nonviolent occupation. This triggered comparable movements and confrontations all across the country. It also contributed to the rapid growth of Mobilization for Survival, an organization founded in 1977 that united hundreds of small, local activist groups in a nationwide campaign against both nuclear power and nuclear weapons. This kind of revolt burgeoned after the near meltdown of the nuclear reactor at Three Mile Island, Pennsylvania, in March 1979.

Other movement activity emphasized halting the nuclear arms race. Peace organizations like SANE, WSP, and the small pacifist groups renewed their anti-nuclear ventures, adding new members along the way. In 1978, Dr. Helen Caldicott, an Australian pediatrician working in the United States, revived a defunct organization, Physicians for Social Responsibility, which soon brought thousands of medical doctors into the anti-nuclear struggle. Through the Plowshares movement, religious pacifists—many previously active in the struggle against the Vietnam War—staged civil disobedience actions at nuclear weapons production facilities. Feminists began to critique the arms race as a male obsession and argued that it was time to "take the toys away from the boys." Organized by the American Friends Service Committee, a small protest campaign against the nuclear weapons plant in Rocky Flats, Colorado, grew into a mass movement. When the U.N. Special Session on Disarmament opened in May 1978, an estimated 20,000 anti-nuclear demonstrators turned out for the event.

Moreover, plans were afoot for a dramatic expansion of the movement. After years of addressing peace and disarmament groups, Randy Forsberg, a young defense analyst, became convinced that they needed a common focus to maximize their strength. Therefore, she drew up a proposal which she felt that they—and the American public—would endorse: a bilateral halt to testing, production, and deployment of nuclear weapons. Most major peace groups did rally behind this "Nuclear Freeze" idea.

In the following years, the Nuclear Weapons Freeze Campaign grew dramatically. The Freeze mobilized unprecedented numbers of Americans, including a million that turned out for a June 1982 anti-nuclear rally—the largest demonstration up to that point in U.S. history. The Freeze also was endorsed by most mainstream religious denominations, dozens of major labor unions, and more than 370 city councils. Adopted as part of the 1984 Democratic Party campaign platform, the Freeze, polls reported, had the support of from 70 to 80 percent of Americans.

Once again, much the same occurred in other nations, where millions of people participated in anti-nuclear demonstrations. In Communist lands, where independent nuclear disarmament groups could not operate freely, they nevertheless carried on spirited campaigns, despite fierce repression by the authorities.

The surge of anti-nuclear activism in the late 1970s and early 1980s had important effects. It not only garnered widespread public backing, but transformed government policy. In response to popular protest, the Carter administration scrapped plans for the neutron bomb and pledged to cancel plans for deployment of cruise and Pershing II missiles if the Russians would agree to withdraw their SS-20 missiles. Meanwhile, nuclear power plant construction ground to a halt. The impact upon the Reagan administration was even more pronounced. At the time of Reagan's election in 1980, he had opposed every nuclear arms control and disarmament treaty negotiated by his Democratic and Republican predecessors.

Furthermore, he championed a massive nuclear buildup and talked glibly of waging nuclear war. But, under massive pressure from the anti-nuclear campaign, Reagan soon came around to championing and implementing nuclear disarmament programs. Starting in April 1982, he also began declaring publicly that "a nuclear war cannot be won and must never be fought." He added, "To those who protest against nuclear war, I can only say: 'I'm with you!' "

Despite these achievements, the anti-nuclear movement had a number of weaknesses. Although many Americans were uneasy about nuclear weapons, they were also frightened at the prospect of attack by other nations and, therefore, sometimes were reluctant to embrace nuclear disarmament. Furthermore, the movement had difficulty maintaining a consistent level of mobilization because progress toward nuclear disarmament undermined the sense of nuclear danger upon which the movement was based. Movement mobilization was also hard to sustain because anti-nuclear campaigners had competing priorities.

Nevertheless, the movement exhibited considerable strength, for its fundamental message was irrefutable: nuclear war would be a disaster. Indeed, even the development of "peaceful" nuclear power seemed likely to produce very dangerous consequences. For these reasons, the anti-nuclear campaign was able to win substantial popular support in American life, to curb the nuclear arms race, and to prevent nuclear war.

WOMEN STRIKE FOR PEACE, *A Letter to Nikita Khrushchev* (1962)

In mid-1962, the Washington, DC branch of Women Strike for Peace—which coordinated the nationwide WSP organization—sent the following appeal to the Soviet Premier.

May 14, 1962

Dear Mr. Khrushchev:

The peoples of the world wait—helpless and almost hopeless—as they watch the tests and counter tests by the U.S.A. and the U.S.S.R. spew their deadly poisons into our atmosphere.

We . . . have unceasingly protested our government's resumption of nuclear testing in the atmosphere. We had hoped that our president would take the initiative in turning from an arms build-up to measures which would lead to peace and a reduction of armaments.

With the resumption of tests by the U.S., the initiative in calling a halt to this deadly nuclear buildup-up now passes to you.

Source: Letter from Kay Johnson to Nikita Khrushchev, May 14, 1962, Box 2, Series I, Women Strike for Peace Records, Swarthmore College Peace Collection, Swarthmore, PA.

Only the U.S.A. and the U.S.S.R. can break this frightful nuclear spiral. We urgently appeal to you to end now this competition in death. We fear that another series of tests by your government will only provoke ours to further tests. Thus there will be no gain by either side.

Will you not renounce this futile method, which can defend nothing, and which, even without war, is poisoning our planet?

Some leader must have the courage to put the welfare of mankind above national struggles for power. Will you not embark upon this bold course before it is too late—before accident or design has turned out world into a flaming funeral pyre?

Respectfully,

(Mrs.) Kay Johnson
Secretary

Women Strike for Peace
Washington, D.C.

HOMER JACK, *What SANE Is and Is Not* (1962)

In late 1962, this essay by Homer Jack, SANE's executive director, appeared in the nuclear disarmament organization's newsletter.

SANE is not gradualist. We believe that disarmament must come today—or tomorrow we will die. Great problems demand grand answers. . . . There must be bold, courageous moves. However, we believe in the educative, political, legislative process throughout. We do not advocate civil disobedience.

SANE is not partisan. We believe no one political party holds a monopoly of political virtue, especially regarding disarmament and peace. We differ from some of our friends who believe only in the political process. We believe in both education and politics. . . .

SANE is not elitist. We work with policy-makers and the so-called influentials, but we know how impotent we are in Washington or even at the U.N. unless we are backed up in depth by the real influentials in our democracy: the people in the districts and wards, in the churches and synagogues and unions, in local SANE committees throughout America.

SANE is not sentimental. We feel deeply, and act strongly, but try to follow feeling with fact, reason and research. We want peace, yes; but we really seek peace plus—plus freedom, plus justice. . . .

SANE is not unilateralist. We do not believe that the U.S. should disarm alone. We believe in phased, inspected disarmament made by mutual agreement among all

---

Source: Homer A. Jack, "What SANE Is and Is Not," *Sane World*, December 15, 1962.

nations. However, SANE does support political and military initiatives by the U.S. to break the present impasse and to dramatize our desire to convert the arms race into a peace race.

SANE is not pacifist. We are pragmatic, not absolutist. We believe that modern war does not work and that other methods are needed to allow change, yet keep the peace in the modern world. . . . However, there is room in SANE for individual pacifists and there are a number among our members and leaders.

. . . We have faith in the democratic process. We are heard and we mean to continue to be heard. We do not feel hopeless. We are not fatalistic. We want to succeed, but we are not tied to success—at least in immediate terms. If we can succeed only in postponing the final holocaust during our generation by abolishing nuclear tests, by minimizing the risks of accidental war, by beginning the process of general disarmament, by leaving the world a . . . more hopeful place for our children, we shall have "succeeded" to some degree.

SAMUEL DAY, *We Re-Set the Clock* (1974)

Despite nuclear arms control agreements in the 1960s and early 1970s, the nuclear arms race continued. Therefore, in September 1974, Samuel Day—editor of the *Bulletin of the Atomic Scientists*—wrote the following editorial explaining why the editors of that anti-nuclear publication had decided to move forward the hands of their doomsday clock.

For twenty-seven years the clock of the *Bulletin of the Atomic Scientists* has symbolized the threat of nuclear doomsday hovering over mankind. The minute hand, never far from midnight, has advanced and retreated with the ebb and flow of international power politics, registering basic changes in the level of the continuing danger in which people have lived since the dawn of the nuclear age.

Two years ago the minute hand was pulled back to 12 minutes to midnight as a consequence of the signing of the first arms control agreements which emerged from the Strategic Arms Limitation Talks between the United States and the Soviet Union. This was an event which seemed to usher in a new era of sanity in superpower nuclear arms policies. In recognition that our hopes for an awakening of sanity were premature and that the danger of nuclear doomsday is measurably greater today than it was in 1972, we now move the clock forward to 9 minutes to midnight.

We do not thereby venture a prediction as to when, or even whether, a nuclear holocaust may come, or to imply that the likelihood of its occurrence can somehow be closely calibrated. We offer instead an assessment and a warning. Our assessment is that in these past two years . . . the international nuclear arms race has gathered

---

Source: Samuel H. Day, Jr., "We Re-set the Clock," *Bulletin of the Atomic Scientists*, September 1974: 4–5.

momentum and is now more than ever beyond control. Our warning is that so long as control continues to elude us civilization faces a growing risk of catastrophe.

Despite the promise of the 1972 [SALT] accords, it is now apparent that the two nuclear superpowers are nowhere near significant agreement on strategic arms limitations. The failure was manifest at the recently concluded summit conference in Moscow. This in itself is cause for concern in view of the arms buildup which has continued during the course of the negotiations, and particularly since 1972. In anticipation of limitations agreements that have never come to pass or were of little consequence, more and more weapons have been built and tested, and more and more weapons systems have been developed and deployed. Far from restraining the forces which it was intended to curb, SALT has sustained and nourished them, providing acceptable channels for conducting business as usual.

This subtle undermining of mankind's hope for a saner world has been aptly characterized by Alva Myrdal, the former Swedish representative to the U.N. disarmament talks at Geneva and at the United Nations: "The so-called 'disarmament agreements' that we have obtained are either nonarmament agreements or mere cosmetic devices. They have been used to stall for time, and to make people believe that something has been achieved."

Thus we find that the United States today, while talking peace, is developing new generations of nuclear weapons and delivery systems, each more terrifying, more efficient, and more lethal than the last, and that the situation in the Soviet Union is much the same. We find policy-makers on both sides increasingly ensnared, frustrated and neutralized by domestic forces having a vested interest in the amassing of strategic inventories. The worldwide arsenal of nuclear warheads continues its astronomical upward spiral. It ranges from hydrogen bombs capable of destroying great cities at a single blow to artillery shells with yields so indistinguishable from those of conventional explosives that their use would blur the distinction between nuclear and non-nuclear hostilities. We find, with the passage of time, a growing tendency to conventionalize the concept of resort to nuclear arms in contingency plans for war, both in the United States and the Soviet Union, as well as in other powers which have achieved nuclear weapons capability. The "narcoticizing" of policy-makers, and the public itself, to the implications of nuclear armaments is a source of growing peril to the world.

To the threats from the established nuclear powers we must now add the new threat of continued proliferation of the nuclear powers themselves. India's explosion of a nuclear device in May further broadened the geographical and political base for nuclear weaponry. It loosened another restraint on nuclear weapons development and raised anew the spectre of the spread of nuclear arms to other governments and regions. India's decision to join the "nuclear club" may have set in motion a train of reaction which could greatly enhance the chances of a local dispute igniting a nuclear conflagration.

Whether nuclear fission is put to peaceful or warlike use depends as much on the intentions of the user as on the nature of the technology. That is why the prospective introduction of nuclear reactors into the Middle East, announced in June by the United States, must be viewed with misgivings. Although the need of that area for greater economic development is undeniable, the introduction of a technology having nuclear weapons potential . . . will remain fraught with danger until a greater measure of political stability has been achieved.

Indeed, the adaptability of nuclear fuels for use as weapons poses a growing danger to all peoples in these times of increasing reliance on nuclear energy to meet the power demands of industrial societies that are increasingly vulnerable to the disruptive acts of desperate individuals and organizations. The nuclear trigger which threatens the lives of millions, if not the peace of the world, is no longer within the grasp of just a very few. The failure of governments to face this ugly fact constitutes another measure of the increasing danger in which we all live.

Taken together, these considerations impel the forward movement of the *Bulletin* clock.

. . . . But we remain hopeful that society has within itself the collective wisdom to adapt its institutions for the successful accommodation of nuclear power. The record of governments to date is far from reassuring. But governments are the creatures of society, not its masters, and their shortcomings are not irremediable. It behooves us, as peoples of all nations, to look to the improvement of our imperfect institutions, to demand a higher level of performance and accountability from those who exercise power, and to remember, above all, that time is running out.

MOBILIZATION FOR SURVIVAL, *No More Hiroshimas!* (1977)

In 1977, Mobilization for Survival produced the following leaflet, announcing its founding and program.

32 years after the first nuclear bomb destroyed Hiroshima . . . , groups in the United States . . . announce the MOBILIZATION FOR SURVIVAL. All are part of an international movement challenging the nuclear powers. . . .

Every nation has said it wants disarmament. And yet every powerful nation has gone ahead and spent more money on weapons. In the 32 years since Hiroshima all the talk of peace and disarmament has not dismantled a single nuclear bomb. Instead we now have ten thousand of them—many times more powerful than the Hiroshima bomb.

Since governments have not moved, the people must. Each country insists that nuclear weapons are necessary for defense. We say those weapons defend no one and threaten hundreds of millions of people in all these countries. We are committed to abolishing all nuclear weapons in every nation before those weapons destroy us.

LET EVERY GOVERNMENT HEAR US CLEARLY. We shall support every action by any government to end the arms race. We will oppose every action by any government, including our own, to continue the arms race and increase the nuclear

---

Source: Mobilization for Survival, "No More Hiroshimas!" (1977), Mobilization for Survival Records, Swarthmore College Peace Collection, Swarthmore, PA.

stockpiles. . . . We will break the guns, dismantle the bombs, and close down the missile sites. . . .

Let the hundreds of billions spent for death be spent for life: for healing the sick, housing the homeless, feeding the hungry, caring for children, tending the elderly. . . .

ZERO NUCLEAR WEAPONS. BAN NUCLEAR POWER.
STOP THE ARMS RACE. FUND HUMAN NEEDS.

NUCLEAR FREEZE CAMPAIGN, *Call to Halt the Nuclear Arms Race* (1980)

In March 1980, the Nuclear Freeze campaign produced this first summary of its program.

The United States and the Soviet Union should immediately and jointly stop the nuclear arms race. Specifically, they should adopt an immediate, mutual freeze on all further testing, production and deployment of nuclear weapons and of missiles and new aircraft designed primarily to deliver nuclear weapons.

The horror of a nuclear holocaust is universally acknowledged. Today, the United States and the Soviet Union possess 50,000 nuclear weapons. In half an hour, all cities in the northern hemisphere can be destroyed. Yet over the next decade, the USA and USSR plan to build over 20,000 more nuclear warheads, along with a new "generation" of missiles to deliver them at long range. . . .

A freeze would hold constant the existing nuclear parity between the United States and the Soviet Union. . . . Later, following the immediate adoption of the freeze, its terms should be negotiated into the more durable form of a treaty.

Stopping the US-Soviet nuclear arms race is the single most useful step that can be taken now to reduce the likelihood of nuclear war and to prevent the spread of nuclear weapons to more countries. This step is a necessary prelude to creating conditions in which:

—the freeze can be extended to other nations;

—the nuclear arsenals on all sides can be drastically reduced or eliminated; and

—the threat of use of nuclear weaponry can be ended.

Only these more far-reaching measures can make the world truly safe from nuclear destruction.

Source: "Call to Halt the Nuclear Arms Race," March 1980, Box 15, Nuclear Weapons Freeze Campaign Records, Western Historical Manuscript Collection, Thomas Jefferson Library, University of Missouri-St. Louis, St. Louis, MO.

8

Anti-War Activism

—KENNETH J. HEINEMAN

Shortly after the end of World War II, U.S. President Harry S. Truman, with bipartisan support from Congress, organized labor, intellectuals, Hollywood, and the news media embraced a policy of communist containment. First in Western Europe, and then in Asia, Africa, and Latin America, the United States provided diplomatic, economic, and, on occasion, military aid to countries resisting Soviet Russian and communist Chinese expansion. Three times in the course of what journalist Walter Lippmann dubbed "the Cold War" (1946–1991), the United States and its communist rivals—as well as their proxies—faced off in major military engagements: Korea (1950–1953), Indochina (1965–1975), and Afghanistan (1979–1989).

In spite of the bipartisan consensus on U.S. Cold War foreign policy in the 1940s and 1950s, there remained pockets of dissent across the ideological spectrum. Republican isolationists, Democratic liberals who were uncomfortable with allying with anti-communist dictators, and disaffected radicals voiced their opposition to the policy of communist containment. The deepening crisis of the Vietnam War in the 1960s swelled the ranks of such critics.

In 1960, undergraduates and faculty at Lake Forest College, an exclusive suburban Chicago school, established the Student Peace Union (SPU). The Student Peace Union took a "Third Camp" position, meaning that its members regarded the United States and the Soviet Union as equally at fault for perpetuating the nuclear arms race. By 1963, the SPU had grown from 100 members to 3,500 and had established affiliates at Harvard and the University of Chicago.

Shaken by the 1962 Cuban Missile Crisis and the prospect of a nuclear Third World War, the SPU asserted that Cold War Democrats—rather than the Soviets—were the chief threat to world peace. In what would become a distressing pattern for Cold War Democrats in the 1960s, Republicans almost always received less faculty and student-activist criticism. There were at least two reasons for this phenomenon. First, most SPU members came from either Democratic or socialist households. They therefore expected better behavior from their "family" elders. Second, conservatives, when they even entered the mental world of progressive activists, were regarded as beyond redemption given their purported racism and militarism.

Another activist youth organization appeared at the beginning of the 1960s—one that demonstrated greater appeal and staying power than the Student Peace Union. In 1962, the Students for a Democratic Society (SDS) held its founding convention in Port Huron, Michigan. Tracing its ancestry to the 1930s-era Student League for Industrial Democracy (SLID), SDS initially advanced a social democratic critique of U.S. capitalism and opposition to overseas military intervention. University of Michigan activist Tom Hayden wrote SDS's founding document, "The Port Huron Statement."

While SDS initially organized at elite schools such as Chicago, Harvard, Michigan, and Swarthmore, it spread to less academically prestigious campuses, including Penn State and Kent State. SDS was an organization of middle to upper-middle-class liberal arts majors from predominantly secular Protestant and Jewish households. Few Catholics and African Americans could be found. One-third of SDS's members were "red diaper babies," the children of 1930s socialists and communists. The remainder overwhelmingly came from Democratic families. These demographic features meant that the media-designated "generation gap" of the 1960s could more accurately be described as a civil war among factions of the Democratic Party and the Left.

With the escalation of the Vietnam War, the peace movement grew but became more internally divided. Two tracks of anti-war protest soon emerged. The first protest track was campus-based and, on more than a few occasions, witnessed violent confrontations with university administrators, law enforcement officials, and representatives of the military and corporations involved with defense contracting. A second protest track largely existed off-campus, often among established white-collar professionals and intellectuals. These activists sought through nonviolent rallies, petitions, and political mobilization to move the Democratic Party away from its Cold War foreign policy.

Much contemporary news media and subsequent scholarly attention focused on the first protest track. The specter of military service in Vietnam after graduation—or after flunking out—fed the ranks of campus peace protestors, as well as contributed to youthful alienation from a Democratic Party committed to the policy of communist containment. Further, dissenters were disturbed by the mounting American and Vietnamese casualties and frustrated that the war continued without reaching a successful conclusion. The emphasis of the American news media on images of seemingly pointless death and destruction in Vietnam also eroded public support for the war and boosted protest ranks.

Following U.S. President Lyndon Johnson's decision to bomb North Vietnam in February 1965, the Swarthmore SDS mobilized 300 protestors, representing one-third of the college's student body. After Johnson introduced combat troops into South Vietnam in March 1965, the national SDS organized a Washington, DC, peace rally of 15,000 in April 1965. At a larger November 1965 anti-war rally in Washington, Carl Oglesby, the national president of SDS, moved beyond criticism of Johnson's escalation of the Vietnam War. Oglesby condemned Cold War Democrats since Harry Truman for trampling upon the nationalist aspirations of Africans, Asians, and Latin Americans in the name of communist containment.

Campus-based anti-war groups spent much of 1966 in educational and organizational activities. Such preparation work paid off in 1967 as students and some faculty participated in two major protests. In the first protest wave, SDS tried to prevent Dow Chemical recruiters from meeting with student job-applicants, because the company manufactured napalm that the U.S. military used in Vietnam. At schools such as Wisconsin and SUNY-Buffalo, a few hundred SDS members blocked access to Dow recruiters and engaged in running battles with police officers. SDS and university officials accused each other of instigating violence. Carl Davidson, the national vice president of SDS, contended that whatever student-generated violence might come from such protests was morally justified given Dow's role in the Vietnam War.

The second significant student-led anti-war protest of 1967 took place in October when 100,000 youths marched on the Pentagon in order to "Confront the Warmakers." For the first time in American history, student radicals faced off against U.S. soldiers and U.S. marshals. The American news media did not know what to make of protestors who claimed that their harmonic energy would levitate the Pentagon and excise its evil spirits.

By 1968, SDS had grown to 100,000 members and figured prominently in many campus protests against university military research, the draft, and the Vietnam War. In the spring of 1968, Columbia SDS, protesting university military research and racist policies toward the neighboring black community, seized campus buildings. Inspired by the intense New York-based national news media coverage of the Columbia confrontation, thousands of campus activists attempted to take over buildings at their universities.

President Johnson emerged from the spring of 1968 a broken man, unwilling to stand for re-election and seeking ways to extricate the United States from Vietnam. The North Vietnamese Tet Offensive in January 1968, while ultimately a U.S. military victory, had been a public relations and political disaster at home. Johnson had been dismayed by the sight of academics, clergy, journalists, and suburban middle-class professionals—nearly all of which were Democrats—turning against him and American Cold War foreign policy. Martin Luther King, Jr.'s public stance against the war in 1967, followed by his assassination in the spring of 1968 which sparked riots in over 100 cities, only added to Johnson's sense of despair.

Johnson also faced a serious challenge for re-nomination from New York senator Robert F. Kennedy who criticized both the Vietnam War and student radicals. Kennedy's stance attracted the support of many Democrats weary of campus disruption and a seemingly unending war. Johnson's decision not to seek re-election, and Kennedy's assassination in June 1968, paved the way for vice president Hubert Humphrey to receive the Democratic presidential nomination.

In that summer of 1968, nearly 15,000 protestors answered the call by SDS founders Tom Hayden and Rennie Davis, among others, to gather in Chicago and disrupt the Democratic National Convention. With 525,000 U.S. troops in South Vietnam and some 30,000 Americans killed, radicals were out of patience. Their goal was embarrass—Humphrey whom radicals correctly regarded as an unrepentant Cold Warrior.

While the resulting battles between Chicago police officers and student radicals did not prevent Humphrey's nomination, the televised images of youth battling police disgusted millions and undermined the Democrats at the polls in 1968. At the same time, many college-educated suburbanites blamed only the Chicago police for the violent street clashes and vowed to wrest control of the Democratic Party away from its anti-communist labor and political leaders. Among such Democratic activists was Molly Yard of Pittsburgh, a future leader of the National Organization for Women (NOW). By 1968, women's rights activists and civil rights leaders had also become central players in the anti-war movement and the issue was no longer the preserve of college students. Not only did well-known civil rights figures like Martin Luther King, Jr., decide to speak out against the war, but so also did feminist icon Gloria Steinem and famous movie actress Jane Fonda.

A year later, in 1969, movement attentions were suddenly consumed with a dramatic trial in which the so-called "Chicago Seven," Tom Hayden, Davis, and five other radical activists stood accused of formenting the rioting that accompanied the 1968 Democratic National Convention. But rather than unify movement activists, as the Chicago Seven trial proceeded internal tensions over tactics grew more glaring and large anti-war organizations such as SDS split apart. One faction, called the Revolutionary Youth Movement (or Weathermen) believed that terrorist acts were acceptable strategies for ending the war. A second faction, influenced by the Maoist Progressive Labor Party, saw the anti-war issue as too limited in scope and sought to go into factories and organize white workers into a revolutionary vanguard that would overthrow American capitalism. It is worth noting, however, that the anti-war movement had grown far beyond SDS and that the majority of protestors, including many who stayed in SDS embraced nonviolent activism.

The greatest uprising of anti-war activists took place in response to the slaying of four Kent State students by the Ohio National Guard on May 4, 1970. Four million students had gone on strike nationally there to protest U.S. President Richard Nixon's decision to bomb Cambodia despite his campaign promises not to take the war into neighboring countries. However, once it became clear that the incursion into Cambodia was not going to lead to escalation of the Vietnam War, such massive student protests evaporated.

In fact, after 1970, the anti-war movement more broadly was losing steam for a number of reasons. First, President Richard Nixon introduced a policy of "Vietnamization," steadily replacing U.S. troops with South Vietnamese forces. Vietnamization reduced American casualties and draft calls, as well as lessened the prominence of the "war issue" in national politics. Second, Nixon instituted the lottery in 1969, which, by eliminating college deferments and assigning young males a number based upon their birth dates, reduced student anxiety. With lowered troop levels in Vietnam, students knew that they were not going to be drafted if they were among the four-fifths of youths who had a lottery number higher than 80. The 1970 Cambodian incursion had re-ignited student fears of military escalation of the war, but only briefly.

The anti-war movement of the 1960s and early 1970s demonstrated one area of great strength: the ability to recruit America's best educated and most prosperous. Many such recruits found (or would find) employment in the nation's "culture"-making professions, exercising enormous influence within the news and popular media, advertising, and universities. Given their education and sources of employment, such activists had their opinions amplified more loudly than their actual numbers justified.

Paradoxically, however, the very strength of the anti-war movement proved to be its greatest weakness in the electoral arena. Working-class whites and southerners resented seeing "their" party taken over by a "cultural elite" that, they believed, held patriotism and moral conservatism in contempt. No Democrat could expect to gain entry into the White House without distancing him or herself in the general election from the protest movements of the 1960s. At the same time, no Democrat seeking the presidency could win bi-coastal primaries without appealing to the activist voter base that came out of the anti-war and women's liberation movements of the 1960s.

The cultural legacies of the anti-war movement and 1960s protest were just as complicated and profound as their political legacies. For instance, while the radical campus tide receded after 1970, student support for lifestyle liberation remained high. A 1972 Minnesota poll of students showed that 62 percent did not believe state governments should criminalize gay intercourse. Sixty-five percent of the public thought otherwise. In 1973, a Gallup Poll reported that 34 percent of youths supported the legalization of marijuana, compared to 7 percent of their elders. Other surveys concluded that by 1972 half of America's youths between 18 and 25 had smoked dope, compared to just 4 percent in the early 1960s. College students helped drive those numbers upward, with 70 percent of students at the University of Kansas having smoked marijuana.

CARL DAVIDSON, *The New Radicals and the Multiversity* (1966)

Carl Davidson, a Penn State graduate and son of an auto mechanic, attained the vice presidency of the Students for a Democratic Society on the basis of this 1966 exhortation for increased anti-war militancy in the nation's Heartland. In 1967, campuses outside the elite institutions of the East and West coasts heeded Davidson's call to disrupt violently, if necessary, the efforts of Dow Chemical representatives to recruit on campus.

Perhaps the single most important factor' for the student power movement to keep in mind is the fact that the university is intimately bound up with the society in general. Because of this, we should always remember that we cannot liberate the university without radically changing the rest of society. The lesson to be drawn is

Source: Carl Davidson, "The New Radicals and the Multiversity," in Massimo Teodori, ed., *The New Left: A Documentary History*, Indianapolis: Bobbs-Merrill, 1969, pp. 323–335.

that any attempt to build a student movement based on "on-campus" issues only is inherently conservative and ultimately reactionary. Every attempt should be made to connect campus issues with off-campus questions. For example, the question of ranking and university complicity with the Selective Service System needs to be tied to a general anti-draft and "No Draft for Vietnam" movement. The question of the presence of the military on the campus in all its forms needs to be tied to the question of what that military is used for—fighting aggressive wars of oppression abroad—and not just to the question of secret research being poor academic policy. Furthermore, the student movement must actively seek to join off-campus struggles in the surrounding community. For example, strikes by local unions should be supported if possible. This kind of communication and understanding with the local working class is essential if we are ever going to have community support for student strikes.

If there is a single over-all purpose for the student power movement, it would be the development of a radical political consciousness among those students who will later hold jobs in strategic sectors of the political economy. This means that we should reach out to engineers and technical students rather than to business administration majors, education majors rather than to art students. From a national perspective, this strategy would also suggest that we should place priorities on organizing in certain *kinds* of universities—the community colleges, junior colleges, state universities, and technical schools, rather than religious colleges or the Ivy League.

CARL OGLESBY, *Trapped in a System* (1965)

The son of a southern-born tire worker and one-time Kent State student, Carl Oglesby ascended to the presidency of the Students for a Democratic Society. At this anti-war rally in the fall of 1965, Oglesby argued that the Vietnam conflict was more than a misguided product of President Lyndon Johnson's administration. Rather, the fundamental problem was a Cold War Democratic Party that had stifled revolutionary movements since the presidency of Harry Truman and which differed little from the equally anti-communist Republican Party.

Seven months ago at the April March on Washington, Paul Potter, then President of Students for a Democratic Society, stood in approximately this spot and said that we must name the system that creates and sustains the war in Vietnam—name it. Describe it, analyze it, understand it, and change it. Today I will try to name it—to suggest an analysis which, to be quite frank, may disturb some of you—and to suggest what changing it may require of us.

Source: Carl Oglesby, "Trapped in a System," in Massimo Teodori, ed., *The New Left: A Documentary History*, Indianapolis: Bobbs-Merrill, 1969, pp. 182–188.

We are here again to protest again a growing war. Since it is a very bad war, we acquire the habit of thinking that it must be caused by very bad men. But we only conceal reality, I think, by denouncing on such grounds the menacing coalition of industrial and military power, or the brutality of the blitzkrieg we are waging against Vietnam, or the ominous signs around us that heresy may soon no longer be permitted. We must simply observe, and quite plainly say that this coalition, this blitzkrieg, and this demand for acquiescence are creatures, all of them, of a Government that since 1932 has considered itself to be fundamentally *liberal*. The original commitment in Vietnam was made by President Truman, a mainstream liberal. It was seconded by President Eisenhower, a moderate liberal. It was intensified by the late President Kennedy, a flaming liberal. . . . They are not moral monsters. They are all honorable men. They are all liberals.

But so, I'm sure, are many of us who are here today in protest. To understand the war, then, it seems necessary to take a closer look at this American Liberalism. Maybe we are in for some surprises. Maybe we have here two quite different Liberalisms: one authentically humanist; the other not so human at all. Not long ago, I considered myself a liberal. And if someone had asked me what 1 meant by that. I'd perhaps have quoted Thomas Jefferson or Thomas Paine, who first made plain our nation's unprovisional commitment to human rights. But what do you think would happen if these two heroes could sit down now for a chat with President Johnson and McGeorge Bundy? They would surely talk of the Vietnam war. Our dead revolutionaries would soon wonder why their country was fighting against what appeared to be a revolution. The living liberals would hotly deny that it is one: there are troops coming in from outside, the rebels get arms from other countries, most of the people are not on their side, and they practice terror against their own. Therefore, *not a* revolution. What would our dead revolutionaries answer? They might say: What fools and bandits, sirs, you make then of us. Outside help?

Do you remember Lafayette? Or the 3,000 British freighters the French navy sunk for our side? Or the arms and men we got from France and Spain? And what's this about terror? Did you never hear what we did to our own loyalists? Or about the thousands of rich American Tories who fled for their lives to Canada? And as for popular support, do you not know that we had less than one-third of our people with us? That, in fact, the colony of New York recruited more troops for the British than for the revolution? Should we give it all back?

Revolutions do not take place in velvet boxes. They never have. It is only the poets who make them lovely. What the National Liberation Front is fighting in Vietnam is a complex and vicious war. This war is also a revolution, as honest a revolution as you can find anywhere in history. . . . But it doesn't make any difference to our leaders anyway. Their aim in Vietnam is really much simpler than this implies. It is to safeguard what they take to the American interests around the world against revolution or revolutionary change, which they always call Communism—as if that were that. . . .

Can we understand why the Negroes of Watts rebelled? Then why do we need a devil theory to explain the rebellion of the South Vietnamese? Can we understand the oppression in Mississippi? Or the anguish that our Northern ghettos make epidemic? Then why can't we see that our proper human struggle is not with Communism or revolutionaries, but with the social desperation that drives good men to violence, both here and abroad?

ROBERT F. KENNEDY, *What Can the Young Believe?* (1967)

The brother of slain Democratic president John Kennedy, and a former U.S. Attorney General, Robert Kennedy grew increasingly disturbed by mounting casualties from Vietnam, as well as escalating campus and urban unrest and broke with President Lyndon Johnson in 1967. Weighing the feasibility of challenging Johnson in the 1968 Democratic presidential primaries, Kennedy sought support from the Americans for Democratic Action, an organization born in 1947 of the Cold War that, like the New York senator, was revising its commitment to communist containment.

More and more of our children are almost unreachable by the familiar premises and arguments of our adult world . . . What are they dissenting from—and what do they tell us about ourselves? They begin, of course, with the war in Vietnam. We are not talking about all our young people; after all, Vietnam is a young man's war. The men who fight and die there, with bravery and endurance equal to any in our history, are young. There are others, as I have seen on many campuses, who are in favor of escalation . . . But when a hundred student body presidents and editors of college newspapers; hundreds of former Peace Corps volunteers; dozens of present Rhodes scholars question the basic premises of the war, they should not and cannot be ignored.

These students oppose the war for the brutality and the horror of all wars, and for the particular terror of this one. But for our young people, I suspect, Vietnam is a shock as it cannot be to us. They did not know World War II, or even Korea. And this is a war surrounded by rhetoric they do not understand or accept; these are the children not of the cold war, but of the thaw. Their memories of communism are not of Stalin's purges and death camps, not even the terrible revelations of the Twentieth Party Congress, or the streets of Hungary. They see the world as one in which communist states can be each others' deadliest enemies or even friends of the West, in which communism is certainly no better, but perhaps no worse, than many other evil and repressive dictatorships all around the world—with which we conclude alliances when that is felt to be in our interest.

Even as the declared foreign policy of our government is to "build bridges" to this new communist world, they see us, in the name of anti-communism, devastating the land of those we call our friends. However the war may seem to us, they see it as one in which the largest and most powerful nation on earth is killing children (they do not care if accidentally) in a remote and insignificant land.

We speak of past commitments, of the burden of past mistakes; and they ask why they should now atone for mistakes made before many of them were born, before almost any could vote. They see us spend billions on armaments while poverty and ignorance continue at home; they see us willing to fight a war for freedom in Vietnam, but unwilling to fight with one-hundredth the money or force or effort to

Source: Robert F. Kennedy, "What Can the Young Believe?" *The New Republic*, March 11, 1967: 11–12.

secure freedom in Mississippi or Alabama or the ghettos of the North. And they see, perhaps most disturbing of all, that they are remote from the decisions of policy; that they themselves frequently do not, by the nature of our political system, share in the power of choice on great questions shaping their lives. . . .

It is not enough to understand, or to see clearly. Whatever their differences with us, whatever the depth of their dissent, it is vital—for us as much as for them—that our young feel that change is possible; that they will be heard; that the cruelties and follies and injustices of the world will yield, however grudgingly, to the sweat and sacrifice they are so ready to give. If we cannot help open to them this sense of possibility, we will have only ourselves to blame for the disillusionment that will surely come. And more than disillusionment, danger; for we rely on these young people more than we know: not just in the Peace Corps, though the Peace Corps has done more for our position around the world than all our armed forces and foreign aid; not just in civil rights, though our youth have done more toward a solution of that problem than all the power and panoply of government; we rely on our youth for all our hopes of a better future—and thus, in a real and direct sense, for the very meaning of our own lives.

JANE FONDA, *Broadcast Over Radio Hanoi to American Servicemen Involved in the Indochina War* (1972)

Movie star Jane Fonda made national and international headlines during the Vietnam War when she travelled to North Vietnam and spoke out against the U.S. military presence there. Although the anti-war movement came to see Fonda as a hero, she became one of the most reviled of all celebrities by much of mainstream America as well as U.S. military.

This is Jane Fonda. During my two week visit in the Democratic Republic of Vietnam, I've had the opportunity to visit a great many places and speak to a large number of people from all walks of life—workers, peasants, students, artists and dancers, historians, journalists, film actresses, soldiers, militia girls, members of the women's union, writers.

I visited the (Dam Xuac) agricultural co-op, where the silk worms are also raised and thread is made. I visited a textile factory, a kindergarten in Hanoi. The beautiful Temple of Literature was where I saw traditional dances and heard songs of resistance. I also saw unforgettable ballet about the guerrillas training bees in the south to attack enemy soldiers. The bees were danced by women, and they did their job well.

Source: Jane Fonda, "Broadcast Over Radio Hanoi to American Servicemen Involved in the Indochina War," August 22, 1972—The following was submitted in the U.S. Congress House Committee on Internal Security, Travel to Hostile Areas. [HR16742, 19–25 September 1972, p. 761]

In the shadow of the Temple of Literature I saw Vietnamese actors and actresses perform the second act of Arthur Miller's play All My Sons, and this was very moving to me—the fact that artists here are translating and performing American plays while US imperialists are bombing their country. . . .

It was on the road back from Nam Dinh, where I had witnessed the systematic destruction of civilian targets—schools, hospitals, pagodas, the factories, houses, and the dike system. . . . One thing that I have learned beyond a shadow of a doubt since I've been in this country is that Nixon will never be able to break the spirit of these people; he'll never be able to turn Vietnam, north and south, into a neo-colony of the United States by bombing, by invading, by attacking in any way . . . every bomb that is dropped only strengthens their determination to resist.

I've spoken to many peasants who talked about the days when their parents had to sell themselves to landlords as virtually slaves, when there were very few schools and much illiteracy, inadequate medical care, when they were not masters of their own lives.

But now, despite the bombs, despite the crimes being created—being committed against them by Richard Nixon, these people own their own land, build their own schools—the children learning, literacy—illiteracy is being wiped out, there is no more prostitution as there was during the time when this was a French colony. In other words, the people have taken power into their own hands, and they are controlling their own lives.

And after 4,000 years of struggling against nature and foreign invaders—and the last 25 years, prior to the revolution, of struggling against French colonialism—I don't think that the people of Vietnam are about to compromise in any way, shape or form about the freedom and independence of their country, and I think Richard Nixon would do well to read Vietnamese history, particularly their poetry, and particularly the poetry written by Ho Chi Minh.

UNITED WOMEN'S CONTINGENT, *March on Washington Against the War* (1971)

The longer that the Vietnam War continued, more and more women became involved in the anti-war movement. The following is a flyer that calls for a massive women's march against the war. This march was endorsed by politically radical and liberal women alike.

On April 24, peaceful, massive demonstrations for immediate withdrawal will take place in Washington, DC and San Francisco. Women—from campuses, Black, Puerto Rican, Chicano and Asian-American groups, trade unions, religious groups,

---

Source: Flyer. United Women's Contingent: March on Washington Against the War, April 24, Documents from the Women's Liberation Movement, An Online Archival Collection Special Collections Library, Duke University. http://scriptorium.lib.duke.edu/wlm/united/.

the women's liberation movement—will join together and march as a united women's contingent. Last August 26th, the 50th anniversary of women's suffrage, tens of thousands of women poured into the streets to demonstrate for our right to control our lives. On April 24th, we will take the strength of women, which we showed to the world last August, and link up with all other people who say this war must end now.

. . . There are many reasons why it is essential that we relate to the April 24 demonstrations as women. First, women have played a leading role in the antiwar movement since the first teach-ins and demonstrations. Yet the press and media imply that the antiwar movement is led entirely by men. This is a misconception that must be corrected. We have participated in and been key organizers of every anti-war march, just as we have been perhaps the most effective force in every movement for social change, in the history of the world. . . .

Women in this country are challenging the right of the U.S. government to wage a war of slaughter and destruction in Indochina while it denies the needs of women at home. One million children are left uncared for, while their mothers work, because there are no child care facilities. Seven thousand women die every year of illegal abortions. Millions of dollars of profit is made every year by paying women less than men in the exact same job. Thousands of women are shut out of higher education because there's not enough money to provide scholarships and loans. We are told that there is no money for child-care centers or for abortion services; that the economy cannot meet the demands of women for equal and decent jobs; that high schools and universities cannot provide equal education for women. All this while Nixon spends billions of dollars on bombs, B-52s and "Vietnamization."

. . . Recent polls show that 78% of the women in this country want an end to the war. We must galvanize that antiwar sentiment into mass participation of women to activate them into the planning and participation in them demonstrations. The action of our sisters around demands for the control of our own lives, combined with our outrage at the latest action of the U.S. government in Southeast Asia, indicate the potential for the largest participation of women ever, in the April 24th demonstrations. . . .

<u>PARTIAL LIST OF N.Y. ENDORSERS OF THE UNITED WOMEN'S CONTINGENT</u> (Organizations listed for identification purposes only) MYRNA LAMB playwright; BARBARA LOVE Gay Liberation Front; MAE MASSIE Civil Rights Director for IUE; SUSAN MILLER Episcopal Peace Fellowship; WOMEN'S STRIKE COALITION; KATE MILLETT feminist writer; LONG ISLAND UNIVERSITY WOMEN'S LIBERATION FRONT; PAULINE ROSEN Women Strike for Peace; BARBARA DANE folksinger; GLORIA STEINEM feminist writer; BETTY FRIEDAN feminist writer; QUEENS COLLEGE WOMEN'S LIBERATION: COLUMBIA WOMEN'S LIBERATION; N.Y.U. WOMEN'S LIBERATION; HOFSTRA WOMEN'S LIBERATION; RENEE BLAKKAN Guardian; MYRNA BURKHOLDER Women In City Gov't; RUTH GAGE-COLBY Women's Int'l League for Peace & Freedom; ELIZABETH FISHER; APHRA writer; DORIS L. SASSOWER Professional Women's Caucus; DOROTHY ELDRIDGE N.J. SANE; SARAH DOELY Church Women United; LUCILLE IVERSON Radical Feminists; CLARA DE MIHA Jeanette Rankin Brigade Rank and File—and others.

9

The Asian American Movement

—Daryl J. Maeda

The Asian American movement emerged from the political ferment of the late 1960s and was formed when Asians of various ethnicities in the United States banded together to fight for racial justice. Although Asians had been in the United States in large numbers since the mid-1800s, they had not previously formed strong interethnic coalitions; instead, various Asian nationalisms had divided Asians in the United States, and the few multiethnic alliances they did form were fleeting. Because of numerous bans on Asian immigration enacted from 1875 through 1934, by the mid-1960s the majority of Asian Americans were native-born citizens and most Asian American youth spoke English and were immersed in American popular culture. Some Asian Americans were drawn into the social movements of the 1960s—including the civil rights, Black Power, and anti-Vietnam War movements—and many others became convinced that fundamental changes were necessary to achieve justice for Asians and other people in the United States and abroad.

The Asian American movement was a loosely organized coalition of groups and individuals spanning the nation, with epicenters in major cities on the coasts and in college towns. It addressed issues including education, housing, healthcare, workers rights, culture, and the war. Three points distinguished the movement from previous modes of politics among Asian Americans: first, it pulled together Asians of various ethnicities by arguing that Asians, regardless of ethnicity or national origin, shared common experiences of racism in the United States; second, it sought to build alliances between Asian Americans and other people of color in the United States; and third, it conceptualized the linkage between Asians in the United States to those in Asia as one of a shared relationship to U.S. imperialism rather than common biology or culture.

The beginnings of the Asian American movement can be traced to the late 1960s, when the Black Power and anti-war movements were blooming. The Asian American Political Alliance (AAPA, the first organization to use the term "Asian American") was formed at University of California, Berkeley, by Yuji Ichioka, who started the group by contacting all of the people with Asian surnames on the roster of the progressive Peace and Freedom Party. AAPA chapters, which borrowed the name but were not organizationally affiliated, were formed at Yale University, Columbia University, and elsewhere across the nation. In 1968 and 1969, Asian Americans participated in student strikes for Ethnic Studies at San Francisco State College and University of California, Berkeley. In both cases, Asian American organizations were part of multiracial coalitions called the Third World Liberation Front. While the strike at San Francisco State was the longest student strike in American history, it was part of a wave of student strikes across the United States and abroad during the late 1960s, in which students demanded social justice and protested the war in Vietnam; strikers often clashed not only with administrators, but also the police.

While AAPA began on campus, the Red Guard Party emerged from San Francisco's Chinatown in 1969. The Red Guards adopted programs of self-determination modeled on the Black Panther Party's ideology and rhetoric; they decried police brutality, demanded fair employment, decent housing, and social services, opposed the war in Vietnam, and viewed racism against Asian Americans as similar to that against blacks, Latinos, and American Indians. In New York City, Asian Americans for Action (AAA) was initially organized in 1969 by Kazu Iijima and Minn Matsuda, two Nisei (second-generation Japanese American) women who had been political radicals before they were interned during World War II. These pioneers revived their prewar radicalism and connected with the growing political awareness of the younger generation (including Kazu's son Chris) to form a multi-ethnic Asian organization that opposed U.S. militarism in Asia and racism at home. They were joined by Yuri Kochiyama, another Nisei woman, who was famously associated with Malcolm X and cradled his head when he was assassinated. Avowedly communist groups, including I Wor Kuen (into which the Red Guard Party merged in 1971) and Wei Min She admired Mao Tse Tung as the most globally prominent opponent of U.S. imperialism; they sought to find common ground with other "Third World" radicals in trying to better the lives and working conditions of Asian Americans and other people of color in the United States.

Opposition to the Vietnam War was critical to the Asian American movement. Asian American organizations participated in many of the large-scale anti-war protests of the 1970s, often by forming Asian Contingents that marched and rallied together under the flags of left Asia, including North Vietnam, the People's Republic of China, and North Korea. They felt that it was vital for Asian Americans oppose the war as an anti-Asian genocide that followed in the steps of the U.S.-Filipino War, the atomic bombing of Hiroshima and Nagasaki, and the Korean War. Among Filipino Americans, one of the most pressing issues was opposition to the dictatorship of Ferdinand Marcos in the Philippines. The Union of Democratic Filipinos (Katipunan ng mga Demokratikong Pilipino, or KDP) opposed Marcos as both anti-democratic and complicit with U.S. imperialism.

As the anti-Marcos movement demonstrates, the Asian American movement was not motivated by uncritical Asian pride. Rather, its participants drew inspiration from Asian leaders such as Mao and Ho Chi Minh whom they believed exemplified the ideals self-determination and equality. Furthermore, they understood that while there were differences among Asian nationalities and ethnicities, Asians in the United States and in Asia were bound together by a relation of subjugation to American racism and imperialism.

Participants from across the spectrum of the Asian American movement objected strenuously to the depiction of Asian Americans as a "model minority" who had escaped from prejudice through hard work and education. Instead, they emphasized that Asian Americans continued to suffer from discrimination, poverty, and exploitation. The International Hotel, the last vestige of San Francisco's Manilatown, was the site of a bitter battle from 1968 to 1977 in which Asian Americans and their allies fought developers who wished to raze the building. The hotel provided affordable housing and a sense of community to elderly Filipino and Chinese bachelors, former migrant workers who were the source of the cheap labor indispensable to the agricultural industry and became disposable once their labor was extracted. Students trekked to the hotel to renovate its deteriorating edifice and organizations including Asian Community Center and Chinese Progressive Association established offices there. Despite their best efforts, however, the tenants were evicted and the hotel was destroyed.

A wide array of cultural workers explored Asian American identity in music, visual arts, literature, poetry, and drama. Joanne ("Nobuko") Miyamoto, Chris Iijima, and Charlie Chin performed as the folk trio A Grain of Sand at rallies, protests, and conferences across the nation and in 1973 recorded the self-titled album, *A Grain of Sand*, which expressed their opposition racism, capitalism, and imperialism, along with their solidarity with blacks, Latinos, and American Indians. Organizations such as Basement Workshop in New York City and Kearny Street Workshop in San Francisco provided resources and opportunities for artists and encouraged community participation in the arts. Theater companies in Seattle, San Francisco, and Los Angeles developed and staged Asian American plays and fostered Asian American talent. Frank Chin emerged as a prominent, but controversial writer and critic. Although numerous Asian American organizations produced newsletters, newspapers, and magazines, the most influential and widely read movement periodical was *Gidra*, a newspaper published monthly in Los Angeles from 1969 to 1974. Its exuberant graphic design expressed the humorous and joyful spirit of the 1970s, but *Gidra* also reported seriously on Asian American perspectives on issues such as the war, Asian American studies, fair housing and wages, and drug abuse within the Asian American community; furthermore, it highlighted the activities of other "Third World" activists, such as the American Indian takeover of Alcatraz Island.

Asian American women played pivotal roles in the movement. Pat Sumi was a well-known anti-war activist who toured with Eldridge Cleaver across China, North Korea, and North Vietnam; upon her return, she spoke to Asian American groups across the United States and helped to organize a conference between Indochinese and North American women in Vancouver, Canada, in 1971.

Similarly, Evelyn Yoshimura also traveled through China and published reports with *Gidra* in 1972 and 1973. Carmen Chow was a driving force of I Wor Kuen after the merger with the Red Guard Party. Despite the visibility of a few individuals, many Asian American women felt that they were relegated to performing menial tasks, that their issues were not considered important, and that Asian American men viewed them as sexual property. Asian American women addressed sexism within the movement by pursuing projects that addressed their particular needs, including drug abuse among young women and domestic abuse, educating men about sexism, and building sisterhood with each other. The Asian American women's movement viewed itself as integrally connected with the larger movement and argued that Asian American liberation could not take place without women's liberation.

The Asian American movement drew much of its strength from its diversity and flexibility. It encompassed groups and individuals with a wide array of ideologies and political commitments ranging from liberalism to avowed communism. All participants agreed, to varying degrees, that Asians of all ethnicities suffered from common racism and that coalescing together provided an effective means for combating that racism. However, tensions between and within groups detracted from the movement's effectiveness, especially as the 1970s progressed. Like much of the new communist movement, Asian American radicals turned increasingly toward party-building and political consolidation with other like-minded groups, including those composed of leftists from other racial minorities. I Wor Kuen allied with Chicanos of the August Twenty-ninth Movement in 1978 to form the League of Revolutionary Struggle (LRS), while Wei Min She entered the Revolutionary Union. Excessive devotion toward achieving ideological correctness embroiled these organizations in bitter internecine conflicts, and disproportionate efforts at party-building inhibited their ability to build grassroots connections to communities. On the left, Asian American radicals sometimes overly romanticized communist Asian nations such as the People's Republic of China and North Vietnam and leaders including Mao and Ho Chi Minh and underestimated the degree of internal conflict and political repression within these nations. Adopting democratic centralism (which was more central than democratic) as an organizing principle led some groups into undue rigidity.

But rather than disappearing with a trace, the Asian American movement left lasting legacies that continue to impact American ideas about race and ethnicity and improve the lives of people of Asian ancestry in the United States. To begin with, the very idea of Asian Americans as a racial bloc encompassing multiple ethnicities, which is now recognized by the federal government and has become part of commonplace understandings of race among Americans, was pioneered in the 1960s and 1970s by the movement. Furthermore, cultural, educational, and social service institutions begun by the movement—including theatrical companies, arts organizations, historical societies and museums, Asian American studies programs, immigrant service providers, and legal aid advocates—continued to serve the needs of the community throughout the twentieth century and are still flourishing in the twenty-first century. Finally, the Asian American movement brought attention to ongoing problems of racial inequality and showed the importance of building coalitions and alliances across lines of ethnicity, race, and gender.

KILLER FAWN, *In the Movement Office* (1971)

This 1971 skit by Killer Fawn (Linda Iwataki) illustrates women's frustration with sexism within the Asian American movement.

SISTER: (walking in) What do you think of women's liberation?

BROTHER 2: Well, Chairman Mao says "Unite and take part in production and political activity to improve the economic and political status of women."

BROTHER 1: Far out. Hey man, we better start getting the conference together. (all sit)

BROTHER 2: Yeah, I been thinking about that. Hey, did you dig on the article brother Alan put out? It runs down some heavy shit!

BROTHER 1: Right on! Let's put it on a stencil and run it off for the conference. Here, sister, can you type it up (hands it to her without waiting for her to answer) . . . and do this one on illegal search and seizure, too.

SISTER: Here's an article that Yuki wrote on women. It's really heav . . .

BROTHER 1: Yeah, that illegal search and seizure is important because the students need to get their shit together as far as legal matters are concerned. Hey, before you start typing, can you get me some coffee?

BROTHER 2: Me too. I take two sugars. (she gets up without saying anything, goes to get the coffee. Brothers look her up and down.)

BROTHER 2: When do you think we should have it? During Christmas vacation?

BROTHER 1: Yeah, righth on. Let's try the first weekend. Maybe we can get the Center. Hey sister, can you call the Center right now and get a confirmation?

SISTER: (bringing back the coffee) We can't use the Center anymore. Remember what happened last . . .

BROTHER 2: Oh shit! We can't use the Center. Last year someone left cigarette burns in the furniture and those s.o.b.'s aren't letting anyone use it on weekends.

SISTER: The first weekend of Christmas vacation might be rough for the students because papers and . . .

BROTHER 1: Fuck that shit! If they place their priorities on a bullshit paper, fuck 'em.

BROTHER 2: Right on! Hey, I got a meeting now. Can you get some press releases out and start contacting people for a general meeting? Thanks baby, you're a righteous sister.

Source: Printed in *Gidra*, January 1971.

BROTHER 1: Yeah, I got to split now, too. I have to go out in the field and do some people's work. I'll try to help you if I get back in time. But I know you can take care of business, baby. (both split)

SISTER: (alone and pissed off) What's going on! I got a goddamn meeting, too! The people's work . . . What the hell do they think this is!!

ASIAN AMERICAN POLITICAL ALLIANCE, *AAPA Perspectives* (1969)

The Asian American Political Alliance was the first organization to use the term "Asian American." Its first chapter was formed out of the larger New Left in Berkeley and subsequent chapters arose spontaneously in other locales. This statement demonstrates AAPA's understanding of the deep linkages between racism in the United States and imperialism abroad.

We Asian Americans believe that we must develop an American Society which is just, humane, equal and gives the people the right to control their own lives before we can begin to end the oppression and inequality that exists in this nation.

We Asian Americans realize that America was always and still is a White Racist Society. Asian Americans have been continuously exploited and oppressed by the racist majority and have survived only through hard work and resourcefulness, but their souls have not survived.

We Asian Americans refuse to cooperate with the White Racism in this society which exploits us as well as other Third World people, and affirm the right of Self-Determination.

We Asian Americans support all oppressed peoples and their struggles for Liberation and believe that Third World People must have complete control over the political, economic, and educational institutions within their communities.

We Asian Americans oppose the imperialistic policies being pursued by the American government.

PAT SUMI, *Third World People: Shoulder to Shoulder* (1974)

Pat Sumi was a prominent Asian American anti-war activist who traveled to North Korea and North Vietnam. She delivered this speech at the University of Michigan on February 21, 1974. Sumi appeared alongside the black radical Angela Davis, Clyde Bellecourt of the American Indian

Source: Printed in *Asian American Political Alliance Newspaper*, vol. 1, no. 5 (Summer), 1969.
Source: Printed in *Gidra*, April 1974.

Movement, and Ramsey Muniz of La Raza Unida Party in Texas. In this speech, Sumi demonstrates the connections that Asian American radicals saw between their movement and those of other Third World peoples in the United States and abroad through opposition to capitalism.

130 years ago, when the first Chinese laborers arrived on the West Coast, America was still a young agricultural country. The outmoded system of slavery still flourished in the Southern plantations . . . .

130 years ago, the nations of Asia—China, Japan, Korea, and the Philippines—groaned under the weight of decaying feudalism and European imperial penetration.

And 130 years ago, two relatively unknown political economists named Karl Marx and Friedrich Engels served notice to a skeptical but soon to be revolutionary Europe, that capitalism would soon be swept away by the combined might of the world's peoples.

. . . .We Asian American people have not remained apart from this great era of historical change. . . .

What made us leave our homelands? What brought us Asian American people to the United States? It was none other than the great 19th century dynamic of imperialism and colonialism—an imperialism and colonialism fueled by the African slave trade, the robbery of Latin America, and the confiscation of Native American land. Therefore, from the beginning, our existence as Asian American people was conditioned by the very same social and historical factors which conditioned the lives of other Third World peoples in this country.

. . . .We Asian American young people are finding great strength and courage for the trails ahead of us by understanding our heritage as part of the Third World working people. Who can fail to be moved by the quiet dignity of our mothers cooking, cleaning, and sewing to save money for our education? Who can fail to feel humble at the magi and stoic strength that brings for food and flowers for the people's livelihood? Who can fail to be moved when an old Filipino farm worker in his 70's says that the most important lesson he has learned is that young people of all races must work together for the people's sake?

Our lives, along with the lives of all Third World peoples of the world have been conditioned by imperialism. Therefore, our struggles to liberate the Asian, African and Latin American peoples from imperialism. Our lives have been conditioned by racism. Therefore, our struggles as Asian Americans must be part of the struggle to end racism and win genuine equality for all people. And most of all, our lives as Asian Americans have been conditioned by the most brutal exploitation. Therefore, our struggle must be merged with the great world wide struggle against exploitation and for building a society free from exploitation.

The unity of Third World people in America: what does it mean to Asian Americans? It is a window to look back on the past and see ourselves as an integral part of America's transformation into a rich and powerful industrial state. It is a window to see ourselves as part of the long and glorious tradition of slave rebellions, workers' strikes, civil rights movements, and anti-imperialist struggles of the American people's history.

And most of all, the unity of Asian Americans with Third World people in America is the only door through which we can enter the future. The history of the past 130 years, 130 years of blood and sweat, teaches us that only through the unity of the poor and disenfranchised, only thorugh the unity of the racially oppressed, only through the unity of the exploited, can people be victorious. 130 years ago, Karl Marx and Friedrich Engels said that capitalism and imperialism would be overthrown by the might of the world's peoples. Today, all the world's people are learning that it is possible, that it is necessary, and that a glorious future awaits us at the end. We Asian American people are determined to be a part of that future.

We Asian, Black, Brown and Native American people are determined to end exploitation and become masters of our society. We who are exploited and oppressed will build a future for our children such that our parents and grandparents hardly dared to dream of. The future is ours. Through unity we shall win!

RODAN, *U.S. Savages* (1971)

Rodan was an Asian American movement newspaper published out of San Francisco. This article argues that Asian Americans should identify with Indochinese people as fellow Asians and oppose the war on the basis of Asian solidarity.

Brothers and sisters, are we not also Asians? Do we not relate to those people who are being tortured and murdered? We are also "gooks" by birth. You and I are no different from those subhuman creatures called Vietnamese. Take a look in the mirror, you have dark hair and dark eyes. You are part of the Third World people and the United States is destroying our kin in Asia. If you don't feel sick after this report, then you are a savage animal. If you do feel sick for the brothers and sisters, then let your rage be known. If you don't, then you and I will be their next victims. Try and remember what happened to the quiet Japanese Americans in World War II. They were like the enemy. They had slanted eyes, black hair, brown eyes, and dark skin. All the necessary features that made them the enemy. Today, the United States is continuing its destruction of the Asian people. They are widening the war by their incursions into Laos and Cambodia. . . . . And if war breaks out with China, then it will be possible that the Chinese Americans will suffer the same fate as did the Japanese Americans in World War II. The repression may even be worse, and include all people of Asian descent. Since all Asians have been identifying with one another, regardless of nationality, then we will all become the enemy to the US imperialist. We have been working together politically, economically and culturally to free ourselves from the oppression that is given to all Third World people. Therefore, the US will be forced to repress all Asian Americans, because we will not

Source: Rodan, March 1971.

be separated. We are all in the same bag, so we must become truly united and begin to raise our voice as one. . . . . See this country for what it really is. It is destroying the people of Vietnam by torture and murder. It will do the same to us.

RED GUARD PARTY, *Our Political Program* (1969)

In this program, which was modeled after the Black Panther Party's 10-point plan, the Red Guards place Asian Americans (referred to as "Yellow people") within a racial paradigm that aligns them with other people of color as exploited and suffering from discrimination.

1. We want freedom. We want power to determine the destiny of our people, the Yellow Community.

   We believe that Yellow people will not be free until we are able to determine our destiny.
2. We want decent housing, fit for shelter of human beings.

   We believe that if the white landlord will not give decent housing to our Yellow community, then the housing and the land should be made into cooperatives so that our community, with government aid, can build and make decent housing for its people.
3. We want education for our people that exposes the true nature of this decadent American society. We want education that teaches us our true history and our role in the present-day society.

   We believe in an educational system that will give to our people a knowledge of self. If a man does not have knowledge of himself and his position in society and the world, then he has little chance to relate to anything else.
4. We want all Yellow men to be exempt from military service.

   We believe that Yellow people should not be forced to fight in the military service to defend a racist government that does not protect us. We will not fight and kill other people of color in the world who, like Yellow people, are being victimized by the white racist government of America. We will protect ourselves from the force and violence of the racist military, by whatever means necessary.
5. We want an immediate end to POLICE BRUTALITY AND MURDER of Yellow People.

   We believe we can end police brutality in our Yellow community by organizing Yellow self-defense groups that are dedicated to defending our Yellow community from racist police oppression and brutality. The Second Amendment

---

Source: Red Guard Community Newspaper, March 12, 1969, p. 6. Reprinted in Fred Ho et al., eds., *Legacy to Liberation: Politics and Culture of Revolutionary Asian/Pacific America*, Boston: AK Press, 2000, pp. 401–403.

to the Constitution of the United States gives a right to bear arms. We, therefore, believe that all Yellow people should arm themselves for self defense.

6. We want freedom for all Yellow men held in federal, state, county and city prisons and jails.

   We believe that all Yellow people should be released from the many jails and prisons because they have not received a fair and impartial trial.

7. We want all Yellow People when brought to trial to be tried in court by a jury of their peer group or people from their Yellow communities, as defined by the Constitution of the United States.

   We believe that the courts should follow the United States Constitution so that Yellow people will receive fair trials. The 14th Amendment of the U.S. Constitution gives a man a right to be tried by his peer group. A peer is a person from a similar economic, social, religious, geographical, environmental, historical and racial background. To do this the court will be forced to select a jury from the Yellow community from which the Yellow defendant came. We have been, and are being tried by all-white juries that have no understanding of the "average reasoning man of the Yellow community."

8. We want adequate and free medical facilities available for the people in the Yellow community.

   We know that Chinatown has the highest density area next to Manhattan. It also has the highest TB and sickness rate in the nation.

9. We want full employment for our people.

   We believe that the federal government is responsible and obligated to give every man employment or a guaranteed income. We believe that if the white American businessmen will not give full employment, then, the means of production should be taken from the businessmen and placed in the community so that the people of the community can organize and employ its people and give a high standard of living. There are thousands of immigrants coming into Chinatown every year and it is impossible for them to find gainful employment.

10. We demand that the United States government recognize the People's Republic of China.

    We believe that MAO TSE-TUNG is the true leader of the Chinese people; not CHIANG KAI SHEK. The government of the United States is now preparing for war against the Chinese People's Republic and against the Chinese people. The racist government of the United States has proven that it will put only peoples of color in concentration camps, Japanese were placed in concentration camps; therefore, it is logical that the next people that will be going are the Chinese people; because the United States is gearing its war time industrial complex for war against China.

10

Chicano Activism

—MATT GARCIA

Mexican Americans participated in the "civil rights movements" of the 1960s and 1970s in a way that transformed popular notions of social justice to include issues of land and labor rights in addition to the familiar concerns of equality in education and access to government. The Black Civil Rights Movement and the ensuing Black Power movement also shaped the consciousness of young Mexican Americans who began to embrace a nonwhite, politicized identity known as "Chicano." After years of employing gradual and cooperative pressure on local, state and federal officials, Chicanos began to experiment with more direct action and protest, challenging the intentions and interests of the government to remedy the problems facing their communities. Whereas previous groups such as the League of United Latin American Citizens (LULAC) and the GI Forum sought to work within the system to end discrimination and segregation during the 1940s and 1950s, new groups such as the United Farmworkers Union, La Alianza Federal de las Mercedes (New Mexico), El Centro de Acción Social y Autónomo/the Center for Autonomous Social Action (CASA), the Brown Berets, United Mexican American Students (UMAS), and La Raza Unida Party became much more assertive and considered a wider range of strategies to achieve their goals in the 1960s and 1970s. In addition to more strident political expression, this generation of activists also employed and inspired artistic expression that articulated a new, nonconformist, nonwhite identity that sought equality and racial justice for Mexicans living in the United States. The Chicano movement, therefore, was a multifaceted social movement that articulated a new politics and a new place for Mexican people within the U.S. national culture.

The Chicano movement has largely been described as having four primary components: the struggle for homelands formerly held in common by Mexican people in the rural Southwest; the farm workers movement and the debate over Mexican immigrant rights; the urban youth movement in the Southwest, including protests against the Vietnam War and advocacy for educational reform; and finally, the articulation of radical political thought and the formation of a Mexican American political party, La Raza Unida Party. Within each of these movements, Mexican American women articulated a politics of racial solidarity while challenging the patriarchal notions of leadership and work within social organizations. Their challenges coalesced into a politics of "Chicana feminism" that expressed both support and criticism of the Chicano movement and the women's movement of the period.

Advocates for the land grant movement in the rural Southwest initiated much of the change toward a more assertive and at times militant attitude and strategy among Mexican Americans. Embittered by the U.S. government's imposition of stricter codes regulating land use on *Hispano* (New Mexicans of Mexican descent) farmers, villagers in northern New Mexico formed La Alianza Federal de las Mercedes (Federal Alliance of Land Grants) led by Reies López Tijerina, a Pentecostal preacher with a knowledge of property law. Under Tijerina, La Alianza sought to take back the territory lost under the 1848 Treaty of Guadalupe Hidalgo by re-occupying land that had formerly been held in common under the *ejido* system—a system that allowed people to share grazing lands for their livestock. In the Tierra Amarilla area of northern New Mexico, Anglo farmers, supported by the federal government, had supplanted the *ejido* system by fencing off territory for their livestock and intimidating Hispano leaders who challenged their grazing practices. Tijerina tapped into the growing militancy of villagers by rallying Hispanos to march and protest the governments' regulations throughout the mid-1960s.

On October 16, 1966, Tijerina and a small contingent of Alianza activists occupied the original *merced* (land grant) called San Joaquín del Río Chama in Kit Carson National Forest, provoking the U.S. government into an armed conflict that resulted in the arrest of Tijerina and five other *aliancistas.* Tijerina remained active while out on bail, though government pressure seriously disrupted the movement. Ultimately, Alianza never realized their goal of reclaiming lost land though their movement initiated a new, more aggressive attitude among Mexican Americans.

The movement for farmworkers' rights consisted of both old and new approaches in labor politics. The struggle for farmworker justice began in the rural farming town of Coachella, California, in 1965 when Filipino workers struck grape farms in an effort to increase their hourly wages and improve their living conditions. By September, the movement had coalesced into a fierce battle between growers and workers, with Mexicans and Filipinos finally joining forces under the common banner of the United Farm Workers union (UFW). After years of heavy losses due to strikes and boycotts, in 1970, growers signed the first United Farm Workers grape contracts. The good feeling, however, did not last long as the International Brotherhood of Teamsters (IBT) union moved in just prior to the 1973 harvest to negotiate "sweetheart contracts" with terms favoring the growers and kickbacks lining the pockets of Teamsters officials. Through outright physical intimidation, the Teamsters declared war on the United Farm Workers, attempting to beat UFW challengers into submission. The extreme violence exhibited by the Teamsters precipitated another cycle of Chávez's now-famous hunger strikes to quell urges of retaliation among his followers. While his strategy of nonviolence ultimately succeeded in winning national and international sympathy for the workers, locally families endured a decade of hardship.

Fissures within the rank and file surfaced in the early 1970s when Mexican immigrants and Filipino workers started abandoning UFW contracts for those administered by the IBT. The challenge of organizing recent and desperate immigrants from

Mexico drove a wedge between some organizers who believed in a *sin fronteras* (open borders) policy advocated by Chicano activist Bert Corona and the El Centro de Acción Social Autónomo (CASA) and those, including César Chávez, who wanted to stamp out all forms of undocumented immigration. Although UFW leaders eventually backed away from their anti-undocumented immigrant position, the issue continued to be a point of contention among farmworkers, UFW organizers, and community activists throughout the 1970s. The abandonment of the union by many Filipino workers also posed a threat to the cohesiveness of the union's core since the UFW in its early days prided itself on attracting a wide array of workers and contributors to *la causa*. The departure of a significant number of Filipinos revealed the fragility of this coalition and a weakness in the UFW armor.

Problems in these organizations notwithstanding, the farmworkers movement and the land grant movement raised the consciousness of the average American about the plight of Mexican people in rural areas and inspired a new generation of urban Mexican American youths to organize their communities and school-aged peers. Youth responded with two inaugural conferences: the National Chicano Liberation Youth Conference in Denver, Colorado, in March 1969 and a meeting of Mexican American students at the University of California, Santa Barbara, in April 1969. In Denver, young people articulated a politics of separatism in *El Plan Espiritual de Aztlán*: "We the Chicano inhabitants and civilizers of the northern land of Aztlán, from whence came our forefathers, reclaim the land of their birth and concentrating the determination of our people declare that . . . Aztlán belongs to those who plant the seeds, water the fields and gather the crops, and not the foreign Europeans." In Santa Barbara, college students designed a plan for implementing Chicano studies programs across the University of California system and launched the student organization MEChA (El Movimiento Estudantil Chicano de Aztlán) in *El Plan de Santa Bárbara*.

Both meetings proved to be inspirational to a new generation, but also produced generative discussions on gender inequality in the Mexican American community. At the Denver conference, for example, women formed a separate workshop to critique their assignments to gender-specific tasks such as typing, cooking, and cleaning, but suppressed a report of dissatisfaction in favor of a message of unity for all Chicanos. Such conformity, however, did not last long as Chicanas wrote about their experiences in the movement and convened meetings on the subject. In 1971, young Mexican American women from various organizations convened the first National Chicana Conference (La Conferencia De Mujeres Por La Raza) in Houston, Texas. Participants distinguished their position from the decidedly middle-class and white-dominated women's movement by articulating a platform and a politics that took into consideration the race- and class-specific concerns of Mexican women living in the United States.

Three other campaigns in urban areas helped define the Chicano movement as it transitioned from the 1960s to the 1970s: the campaign for better high schools in East Los Angeles; protest against the Vietnam War; and the formation of a Chicano political party, La Raza Unida Party, in Crystal City, Texas. In East Los Angeles, high school students formed an organizing committee known as the Young Citizens for Community Action (YCCA) to complain about the lack of college preparatory classes for Mexican students and the denigration of Mexican culture and Spanish language in the curriculum. When the school administration and the local school board ignored their petitions, leaders of the movement, including members of the youth organizations United Mexican American Students (UMAS) and the Brown Berets, orchestrated a walkout of Friday morning classes at Wilson High School on March 1, 1968. The following week, students at Lincoln High School, Garfield High School, and Roosevelt High School left their classrooms as well. The actions of these youths led to a series of walkouts, or "blowouts," in Mexican American communities across the Southwest to protest the poor quality of public education for Mexican youth.

Chicano youth also took to the streets to voice their disapproval of the Vietnam War. Following the Chicano Youth Conference in Denver, the Brown Berets, a paramilitary organization that formed during the school walkouts, began work with a variety of Chicano leaders to create the Chicano Moratorium Committee. Although fraught with tension and conflicting interests, the organization managed to plan one of the largest anti-war marches in the United States on August 29, 1970. Initially, approximately 30,000 marchers peacefully made their way down Whittier Boulevard in the heart of East Los Angeles to Laguna Park. Members of the county sheriffs department and LAPD shattered the nonviolent and festive atmosphere, however, when officers applied force to break up a disturbance at a liquor store nearby. The conflict quickly spiraled out of control leading to a police riot and the beating of marchers. In the melee, a deputy sheriff fired a tear gas projectile into the Silver Dollar Café killing Rubén Salazar, a Mexican American journalist who had written articles sympathetic to the Chicano movement in the *Los Angeles Times*. The riots and the death of Salazar confirmed for many Chicano activists the opinion of Mexicans held by the government, and moved some towards more radical actions or political organizing.

Chicano activists committed themselves to the formation of an all-Chicano national political party, La Raza Unida Party, in the 1970s, building on the regional success of Chicano organizers in Crystal City, Texas. An organization known as Mexican American Youth Organization (MAYO) led by the José Angel Gutiérrez took shape in 1967 to challenge a variety of problems facing Mexican people in Texas. MAYO supported a school walkout in Crystal City, Texas, in 1969 and 1970 that culminated in the school board conceding to many of the student demands. Imbued with confidence and a new "Chicano" identity, MAYO changed their name to La Raza Unida Party (LRUP) with the intent of electing Mexican politicians in Texas. LRUP experienced regional success, especially in Cyrstal City, where in 1970 Gutiérrez and two other LRUP candidates were elected to the school board. Attempts to extend this movement beyond rural Texas, however, failed as a result of the militant cultural-nationalist politics of Gutiérrez that appealed to only the most radicalized Chicano activists.

Taken together, these movements and organizations constituted a new attitude among Mexican Americans in the United States. While few of these organizations succeeded in achieving their goals, the debates they raised and the policies they proposed live on in the curriculum of Chicano studies college programs and the political platforms advocated by some Mexican American politicians. Equally important, the decision of the Chicano generation to take direct action in articulating a sense of discontent with the failure of this country to live up to its principles of liberty and equality for all continues to influence the politics of a new generation of Americans of Mexican and Latin American descent living in the United States today.

MARTA COTERA, *La Conferencia De Mujeres Por La Raza* (1971)

This report of the first National Chicana Conference in Houston, Texas, reveals the development of a feminist consciousness among many women of Mexican descent during the early 1970s. Unlike the Denver conference where women suppressed criticism of chauvinistic behavior of Chicanos, Chicanas insisted on equal participation in the movement and criticized the Catholic church for their stance on abortion. The split from the conference of a group of Chicanas protesting the lack of connections with the local community also demonstrates political differences among women in the movement.

About 500 Chicanas attended a national conference in Houston, Texas, May 28–30, 1971. Approximately 80% of the women were in the 18–23 age bracket from various universities across the United States. The main theme covered throughout the conference was that of clarifying the women's role as Chicanas and in the [Chicano] movement, mainly eliminating the passive role (home and motherhood) the Chicana has always played.

Among one of the main speakers was Julia Ruiz, an assistant professor of social work at Arizona State University. Her topic was "The Mexican-American Women's Public and Self-Image." Central to the speech was the idea that "togetherness can liberate Chicanas." The only choice in this society for Chicana women has been the home and motherhood. Chicanas have to fight together for liberation so that they will have a choice. Chicana women can change the society that places inferior sexist and racist labels on them. Too much hatred has been stamped on Chicana women and it has to be shed.

Workshops were held on identity and movimiento issues. Topics ranged from "marriage Chicana style" to "religion," and "militancy or conservatism—which way is forward?" to "exploitation of women—the Chicana perspective."

A resolution was easily passed that the conference join others from San Antonio in speaking out against the use of "dummy" birth control pills in an experiment conducted on Chicana women, which resulted in ten unwanted babies.

Other resolutions, some of which met controversy, were: "We as mujeres de la Raza [women of la Raza] recognize the Catholic Church as an oppressive institution and do hereby resolve to break away and not go to them to bless our unions, and [give our] support for free and legal abortions for all women who want and need them."

Throughout the whole conference, in the workshops, in group sessions, a lot of personal differences were brought out. By Sunday, on the whole, the conference

---

Source: Conference also known as National Chicana Conference. From *Profile on the Mexican American Woman*, Austin: National Educational Laboratory Publishers, 1976: pp. 224–227.

had divided into two groups. One group staged a walk-out because the conference was being held in a "Gringo" [white] institution [YWCA] and should have been in the "barrio" where the people were. They went to a nearby "barrio" park to finish up their evaluations and resolutions. The other group decided to stay in the YWCA and finish up the conference, making evaluations and résolutions. Last-minute workshops on "strategies for [the future]" were cancelled because of this reason. Two sets of final resolutions and evaluations were finally presented.

La Conferencia de Mujeres por la Raza

Complaints were presented by Group I that no "barrio" people were represented at the conference. Group II remarked that they were, but when they (barrio residents) talked, attention, and respect, were not given to them.

Key Points

1. Chicana women not only want to support the men in the [Chicano] movement, but also want to participate.
2. With further involvement in the movement, marriages have changed; traditional roles for Chicanas are not acceptable or applicable anymore.
3. Chicanas want Chicano and public recognition as a major facilitator in the movement.
4. Education and career opportunities are wanted for Chicanas.
5. There is a tremendous amount of personal and group differences among Chicana women. Some will react, others respond rationally, others just rap a lot and still, no action. We feel, along with other Chicana women at the conference, that it makes no difference how many differences there are between what we think. The most important thing is to look at common problems, to get ourselves together, and even more important [to decide] what we're going to do.

ALFREDO FIGUEROA, *The U.F.W. Anti-Immigrant Campaign and Falling Out with Bert Corona, M.A.P.A., and Other Chicano Groups* (2005)

The following account comes from Alfredo Figueroa who participated in the formation of the United Farm Workers union in southern California. He also belonged to the Mexican American Political Association (MAPA)

Source: This account comes from Figueroa's contribution to the Farmworkers Documentation Project, http://www.farmworkermovement.us/essays/essays.shtml, pp. 29–30.

and called both César Chávez and Bert Corona friends. Here, Figueroa recounts the differences between Chávez and Corona on the issue of U.S. immigration policy and his decision to support an "open borders/sin fronteras" position.

The U. F. W. had been plagued with strikebreakers coming from Mexico for a long time. We spent a lot of time meeting with Mexican Union Officials of C. T. M in Mexicali and reaching out to the general commuting farm worker population. There is a tremendous constant arrival of new immigrants at the border cities who want jobs first, owing to great number of turnovers in the work force.

After the first 3 years of the U. F. W. O. C. Strike in Coachella and Delano, we found out that educating the new immigrant approach was not working out. In 1971 a racist state senator from Northern California was able to pass through legislation—the infamous Dixon Arnett Bill. The bill focused on employer sanctions to stop the hiring of undocumented workers, they would be subject to fines, and the employers were authorized to make the determination of employees having green cards or not. The authority of the Federal I.N.S. was given to the employers, which was totally absurd.

The Mexicans were labeled as parasites and a burden to the Anglo way of life, sort of the same mentality that a lot of the Anglo population still has today against the Mexicans.

What made the whole Dixon Arnett Law Campaign so infamous within the Chicano community was that the U. F. W. O. C. and C. R. L. A. were supporting it and lobbied the legislature for its passage. This was the beginning of major split between Bert Corona, M. A. P. A., C. A. S. A (Cento Acion Social Autonomo) and many other Chicano movement groups whose goals are still: no borders, one indigenous continent. M. A. P. A.'s job was to educate the immigrants, not make them the scapegoats for the racist capitalistic population.

The U. F. W. walked right into the hands of anti-Mexican attitudes of the old A. F. L.-C. I. O. anti-immigrant practice and forgot the basic human rights struggle that an Injury to One is an Injury to All.

This was one instance when Cesar used to say that politics makes strange bedfellows. Bert Corona, C. A. S. A. and the rest of the pro-immigrant groups countered with massive demonstrations. Afterwards the State Supreme Court declared the law unconstitutional, because the enforcement of immigration laws were the jurisdiction of the Federal Government and not the state, nor the self-interest unions.

After 1971 the U. F. W. wanted all the offices to report any undocumented workers in the farms and to report them to the I. N. S. and they wanted monthly tabulations of the numbers reported. During the reporting of the undocumented to the I.N.S. ran into differences with the policies and direction that the U. F. W. was taking. I never reported one single undocumented immigrant; on the contrary I was on the Board of Directors of C. A. S. A. with Bert Corona. We would take our Blythe U. F. W. members to Los Angeles to demonstrate against the Dixon Arnett Law . . . The I. N. S. was and is the most hated Federal Dept of the United States, and we would never become their stoolies. During those years the majority of the officers were Anglo racists from Texas and Virginia. . . . .

After the Dixon-Arnett Bill died, the anti-immigrant groups were able to lobby Congressman Peter Rodino to introduce similar legislation as the Dixon-Arnett Bill at the Federal level. I continue working against the Rodino Bill with C. A. S. A. and Bert was able to organize a national coalition called the National Coalition for Fair Immigration Laws and Practices. Even Ted Kennedy was in favor of the Rodino Bill until Bert Corona and the C. A. S. A. members got to him in Washington and he changed his vote.

RAMON PEREZ MEJIA, *Declaration* (1975)

The following document comes from a deposition with Ramon Perez Mejia, a farmworker in the Coachella Valley, California, in 1975. Mejia was a rank-and-file member of the United Farm Workers and, as he states, was subjected to appeals and threats by the International Brotherhood of Teamsters union to switch his allegiance. The document demonstrates that Mexicans and Filipino workers joined both sides. It also demonstrates the extreme pressure placed on UFW affiliates to join the Teamsters.

My name is Ramon Perez Mejia. I live at Wheatland & Ensign, Richgrove.

I've worked for M. Caratan about seven days. I started to work last Wednesday, May 7. On Saturday, two Teamsters organizers, a young Philippino man and a Mexican girl came to the field with a petition supporting the Teamsters. They also told everyone that we were invited to go to Sacramento. They said food and transportation and housing, if needed, would be provided. We were told that they wanted us to come to Sacramento—that we were to go there to support Teamsters and not the strike. I told the organizers, "I can't go." The foreman told me, "If you don't go or sign our petition, you will have no more work." . . .

When they returned from Sacramento, the same Philippino came to the field. He told me three times "Hey you" and I said "Hey you has a name." He said, "If you don't like the Teamsters what are you doing here?" I told the organizer, "If it doesn't please you, tell the grower to fire me." The Philippino organizer said, "I'll kick your ass." I said, "Why is it that you want to kick my ass?" I told the organizer, "Are you here to make trouble for the worker or cause problems for your Union?" At that point, I was challenged by the organizer to step out of the field and have it out. . . . I asked the organizer why was he angry. The organizer told me "You'd better keep your mouth shut, stupid Mexican."

I declare under penalty of perjury that the foregoing is true and correct. Executed at Delano, California, on May 15, 1975.

Ramon M. Perez

COURT FILING, UFW, *United Farm Workers National Union, AFL-CIO, et al. Plaintiffs, International Brotherhood of Teamsters, et al. Defendants* (1973)

The following document, prepared for a lawsuit against the International Brotherhood of Teamsters (IBT), outlines the violence and threats committed against union officials and workers affiliated with the United Farm Workers in the 1970s. Teamster representatives, frequently referred to as "goons," routinely attacked UFW organizers and workers. The document also captures the level of collusion between growers, packers, and the IBT in their attempt to thwart the United Farm Workers union from continuing their success.

A. On April 24, 1973, at a COACHELLA-IMPERIAL DISRIBUTORS (hereinafter CID) labor camp off Dillon Road, members of the UFWU were attacked and abused by Teamsters and grower personnel, under the direction of AL DROUBIE, a Teamster organizer, and Henry Reider, Vice President and General Manager of CID. The attack included punching, kicking, shoving, throwing of rocks and other hard objects, use of slingshots, sticks, and chains, brandishing of pistols, and verbal threats directed at plaintiffs and members of their class.

By reason of said acts, plaintiffs suffered, in part, as follows:

1. Francisco Magalla was grabbed by the neck and thrown to the ground;
2. Cynthia Bell was struck in the head by a rock;
3. Guadalupe Skates was pushed;
4. Lupe Murguia's car window was broken by a rock thrown at him by Charles Mandalla, a supervisor for Valdora, who threatened him first verbally and with rocks;
5. Marshall Ganz was hit and knocked down by Droubie; in addition, his car was struck with rocks;
6. Tobies Espinosa was kicked in the right hip;
7. Yolanda Serrano's car window was broken by a rock;
8. Bill Encinas was assaulted with a chain and then punched and knocked down;
9. Tom Dalzell was shoved by Droubie, punched and knocked down by another Teamster, and struck by three thrown rocks;
10. Celia Horton was nearly hit by numerous rocks which struck the truck she was in;
11. Bobbie Stewart was grabbed and roughed up;
12. Esquino Prado was hit in the face by DROUBIE;
13. Bernardo Prado was hit on the head by a flagstick;
14. All of these victims and many other UFWU members and supporters present were threatened, intimidated, placed in great fear of their physical well-being and suffered extreme and severe mental anguish and emotional distress.

B. On April 16, 1973, at a MEL-PAK ranch, an automobile emerged from the ranch entrance. A Teamster in the back seat, who plaintiffs are informed and believe was JOHNNY MACIAS, struck Alicia Uribe in the right eye with a hard object and knocked her to the ground. This act took place in full view of and close proximity to many UFWU pickets.

By reason of this act, plaintiffs were injured as follows:

1. Alicia Uribe suffered damage to her right eye, medical expenses, shock, fear, mental anguish and emotional distress, pain and suffering:
2. Other UFWU members present were threatened, intimidated, harassed, placed in great fear of bodily harm, and suffered mental anguish and emotional distress.

C. On April 19, 1973, at a HEGOBLADE-MARGULEAS-TENNECO (hereinafter H & M) ranch, one of the two Gimmian brothers, both of whom are employed in supervisory capacities by H & M, drove a truck into a vehicle in which several UFWU members were riding in full view and close proximity to a UFWU picket line. Gimmian then threatened Fred Chavez and another person with a rock. Then, a number of goons from the Teamsters and H & M charged across the street and knocked Chavez and another UFW member down.

By reason of those acts, plaintiffs, suffered the following injuries:

1. Moises and Aaron Huerta and Chavez, who were in the UFWU vehicle, were physically injured;
2. The Huertas, Chavez, and others were placed in great fear of bodily harm;
3. Chavez and another UFWU member were knocked to the ground and physically injured;
4. Other UFWU members were threatened, intimidated, placed in great fear of bodily harm, and suffered mental anguish and emotional distress. . . .

D. On June 23, 1973, on the location near 57th and Buchanen which is a Moreno Ranch, many Teamsters including Hector Perez, Chuck Farris and Ray an Austrian boy attacked the United Farmworker picketers.

The United Farmworker picketers were abused, harassed, intimidated, frightened and beaten.

By reason of said acts, plaintiffs have been injured as follows:

1. Ricardo Lopez was beaten to near unconsciousness, given a bloody nose and his mouth was busted and had three teeth broken.
2. Hector Perez, Chuck Farris and Ray, of the Teamsters, hit Mr. Tamayo on the head with a lead pipe. When Mr. Tamayo was knocked to the ground, the men proceeded to beat him unmercifully.
3. Frederico Sayer was attacked from behind and hit on head.
4. Felipe Reyes was attacked by a Teamster when Mr. Reyes tried to help a friend that was being beaten by Teamsters.
5. Benito Savabria was attacked and thrown to the ground by one of the black Teamsters.
6. Roy Trevino was brutally beaten with a tree branch that Teamster had. He was beaten while on the ground and was beaten until he became unconscious.

7. Rosario Hernandez was beaten as she fell to the ground while attempting to flee from the Teamsters.
8. Juan Gutierrez was badly beaten up.
9. Man named Jesus was beaten on the head with a lead pipe and his head was split open.
10. Manuel Arredondo was hit with a stick.
11. Juan Rodriguez was beaten up very badly.
12. Carlos Ortiz was hit in the back with a stick.
13. Eliseo Viscara was beaten with pipes by the Teamsters.
14. Other farmworkers had witnessed incident where their fellow brothers and sisters were beaten, kicked, pushed, thrown rocks at, attacked with knives, sticks and threatened with guns. It was witnessed how the Teamsters zeroed in on the teen-agers, women, children and sadly enough on the old people. The Teamsters would attack in groups. There were always at least three Teamsters at one time beating up on a person and once that person was knocked down the Teamsters kept beating and kicking them.
15. On that same day of June 23, 1973, it was heard by Mr. Carlos Ortiz as Mike Falco, a Teamster gave the order for the farmworkers to be attacked.

On the same day of June 23, 1973, at 60th and Buchanan, Mrs. Maria Chavez saw Johnny Macias, a Teamster, carrying a pistol. She then saw and heard him tell the Teamsters to ‘Kill them, kill them’, meaning for the Teamsters to kill the farmworkers. Then she saw how all hell broke loose and people started getting beaten with pipes, poles, and rocks.

11

Consumer Rights Activism

—JÜRGEN RUCKABERLE

The consumer movement is probably the least understood social and political movement of the 1960s and 1970s, yet it significantly shaped American culture and politics. The movement had such an impact in part because it grew from an incredibly rich history dating back to the founding of the United States itself.

Consumption had been an issue that fueled political passions and informed political behavior since the American Revolution. In the middle of the nineteenth century, Americans' actions were still being shaped by the politics of consumption. For example, citizens formed cooperatives in this period in order to obtain goods at a fair price and avoid the exploitative character of capitalism. The first organized consumer movement, however, did not come of age until the late 1890s when the reform efforts of populists and Progressives flourished. Concerned with labor conditions, declining purchasing power of wages, adulterated food, growing numbers of ads, and the rising concentration of industries, groups such as the National Consumers League, muckrakers like Upton Sinclair, and even elected officials ushered in legislation designed to protect consumers such as the Pure Food and Drug Act (1906) and the Federal Trade Commission Act (1914). In the early 1920s, consumers were inundated with aggressive advertising campaigns and, in response, consumer advocates wrote several best-selling books that attacked advertising techniques and promoted independent product testing to provide valuable information for consumers to get their "money's worth."

The Great Depression of the late 1920s and the 1930s undermined the purchasing power of American consumers. To address this issue, President Roosevelt formed a rudimentary welfare state that would increase Americans' economic security by providing them with collective bargaining rights, and he insisted that the federal government be a major player in the economy. In key respects, FDR's "New Deal," as it came to be known, placed the needs of ordinary Americans above those of business interests, and since his plan for economic recovery rested on increasing citizens' ability to buy goods, "consumers" came to play an important role in American society.

Economic growth fueled by ever-growing consumer demand and the defense industries during World War II would keep production numbers high, unemployment low, and improve living standards of Americans into the 1940s and 1950s. By the mid-1950s, rampant consumerism not only fed private indulgence but it also allowed the United States to compete successfully in the ongoing Cold War rivalry with the Soviet Union. In fact, because the extraordinary economic growth of the 1950s was accompanied by, and came to fuel, an increasingly conservative political agenda both at home and abroad, almost overnight the more radical or populist aspects of the consumer movement that had come of age during the New Deal, largely faded away. While consumer advocates tuned down their activism in the 1950s, consumers themselves faced an increasingly complex marketplace in which businesses utilized scholarly studies and easy access to credit to provide access to the American way of life. Studying consumer behavior became the holy grail of marketing experts, psychologists, economists, and new business concepts such as market segmentation allowed advertisers to target specific consumer groups. By the early 1960s, Americans celebrated rising standards of living measured by traditional indicators of consumption: cars, radios, and other appliances.

However, some criticism of rampant materialism and a call for consumer protection did exist in this period. Economist John Kenneth Galbraith, for example, argued that not everyone could participate in the postwar affluence because of the unequal distribution of wealth. Likewise, the Consumers Union (CU) that had been formed during the New Deal remained committed to informing buyers and raising their consciousness about everything from the risks of radioactive fallout and smoking to the importance of auto safety. Its publication, *Consumer Reports*, also provided the public with a valuable tool for smart buying.

Still, while many citizens took to the streets to promote social change in the 1960s and 1970s, at first glance it appears that most Americans just continued to shop and consume the rising number of products being promoted on their television screens and in magazines. For these Americans, citizenship rights directly correlated with the ability to consume and it was their collective purchases that had fed the underbelly of the postwar economic boom. But in ways that they may not have appreciated, the activist culture of the 1960s and 1970s did shape the lives of even the mainstream buying public and, in turn, the power of American consumerism came to inform the actions of not a few activist organizations.

Seeing the rising importance of consumer spending for the national well-being, several liberal politicians sought to forge a renewed alliance between the federal government and consumer groups. Much as their New Deal predecessors had done, they courted mainstream consumers by adopting the activist rhetoric of the day without advocating a particularly radical program for regulating businesses. The "value-for-money" consumer activism that they advocated stressed the efficiency of the economy through federal laws and informed consumers about the "best buy."

President Kennedy, for example, promised to protect the rights of and elevate the position of consumers in the federal government. In 1962, Kennedy announced a consumers' bill of rights— the right to safety, the right to be informed, the right to choose, and the right to be heard. The President and members of Congress also spearheaded legislative efforts to protect consumers by outlining for manufacturers how to label, package, price, and advertise their products. They outlined laws that specified safety conditions for products, cars, highways, and workplaces. They ordered credit institutions to fully disclose financial terms and defined appropriate and acceptable environmental standards for the quality of air, water, and waste.

While the value-for-money wing of the consumer movement in this period was fueled primarily by those politicians who advocated for greater consumer protections, the world's largest independent testing organization, Consumers Union, as well as muckrakers such as Sidney Margolius and other critics of the marketplace, played an important role as well. Together, this top-down movement reached a significant goal in 1964 when President Johnson named Esther Peterson Special Assistant for Consumer Affairs. As a longtime consumer and labor movement activist, Peterson was most outspoken.

Notably, however, any attempt to protect consumers to a meaningful degree met with a fair amount of resistance at the federal level. Ironically, for example, Esther Peterson's public support for a meat boycott that had been called by housewives in Denver, led to her ousting in 1967. Even though Peterson returned to the office under President Carter in the late 1970s, her attempt to establish a more substantial consumer department failed. The business community's strenuous objections to greater regulation often won out over the needs of consumers even when they had a presence in the White House. True, consumers had achieved a great deal in this period, but ultimately even their most celebrated legislative gains were hampered by weak enforcement, by the significant influence of business in regulatory agencies, and by the mounting criticism of free-market advocates.

Still, by the late 1960s, consumerism had entered the public's consciousness and groups representing consumers spread to the state, regional, and national level. National organizations such as CU saw their subscription figures climb to over two million by the early 1970s. CU also increased its efforts to support a growing movement of politically mainstream consumers. CU supplied funds to establish and support small grassroots consumer groups. In 1967, CU initiated the formation and growth of the Consumer Federation of America (CFA), a political umbrella over numerous consumer groups. By the early 1970s, CFA claimed over 200 dues-paying organizations. Anti-smoking groups, food safety organizations, and health-care groups complemented the broad consumer agenda. By the late 1960s, most states had created consumer departments.

There was, however, a more radical version of the value-for-money consumer activism that was embraced by liberal politicians in the federal government and groups like CU. Indeed, there were many Americans who felt that only organizations and individuals fully independent of both business and government could conduct the inquiries necessary to protect the public from buying dangerous goods and unscrupulous practices.

Probably the most radical consumer advocate, one who inspired tremendous grassroots support, was Ralph Nader. Nader linked the consumer interest with the public interest and he energized American consumer activism by enlisting young people in his so-called "public interest research groups" or PIRGS. Reaching fame with his 1966 expose of General Motors cars that he claimed were "Unsafe at Any Speed," Nader formed a network of nonprofit organizations working for the public interest. Public Citizen, Congress Watch, the Center for Auto Safety, and the Center for the Study of Responsive Law were only a few such Nader-inspired groups. "Nader Raiders" exposed the manipulation of federal regulatory agencies by industry representatives. They monitored bills, identified legislative outcomes for consumers, and tracked voting records.

Because various social movements in this period also began to use consumer activism to further their political goals, there was a wing of the consumer movement even more radical than that led by Ralph Nader. For example, not only did women who joined the feminist movement find themselves supplying the ground troops for major consumer protests such as the 1966 Denver boycott that soon became a nationwide protest against rising food prices, but they also used the consumer boycott to protest the sale of products or images that they considered sexist.

African Americans who had joined the civil rights movement also used their purchasing power to enhance the struggle for racial justice. For example, African Americans often boycotted stores that relied on black consumers' purchases but would not hire them. As important, the civil rights movement was able to use the consumer boycott to assist in its efforts to desegregate public and private institutions in the American South. In the North, looting white stores and protecting businesses run by "soul brothers" during a number of urban rebellions was yet another way in which consumer consciousness shaped the activism of this period.

One of the most well-known examples of a social movement of the 1960s that both connected with and radicalized the consumer movement was the Chicano movement. Labor leader César Chávez advocated the use of traditional labor strategies such as the strike to improve the condition of Mexican American farmworkers, but the United Farm Workers (UFW) union also used product boycotts to its great advantage. In the early 1970s, consumers all over the world supported the struggling UFW's grape boycott that the union had organized to call attention to issues they faced, ranging from low wages and child labor to the dangerous pesticides being used in agricultural work.

One social movement of the 1960s and 1970s, the environmental movement, took an interest in consumerism not simply because it offered an opportunity to achieve its demands, but also because there were direct links between the production and consumption of goods and the environment that it sought to protect. In 1962, for example, environmental activist Rachel Carson wrote an extremely influential book describing the environmental consequences of the indiscriminate use of pesticides that were used by business to make food products more visually appealing and plentiful for consumers. Notably, through its critique of environmentally unsound business practices, this movement also raised the much larger question of whether mass consumption was itself a sustainable practice.

Ultimately, the consumer movement, in all its facets, had flaws. In terms of its ability to change buying habits, for example, this movement tended to reach only the nation's best-educated and most affluent consumers. In addition, consumer groups were slow to call attention to, and to address, consequences of mass consumption. Perhaps most importantly, even if politicians saw all Americans as consumers, the consumer movement never became a mass movement. Because most in its ranks believed heavily in the tenets of market capitalism, and thus shied away from embracing the political power of consumption, they were never comfortable allying themselves with those activists in the women's movement, civil rights movement, or Chicano movement who most willingly used consumerism as a weapon and an organizational strategy. Without unity of vision, the consumer movement was ultimately unable to withstand the assault on it waged by proponents of the free market and foes of regulation in the late 1970s and 1980s.

But even while free-market advocates clearly eroded the basis of the consumer movement in the 1980s, the movement left an important legacy. The most impressive record of consumer activism is the legion of consumer protection laws passed by Congress in the 1960s and early 1970s. Given the very diverse nature of consumers and the difficulties organizing such fleeting and often incompatible interests, consumer groups did a remarkable job influencing lawmakers, business leaders, and consumers. With limited funds, consumer organizations established an impressive network of professional institutions providing independent information for consumers, lobbying lawmakers, and representing consumers.

UNITED MEXICAN AMERICAN STUDENTS, *Boycott Bulletin* (1969)

Chicano students enrolled at the University of Washington for the first time in 1968. Once there they formed the United Mexican American Students (UMAS) in order to tackle the social problems they faced. Energized by the momentum of the civil rights and farm worker movements, and the general student mobilization on campuses around the nation, they soon adopted a consumer boycott in its efforts to support the United Farm Worker Organizing Committee (UFWOC), which was still trying to secure union recognition from grape growers.

Background: Low pay, long hours, no rest periods, no sanitation facilities, and no grievance procedures is the rule for farm workers. Small children work to help supplement family income. Death from major illnesses is over twice the national rate. Life expectancy in California is 49 years in the Yakima Valley it is 38! To improve conditions the farm workers went on strike in the Delano grape vineyards in September, 1965 and have won contracts with 12 wine grape growers guaranteeing decent wages and other improvements. Struck table grape growers refuse to negotiate with the strikers, allow a union election. They have broken the strikes of over 6000 workers with "green carders" illegally entering from Mexico. . . . the

---

Source: "Seattle Civil Rights and Labor History Project," www.civilrights.washington.edu. http://depts.washington.edu/civilr/mecha_documents.htm#grape.

strikers bring the issue to the people who care, organizing individuals, cities, and institutions to boycott grapes until the growers agree to justice. . . .

At a formal meeting last night, a formal coalition of groups sponsoring the boycott was formed, and a steering committee selected. Representatives were, the United Mexican American Students (UMAS), SDS, BSU, Young Socialists Alliance (YSA), Black and White Concern, the University YMCA Boycott Committee, the Student Assembly (SA), and the ASUW. Other groups supporting the boycott (and individuals) are welcome to join. . . .

The University administration is again selling scab (non-union) California grapes. In doing this, it is undermining the 3.5 year struggle of the United Farm Workers Organizing Committee for the basic right to bargain collectively the UFWOC is leading a sustained struggle for decent wages, living conditions, and the self determination of farm workers. . . . the Administration is acting unilaterally! All dormitories and the Student Assembly voted to boycott grapes. . . . By buying grapes the administration is aiding the politically powerful grape growers. *This is every bit as much a political stand as boycotting grapes. . . .*

Wednesday's picketing of the Husky Den and the cafeteria resulted in a 16% and 30% drop in sales respectively. . . . For the boycott to be successful, all sympathetic people must bring sack lunches or eat the (delicious) alternative food provided. Picketing will continue today from 11 AM until 6:45 PM. We will expand to the Husky Hollow and the Evergreen Room. Food will be provided for the boycotters by the University Y on the second floor. Also, an Open Forum will be held outside the cafeteria. JOIN US!!!!

CONSUMERS EDUCATION AND PROTECTIVE ASSOCIATION, *Our History* (1969)

The Consumers Education and Protective Association (CEPA) was formed in Philadelphia by Max Weiner in 1966. This group organized low-income consumers, provided legal assistance, and used consumer picketing to protest unacceptable business practices.

In September, 1966, CEPA took a giant step forward with the establishment of its monthly newspaper, CONSUMERS VOICE. This little 4-page (sometime 8-page) paper has been a mighty weapon in CEPA's never-ending ballet for consumer protection. CONSUMERS VOICE is an accurate mirror of the situation in which the low-income consumer finds himself today and shows the efforts of the organization in fighting for consumer justice.

Source: From the "Living history" of CEPA in which the monthly publication *Consumers Voice* is introduced. Kansas State University, Richard L. D. and Marjorie J. Morse Department of Special Collections, Consumer Movement Archives, Florence Mason Papers, Box 6, Misc.

CONSUMERS VOICE reflects the action of CEPA. It tells the cases, names the companies involved, reprints the contracts, purchase orders, Sheriff Sale notices, and other documents. It shows the action of the people, the pickets, the demonstrations. It tells of the victories, the homes saved from the Sheriff, the money refunded to victims of swindles, the cars and furniture saved from unfair repossession.

CONSUMERS VOICE is not a dry tract, lecturing people that "you should not have signed that," or "watch out for this and that." It is a lively, living picture of people engaged in a mighty struggle. It reports the issues, events and personalities involved in this great struggle. Where other newspapers make a sensation out of a murder case, a rape or a divorce scandal, CONSUMERS VOICE reports the news of a refund check won from some merchant of a home saved from a Sheriff Sale.

The lessons taught by CONSUMERS VOICE are learned in the market place, where battles are fought and won for the protection of consumers, their families, their money, their possessions, and their dignity as people. [. . .]

Principles of Consumer Organization

As a result of almost three years of daily and continuous battles and campaigns, CEPA has learned a few principles of consumer organization that may be helpful to other individuals and groups interested in establishing similar organizations.

First, the organization must be made up of consumers . . . the people who are facing the problems of the fraud, deceptive sale practices, oppressive collection practices, lax law enforcement. . . .

Second, the consumers must engage in action and must see themselves as having and using their strength to work and win campaigns for consumer justice. . . . The organization establishes its reputation for effectiveness and builds confidence in its ability to tackle the biggest institutions in its fight for consumer justice.

Third, the consumers must have organization. Complaints, grievances, activities, picketing—all must be seen as the organized activity of the consumers. When a complaint is received, the consumer must immediately be informed that his complaint is being handled by an organization, not by an individual, or some big shot . . . It is not the once-in-a-while action . . . which builds up the effective organization that is ready to handle consumer complaints.

NEW YORK TIMES, *Housewives' Friend Esther Peterson* (1966)

This article reports on Esther Peterson, President Johnson's Special Assistant for Consumer Affairs, and her efforts to support a sequence of boycotts that started in Denver and the unfavorable press that she received from several organizations including the Advertising Federation of America who called her the "most pernicious threat to advertising today."

Source: New York Times, November 5, 1966.

Her constituency numbers 197 million Americans, and more of them seem to be getting angrier every day which makes Esther Eggertsen Peterson a happy woman. A picket line? She rubs her hands in glee. A bad bargain? She pounces on it. For Mrs. Peterson is "that woman President Johnson appointed to look out for consumers," which was the only address needed for one man's recent complaint to reach her. She relishes the spreading of boycotts of supermarkets by housewives across the country, protesting high prices and demanding an end to gimmicks, contests, trading stamps and other promotional devices that are believed to drive prices up. . . .

Mrs. Peterson is a former labor organizer and lobbyist, still an Assistant Secretary of Labor (which makes her the highest ranking woman official of both the Kennedy and Johnson administrations), and since January, 1964, the president's special assistant for consumer affairs. . . . Until the recent boycotts, which began in Denver on Oct. 17, Mrs. Peterson found the American consumer unorganized, anonymous and virtually voiceless. . . .

The Peterson's live in an integrated district in North Washington. . . . These days, Mrs. Peterson is getting in the mail such objects as cold cream jars with false bottoms, shrimp that are not as big as those pictured on the package in which they came, and other measures of consumers' discontent. Her mail now numbers 2,000 pieces a day.

CONSUMER ACTION NEWS, *Lemonstration Makes History* (1975)

The nonprofit organization called Consumer Action was founded in 1971 by a student activist and housewife, Kay Pachtner, in San Francisco. The volunteer group began by establishing a consumer complaint hotline to help consumers protect their rights and published studies about deceptive practices by financial institutions.

"Singing 'Swing low, sour chariot, can't even carry me home,' the owners of 50 lemon vehicles paraded their faulty machines past San Francisco's Auto Row in protest of the shabby treatment they say they've received from car dealers.

It was California's—and perhaps the world's—first Lemonstration that was organized by Consumer Action to call attention to what Lemonstration organizer Karen Zahn called 'the national scandal of car buying and car repair,' and was held on Nov. 8 [1975]. Over 60 vehicles and 90 people participated in the demonstration; the non-lemon vehicles carried signs supporting the 'Auto Buyer's Warranty,' which CA has developed as an answer to the lemon car problem. [. . .] 'If Detroit makes a lemon car and by chance I buy it, the problem should be Detroit's and not mine. We're simply asking the industry to stand by its products.' [. . .]

Source: Consumer Action News, November 1975.

JOHN F. KENNEDY, *President Kennedy on Protecting the Consumer Interest* (1962)

By the early 1960s, the White House itself was aware that consumers mattered politically.

To the Congress of the United States:

Consumers, by definition, include us all. They are the largest economic group in the economy, affecting and affected by almost every public and private economic decision. Two-thirds of all spending in the economy is by consumers. But they are the only important group in the economy who are not effectively organized, whose views are often not heard.

The federal Government—by nature the highest spokesman for all the people—has a special obligation to be alert to the consumer's needs and to advance the consumer's interests. Ever since legislation was enacted in 1872 to protect the consumer from frauds involving use of the U.S. mail, the Congress and Executive Branch have been increasingly aware of their responsibility to make certain that our Nation's economy fairly and adequately serves consumers' interests.

In the main, it has served them extremely well. Each succeeding generation has enjoyed both higher income and a greater variety of goods and services. As a result our standard of living is the highest in the world—and, in less than 20 years, it should rise an additional 50 percent.

Fortunate as we are, we nevertheless cannot afford waste in consumption any more than we can afford inefficiency in business or Government. If consumers are offered inferior products, if prices are exorbitant, if drugs are unsafe or worthless, if the consumer is unable to choose on an informed basis, then his dollar is wasted, his health and safety may be threatened, and the national interest suffers. . . .

The march of technology—affecting, for example, the foods we eat, the medicines we take, and the many appliances we use in our homes—has increased the difficulties of the consumer along with his opportunities; and it has outmoded many of the old laws and regulations and made new legislation necessary. The typical supermarket before World War II stocked about 1,500 separate food items—an impressive figure by any standard. But today it carries over 6,000. . . . Additional legislative and administrative action is required, however, if the federal Government is to meet its responsibility to consumers in the exercise of their rights. These rights include:

(1) The right to safety—to be protected against the marketing of goods which are hazardous to health or life.

(2) The right to be informed—to be protected against fraudulent, deceitful, or grossly misleading information, advertising, labeling, or other practices, and to be given the facts he needs to make an informed choice.

Source: http://www.presidency.ucsb.edu/ws/print.php?pid=9108.

(3) The right to choose—to be assured, wherever possible, access to a variety of products and services at competitive prices; and in those industries in which competition is not workable and Government regulation is substituted, an assurance of satisfactory quality and service at fair prices.

(4) The right to be heard—to be assured that consumer interests will receive full and sympathetic consideration in the formulation of Government policy, and fair and expeditious treatment in its administrative tribunals.

To promote the fuller realization of these consumer rights, it is necessary that existing Government programs be strengthened, that Government organization be improved, and, in certain areas, that new legislation be enacted.

RALPH NADER, *We're Still in the Jungle* (1967)

Ralph Nader became one of the nation's most famous consumer advocates in the 1960s when he challenged the General Motors Corporation to make its automobiles safer. This lawyer and author went on to found numerous public interest and consumer advocacy groups and also came to play an active role in changing laws to better regulate American corporations and protect American citizens.

Before he was elected to the House of Representatives in 1958, farmer Neal Smith (D-Iowa) noticed something curious abut the numerous livestock sales he attended. The same buyers seemed to be purchasing all the diseased, sick, and maimed cattle and hogs. The destination of this miserable cargo was slaughterhouses not subject to federal inspection because the meat was sold only within the state. . . . Since 1961, Smith has been trying vainly to secure passage of strong amendments to the Meat Inspection Act—a law which has not been amended substantially since its enactment 61 years ago following publication of Upton Sinclair's The Jungle. . . . It took some doing to cover up meat from tubercular cows, lump-jawed steers and scabby pigs in the old days. Now the wonders of chemistry and quick freezing techniques provide the cosmetics of camouflaging the product and deceiving the eyes, nostrils and taste buds of the consumers . . .

Probably the most effective restraint working to shield these packers and processors from inspection and safety standards is their common interest with both state departments of agriculture and the U.S. Department of Agriculture in promoting the sale of meat products. . . . Upton Sinclair, who at age 88 lives just outside of Washington, is needed once again to tell the Congress that the Jungle is still with us.

Source: Originally appeared in *The New Republic,* July 15, 1967. Reprinted in: *Ralph Nader Reader,* New York: Seven Stories Press, 2000.

RALPH NADER, *The Burned Children: 4,000 Fatal Fabric Fires* (1971)

Ralph Nader's voice was particularly important to the consumer rights movement because he routinely and unapologetically called the nation's attention to the most horrific repercussions of businesses operating without meaningful regulation in the American marketplace. In this piece for the *New Republic,* he awakened the country to the very real hazards of clothing manufacturers selling children's apparel that was, in fact, highly flammable.

A five-year-old boy was playing in the kitchen while his mother was outside putting wash on the clothesline. The next time his mother saw him, the child was running into the yard and his body was totally black. At first she thought he had been playing with ink or paint. But as she got closer, she realized that his pajamas had burned. All that was left of them were the cuffs burning around his ankles. Later she found bits of charred cloth scattered through the house where the child had run wildly after the pajamas caught fire, apparently on the stove, four weeks later the boy died. . . . It is not an isolated case . . . When all fabric fires are included, more than 250,000 people suffer injuries and 4,000 die each year . . . consumers still have little protection against the hazards of flammable fabrics. . . .

The industry has successfully resisted meaningful flammability standards primarily by persuading the Department of Commerce that consumers should bear the burden of protection . . . Passing the burden to the consumer is one of the oldest tricks of the marketplace. In reality, the consumer has almost never been offered a meaningful choice in flammable fabrics. It is virtually impossible to outfit a family and furnish a home in flame-retardant material, even though many fabrics can be made flame-retardant. . . .

Two things are urgently needed if there is to be any change. First the Department of Health, Education, and Welfare is going to have to provide more vigorous data collection on burn injuries and renew its almost dormant research function. . . . Second, concerted consumer pressure will be required if the Department of Commerce is to be moved to enforce the law. Congressional hearings to inquire into the protracted delays in setting standards is one step. Another step is citizen petitions to the Department to activate administrative procedures to set meaningful standards.

Source: Originally appeared in *The New Republic,* July 3, 1971. Reprinted in: *Ralph Nader Reader,* New York: Seven Stories Press, 2000.

12

Disability Rights Activism

—Paul K. Longmore

The Disability Rights Movement is not a single campaign. It is a group of related but distinct movements, each addressing issues of concern to particular disability constituencies. Over time, they adopted increasingly similar perspectives and agendas. Although these movements had a long history, in the 1960s and 1970s they were newly inspired to press for civil rights laws barring discrimination along with court rulings and government resources promoting self-determination and social integration. In the 1970s, they began to ally.

The American Deaf community grew from state residential schools (founded 1817–1870s) that taught in American Sign Language (ASL). In the late nineteenth and twentieth centuries, state political associations and the National Association of the Deaf (founded 1880) fought oralism, a campaign to suppress ASL and require Deaf people to speak. They also resisted discrimination in federal civil service hiring in the 1910s, licensing of drivers in the 1920s, and government work relief projects in the 1930s. In the 1960s and 1970s, they struggled for recognition of ASL as a true language and to develop Deaf culture through such projects as the National Theatre of the Deaf (1967). Their efforts to gain control of Deaf schooling culminated in the March 1988 "Deaf President Now" protest against appointment of a hearing person to head Gallaudet University, the leading institution to educate Deaf people.

Meanwhile, from the 1890s through the early 1960s blind people formed social and political associations. In 1940, several state organizations founded the National Federation of the Blind, with University of California at Berkeley legal scholar Jacobus tenBroek as president. In 1961, other advocates established the competing American Council of the Blind. Resisting domination by sighted professionals, the "organized blind" movement demanded a significant say for blind people in matters affecting them. It also fought restrictive social welfare policies, segregation in sheltered workshops, and discrimination in the larger society. Beginning in the 1930s, it lobbied for local dog guide and white cane laws to ensure blind people's right to use them in public places. These were the first accessibility statutes.

While advocates such as Clifford Beers and advocacy groups of and for mental patients such as the National Committee for Mental Hygiene appeared earlier in the twentieth century, a more activist movement emerged in the 1970s. In 1971, advocates in Boston and New York founded the Mental Patients' Liberation Front and the Mental Patients' Liberation Project. A year later, San Francisco activists launched the Network Against Psychiatric Assault while *Madness Network News* began publication. In 1979, parents of mental patients formed the National Alliance for the Mentally Ill. In 1978, Judi Chamberlin's *On Our Own: Patient Controlled Alternatives to the Mental Health System* became a manifesto of the movement's more militant contingent. Activists opposed forced institutionalization and treatment and fought social stigma and job discrimination. A landmark 1975 U.S. Supreme Court decision, *O'Connor v. Donaldson*, ruled that individuals cannot be involuntarily committed to a psychiatric hospital unless determined to be a threat to themselves or others.

Forced institutionalization was also a central issue in the movement of and for people with mental retardation and other developmental disabilities. In the late nineteenth and early twentieth centuries, many were permanently incarcerated in large prison-like facilities. During the 1960s, advocacy groups campaigned for deinstitutionalization and community-based living. Although the Kennedy administration called for community alternatives, Congress never funded that project adequately. By the early 1970s, advocates became increasingly politicized and civil rights-oriented. In the 1950s, parents founded the Association for Retarded Children (later renamed the Association for Retarded Citizens and then The ARC) to promote deinstitutionalization and mainstream education. The Association of Persons with Severe Handicaps (TASH), organized by special educators in 1975, focused on educational rights. In 1974, People First, a self-advocacy organization of people with cognitive/developmental disabilities, was formed. The movement's greatest impact came through successful lawsuits. In *Wyatt v. Stickney* (1971), a federal district court outlawed institutional "warehousing" without rehabilitation or education. In 1972, exposure of abusive conditions at Willowbrook State School in New York generated extensive media coverage and a lawsuit that brought about transfer of large numbers of people to the community. In *Halderman v. Pennhurst* (1977), advocates demanded correction of harsh conditions at a Pennsylvania institution; a state court ruling helped establish the right to deinstitutionalization and community-based services. Meanwhile, the Developmentally Disabled Assistance and Bill of Rights Act (1975) authorized federal funding of programs serving people with developmental disabilities and set forth their rights in institutions. But these provisions proved useless because of failure to include an enforcement mechanism.

Closely related to this movement was the campaign of parents for their disabled children's educational rights. Beginning in particular states, it ultimately moved to the national level. In two important court rulings in 1972, *Mills v. Board of Education* and *Pennsylvania Association of Retarded Children (PARC) v. State of Pennsylvania*, federal district courts prohibited school districts from excluding children with disabilities from public schools, thus upholding their constitutional right to a free public education. In response, activists in other states filed right-to-education lawsuits. This movement culminated in the federal Education for All Handicapped Children Act (1975) establishing disabled children's right to public schooling in settings as integrated as possible (the "least restrictive environment") and mandating for each such child an "individualized educational program."

Meanwhile, physically disabled activists and their supporters began to integrate higher education. Following World War II, disabled veterans were drawn to accessible and accommodating schools such as the University of Illinois at Champaign-Urbana. By 1961, its student body included 163 students with disabilities, 101 of them wheelchair users. In 1962, Ed Roberts entered the University of California at Berkeley despite the administration's initial rejection of his application because of his physical disability. Over the next several years, other students with major physical disabilities enrolled there. Nicknamed "the Rolling Quads," they became an activist force on the campus and in the Berkeley community. In 1976, Congress amended the Higher Education Act to authorize academic support services to university and college students with disabilities.

In the 1970s, young adults with significant physical disabilities launched the Independent Living Movement (ILM) to promote self-directed community-based living. Between 1972 and 1976, activists established independent living centers in Berkeley, Boston, Houston, Denver, St. Louis, Los Angeles, and Chicago. These were not residential facilities but resource agencies that facilitated personal assistance services and lobbied for civil rights, accessibility, and government resources to support independent living. In the late 1970s, the federal government began to fund the centers. By 1977, 52 were operating in the United States; by the 1990s there were hundreds.

Many disability rights movements made accessibility a prime goal. The Architectural Barriers Act (1968) required that most facilities designed, built, altered, or leased with federal funds be accessible. The first federal law mandating disability rights, it had weak enforcement provisions. In 1973, Congress created the Architectural and Transportation Barriers Compliance Board to oversee compliance with that law and in 1976 mandated that buildings constructed with federal money include access features in their original design. Activists also lobbied for access to public transit. The Urban Mass Transportation Act (1970) and the Federal-Aid Highway Act (1973) declared older and handicapped Americans' right of equal access to mass public transportation systems but their enforcement mechanisms were weak or nonexistent. In response, activists filed lawsuits and engaged in militant actions. In 1972, the Paralyzed Veterans of America and others won a landmark court ruling compelling the Washington, DC, Metropolitan Area Transit Authority to design its new subway system for accessibility. In 1978, Denver activists organized a year-long civil disobedience campaign, blocking buses to force the Regional Transit Authority to buy wheelchair lift-equipped buses. In the 1980s, this local group expanded to become the militant national organization ADAPT (American Disabled for Accessible Public Transit). Accessibility included more than wheelchair lifts. The Deaf community campaigned for captioned television programming. In 1976, the Federal Communications Commission set aside Line 21 on television receivers for closed captioning.

The Rehabilitation Act of 1973 reflected the new civil rights approach. Title V, Sections 501 and 503, mandated affirmative action by federal agencies and government contractors in hiring "handicapped" persons. Section 504 prohibited discrimination against "otherwise qualified handicapped" individuals in federally funded programs. It was the first legal measure barring disability-based discrimination. While this act was the most noted civil rights legislation of this era, Sections 501 and 503 were never enforced and for four years the Nixon, Ford, and Carter administrations delayed issuing regulations to implement 504. Although activists had not participated in drafting 504, their campaign for its implementation became an effective organizing tool of disability rights advocacy. That effort climaxed in April 1977 with protests in ten cities and the three-and-a-half-week occupation of a federal building in San Francisco. The demonstrations compelled the Carter administration to promulgate 504 as an enforceable civil rights statute.

Spurred by advances in diagnostic methods, the movement of and for people with learning disabilities began in the mid-1960s and grew in the 1970s. It too would combat discrimination, which was particularly acute against people with these nonapparent disabilities. It would also advocate for appropriate services and accommodations, such as extended test times for learning disabled students, as enforceable rights.

The several disability rights movements adapted concepts, objectives, and tactics from the civil rights, feminist, consumer, and self-help movements while formulating a distinctive analysis and agenda. Most basic, they redefined "disability" as primarily a social and political, rather than simply a medical and rehabilitative, issue. They explained the social limitations of people with disabilities as, not the inevitable results of impairments, but largely products of social prejudice, institutionalized discrimination, inaccessibility, restrictive public policies, and bureaucratic and professional domination. They asserted that the means necessary for social integration, whether devices and services or access and accommodations, should be enforceable civil rights rather than acts of charity. They demanded legal protection from discrimination and due process in all professional or governmental decision making affecting them. They also challenged the power of professionals, bureaucrats, and the vendors of services and products. Corollary to that contest, they promoted not only individual self-determination and self-advocacy, but also collective empowerment and community self-determination.

Over time during the 1970s, these shared perspectives and parallel agendas began to link the various disability rights movements. The President's Committee on Employment of the Handicapped became an annual meeting ground of disability organizations and constituencies. Disabled in Action (founded in New York City, 1970; with later chapters in Philadelphia, Baltimore, and other northeastern cities) represented a younger generation of activists who used direct action protests and lawsuits. It was cross-disability rather than disability-specific. The American Coalition of Citizens with Disabilities (1974), created to campaign for implementation of Section 504, was the first national cross-disability political alliance. Disabled People's Civil Rights Day, October 20, 1979, involved rallies in major cities to declare solidarity among Americans with disabilities. These developments reflected the beginnings of a sense of cross-disability identification and even cross-disability identity. From the 1970s on, disability rights movements focused on both disability-specific interests and cross-disability concerns.

The role of women in these campaigns varied. The organized blind movement and the Deaf community were dominated by male leaders, while women often took major leadership positions in the Independent Living Movement. Meanwhile, the disability rights movements were (and continue to be) criticized for being overwhelmingly white and middle class. Moreover, in the 1960s and 1970s disability advocacy had little connection with other American movements. There were two exceptions. The 1977 San Francisco 504 sit-in drew support from many community groups, from the Black Panthers to churches to labor unions. Also, during the 1970s, physically disabled feminists challenged both disability rights activists and nondisabled feminists to address disabled women's issues. From the late 1970s on and expanding with the 1980s campaign for passage of a comprehensive Americans with Disabilities Act, disability rights activists worked more and more closely with other civil rights movements.

JACOBUS TENBROEK, *The Right to Live in the World: The Disabled in the Law of Torts* (1966)

Jacobus tenBroek, founding president of the National Federation of the Blind and a prominent University of California Berkeley professor who supported the student Free Speech Movement of the 1960s, wrote landmark studies on civil liberties, the internment of Japanese Americans in World War II, and public policies affecting blind people. By the mid-1960s, he expanded his civil rights advocacy to include people with every sort of disability, as reflected in this excerpt from his classic essay.

. . . Four other extensive legislative programs—the so-called architectural barriers statutes, the programs for the education of disabled children and youth in the regular public schools and colleges, the guide dog laws, and the white cane laws—are built upon an integrationist foundation and necessarily imply an integrationist objective. . . .

From the foregoing, it is abundantly clear that integration of the disabled is the policy of the nation. . . . If the disabled have the right to live in the world, they must have the right to make their way into it and therefore must be entitled to use the indispensable means of access, and to use them on terms that will make the original right effective. A right on such terms to the use of the streets, walks, roads and highways is a rock-bottom minimum. The right to gain access to the world in which they have a right to live must also include, as a part of the same rock-bottom minimum, the right to utilize the common thoroughfares by riding on common carriers. Upon descending from these, the disabled have a right of uninhibited and equal access to places of public accommodation to seek their ease, rest, sustenance, or recreation. . . .

Source: California Law Review 54, 1966: 841–919, quoted from 846 to 848 and 851.

Are humans to be denied human rights? Are persons after all not to be persons if they are physically disabled? Are members of the community to be robbed of their rights to live in the community, their certificates canceled upon development or discovery of disability? These rhetorical questions, the hallmarks of crusade and reform throughout American history, have in our generation become the plea of the disabled as well. As with the black man, so with the blind. As with the Puerto Rican, so with the post-polio. As with the Indian, so with the indigent disabled.

Without legal redress in many areas, and with the frequency of arbitrary action, disabled persons have been turned away from trains, buses, and other common carriers, from lodgings of various sorts, from the rental of public and private housing, from bars, restaurants and places of public amusement, from banks to rent a safety deposit box, from other kinds of banks to give a pint of blood, and from gambling casinos in Nevada, declared by statute as well as by common experience to be places in which the public is accommodated.

GUNNAR DYBWAD, *Toward Human Rights for the Mentally Retarded: A Challenge to Social Action* (1969)

One of the leading figures in the developmental disabilities movement, Gunnar Dybwad challenged dominant thinking to advocate for people with mental retardation as citizens entitled to civil rights protections. This selection is taken from one of his more noteworthy statements.

And thus I return to the draft statement of the revised Standards for Social Service Departments in Institutions for the Retarded. Again stressing that I previously would doubtlessly have been willing to endorse this draft, with the insights I have gained from our young students I find this document wanting because it obviously is more oriented to the maintenance of our establishments than to protection of the rights of individuals, and because it suggests that the retarded person be helped to learn the roles that will enable him to relate constructively to the formal and informal system within the residential facility. . . .

I find the document wanting because it suggests that the social service department helps the family to develop trust in the residential facility and helps the family to engage in a *counselling* relationship which they can explore and communicate troubled feelings and actions in relationship to the retardate and the residential facility, but fails to recognize that there may be no sound basis for developing trust in an institution and that parents may rightfully resent being pushed into a casework-counselling relationship when they try to air grievances and concern about their child's treatment (or lack of it). . . .

Source: Address to the Social Work Division, American Association on Mental Deficiency, San Francisco, California, May, 1969. http://www.disabilitymuseum.org/lib/docs/2261card.htm.

I find the document wanting because it speaks only of needs, not of rights, and because of its lack of recognition of the advocacy role social service must assume on behalf of the retarded person and his family rather than a mere "liaison" role as is suggested. I find the document wanting because it not only fails to recognize the advocacy role of the social worker but fails to take any cognizance of the existence of associations for the mentally retarded which on their part have played a far-reaching advocacy role, granted that this has been done in some localities with less effectiveness than in others. . . .

These rather lengthy introductory remarks were necessary to put into proper perspective a document I want to introduce into this discussion on human rights for the mentally retarded as a challenge to social action. In June of 1967 the International League of Societies for the Mentally Handicapped, which has in its membership over 50 parent sponsored associations around the globe, assembled in Stockholm a Symposium on Legislative Aspects of Mental Retardation. . . .

The Symposium affirmed the following:

"a. The mentally retarded person has the same rights as other citizens of the same country, same age, family status, working status, etc., unless a specific individual determination has been made, by appropriate procedures, that his exercise of some or all of such rights will place his own interests or those of others in undue jeopardy. Among the rights to which this general principle may apply are: the right to choose a place to live, to engage in leisure time activities, to dispose of property, to preserve the physical and psychological integrity of his person, to vote, to marry, to have children, and to be given a fair trial for any alleged offence.

b. The retarded person has furthermore, a right to receive such special training, rehabilitation, guidance and counselling as may strengthen his ability to exercise these rights with the minimum of abridgement.

c. Some persons may be able to exercise all these rights, in due course, even though they are, or may have been, at one time or another, identified as mentally retarded. Others may, as a result of a serious degree of mental retardation, be unable to exercise any of these rights in a meaningful way. There remains a number of retarded persons for whom modification of some or all of these rights may be appropriate.

d. When modification or denial of rights is necessary, certain compensating special or alternative rights should be acquired. In cases where a number of fundamental rights are to be abridged, the special rights include the right to have a guardian appointed, who will have the legal and moral obligation to make necessary decisions on behalf of the retarded person who cannot act for himself."

Let me interpolate here a further provision mentioned in a later section on guardianship.

"e. In respect to any right which it is proposed to deny or modify, the retarded person is entitled to the benefit of special procedures, in accordance with the general legal code of his country, which will ensure that:

1. an evaluation of his social capabilities to exercise the rights in question has been made by persons professionally qualified to do so;
2. both he and members of his family or other interested persons are advised in advance of the process;

3. rights of appeal to higher authorities, and especially the courts are kept open;
4. the benefits of these and related legal provisions are not limited by the economic status of the retarded person;
5. the possibility remains of restoring at a later date any right which is denied, should the circumstances later justify restoration;
6. there is provision for periodic review of the necessity to restrict rights;
7. the physical and psychological integrity of his person is preserved."

. . . We face a strange phenomenon in this country. On the one hand a Presidential Committee for two years in succession has criticized in strongest terms the inhuman treatment to which individuals in many of our State institutions are exposed. To the contrary, we are over and over assured that once we get more money to hire more staff and repair some buildings there is not much to worry about. Those of you who know the conditions in some of the California institutions must, indeed, have marvelled at the nonchalant attitude with which the Director of the Human Relations Agency, Mr. Spencer Williams, glossed over the very conditions which are a matter of such deep concern to the President's Committee and, of course, to countless parents and informed citizens who know so well what Mr. Williams professes not to know. We must recognize, of course, that Mr. Williams' task is in the political area. But what about the Social Service Departments and their professional responsibility? What is their responsibility in the face of flagrant violations of a resident child's or adult's human rights which come to their attention? What about willful concealment of the true nature of a child's death or serious injury, caused by gross negligence of the institutional staff? What about continuing exposure of young children to vicious sexual assaults because of the administration's refusal to take appropriate action?

What about the gross abuse of medication or other medical treatment which when used as a disciplinary measure without doubt constitutes cruel and unusual punishment, outlawed under the Constitution of the United States?

Or the use of residents for peonage, involuntary servitude at long hours, again outlawed by the Constitution?

What about denial or undue restrictions of visitation rights to parents, particularly parents from disadvantaged backgrounds who cannot effectively protest? What about measures deliberately designed to humiliate children such as keeping them naked for punishment or placing a child or adult in a group functioning at a much lower level, again solely for disciplinary reasons?

What about the withholding of a child from schooling—an act which if committed by the parents would result in court action? . . .

These are not hypothetical questions—I am referring to actual happenings in the recent past—not in one State but in several.

And thus it came to pass last week that the Pennsylvania Association for Retarded Children, having in vain communicated by letter, visits and telegrams with the Governor, the Secretary of Welfare, the Director of Mental Retardation and others to bring to their attention clear evidence of gross irregularities, including cases of negligence resulting in death of residents, decided in their Annual Convention by unanimous vote to authorize its Board of Directors to engage counsel to determine what kind of legal action may be taken to compel the State to remedial action.

JUDI CHAMBERLIN, *On Our Own: Patient Controlled Alternatives to the Mental Health System* (1978)

The following excerpt from a manifesto by one of the leaders of the psychiatric patients movement calls for a thorough transformation of the system to recognize the capacities for self-determination of individuals often reckoned incompetent due to a psychiatric diagnosis.

Once it has been decided that a person has a sick mind, enormous social consequences ensue. A finding of mental illness, which is often a judicial, as well as a medical, determination, frequently results in loss of liberty. People labeled mentally ill are usually presumed to be incapable of exercising their decision-making power in their own best interest. . . .

People who are labeled mentally ill become part of a system that deprives them of control over their own life as part of their treatment. Mental hospitals have been called 'total institutions,' in which even such ordinary decisions as when to eat, go to the toilet, and go to bed are made by others. A natural consequence of being subjected to such a regimen is a feeling of depersonalization. . . .

The whole experience of mental hospitalization promotes weakness and dependency. Not only are the lives of patients controlled, but patients are constantly told that such control is for their own good, which they are unable to see because of their mental illness. Patients become unable to trust their own judgment, become indecisive, overly submissive to authority, frightened of the outside world. . . .

[This movement has been] working to change commitment laws, to inform patients about their legal rights, to increase Constitutional guarantees to patients, to end the demeaning and harmful psychiatric system and replace it with true asylums, places to which people can retreat to deal with the pain of their existence. We envision a system in which this pain would not be labeled 'illness' but would be seen as a natural consequence of a system that puts wealth, property, and power above the basic needs of human beings. These asylums . . . would be true alternatives to the present mental health system—voluntary, small, responsive to their communities and to their residents. . . .

Patient-controlled alternatives can provide services to people without the demoralizing consequences of the authoritarian, hierarchical structure of traditional mental health services. When the emphasis is on people helping one another, the gulf between 'patient' and 'staff' disappears. Someone can seek help from others without being thought of as sick or helpless. The same person who seeks help can also offer it. . . .

There are immense practical problems involved in trying to set up patient-controlled alternative facilities and services. Money is difficult to find. Opposition

---

Source: Judi Chamberlin, "On Our Own: Patient Controlled Alternatives to the Mental Health System," New York: Hawthorn Books, 1978, pp. 3, 6, 7, 8.

from professionals, who are accustomed to being in charge and to thinking of patients as incompetent, can be enormous. Ex-patients may be uncertain of their own abilities.

DISABILITY RIGHTS CENTER, *Disabled People's Bill of Rights and Declaration of Independence* (1979)

Disabled Peoples Civil Rights Day, October 20, 1979, was a national day of solidarity, marked by demonstrations in all major cities across the country. It aimed to encourage enforcement of Section 504 and the Education for All Handicapped Children Act. The following declaration was written for that occasion by activists at the Disability Rights Center in Washington, DC.

Preamble

We believe that all people should enjoy certain rights. Because people with disabilities have consistently been denied the right to fully participate in society as free and equal members, it is important to state and affirm these rights. All people should be able to enjoy these rights regardless of race, creed, color, sex, religion or disability.

1. The right to live independent, active and full lives.
2. The right to the equipment, assistance, and support services necessary for full productivity, provided in a way that promotes dignity and independence.
3. The right to an adequate income or wage, substantial enough to provide food, clothing, shelter, and other necessities of life.
4. The right to accessible, integrated, convenient, and affordable housing.
5. The right to quality physical and mental health care.
6. The right to training and employment without prejudice or stereotype.
7. The right to accessible transportation and freedom of movement.
8. The right to bear or adopt and raise children and have a family.
9. The right to a free and appropriate public education.
10. The right to participate in and benefit from entertainment and recreation.
11. The right of equal access to and use of all businesses, facilities, and activities in the community.
12. The right to communicate freely with all fellow citizens and those who provide services.
13. The right to a barrier free environment.
14. The right to legal representation and full protection of all legal rights.
15. The right to determine one's own future and make one's own life choices.
16. The right of full access to all voting processes.

Source: Deborah Kaplan, Disability Rights Center, and other contributors for Disabled People's Rights Day, 1979.

13

Environmental Activism

—Angela G. Mertig

The 1960s and 1970s witnessed a dramatic surge of activism on behalf of environmental causes. This swell in activism and related events is commonly considered the beginning of the contemporary Environmental Movement. Even so, much of the foundation for the Environmental Movement in the United States was laid at the turn of the nineteenth century. In response to the ending of the American frontier and escalating exploitation of natural resources, prominent individuals throughout the mid to late 1800s began clamoring for protection of natural areas and resources. This led to the development of the Conservation Movement, which was divided into preservationists who wished to protect nature for its own sake and for human recreation, and conservationists who advocated wise use and management of natural resources. Environmentally concerned citizens founded several organizations at this time, including the Sierra Club and National Audubon Society. At roughly the same time, several other groups came together in cities to address pressing environmental issues. Their efforts were less widely known but were nevertheless important as they sought to improve urban and industrial environments by creating urban parks or advocating laws to protect workers' safety.

Between the turn of the nineteenth century and the 1960s, groups of conservationists and preservationists persisted and gradually grew in number as they garnered more public support. The 1960s, however, brought new and unprecedented public attention to environmental causes, and the way in which environmental concerns were framed and acted upon changed qualitatively. Growth in environmental activism during the 1960s and 1970s was stimulated by several interrelated forces going on in American society. After World War II, increasing levels of education, affluence, and urbanization led to growing public concern and a greater ability for individuals to take action on behalf of the environment. Environmental issues became central to Americans' quest for a higher quality of life. Greater affluence also brought an increase in leisure time which allowed people to spend more time in the "great outdoors," which, in turn, led many to desire protecting it from development and pollution. Evidence of environmental decline was becoming increasingly publicized and was especially manifest when a dramatic oil spill ruined the beautiful shoreline of Santa Barbara in 1969. At the same time, newly retrieved pictures from outer space showed Earth as a fragile, beautiful, and unique planet in the midst of dark, empty space. The growth of television and other media played an increasingly important role in fostering public perceptions of the environment as a social problem.

Scholars of environmentalism use various events to mark the rise of the modern Environmental Movement. Four events in the 1960s signified a change in how environmental issues were presented and addressed. The first was publication of Rachel Carson's *Silent Spring* in 1962. She detailed the harmful consequences of the new chemicals being developed by post–World War II industry. Not only did she emphasize the importance of a relatively new environmental issue, but she utilized a scientific and ecological perspective in presenting her arguments. Carson's book, along with a growing field of environmental research and popular literature, had a major influence on public perceptions of environmental issues.

The second event was a passionate fight in 1966 and 1967 to protect the Grand Canyon. Previously, both the Sierra Club and the Wilderness Society defeated attempts to build dams in Dinosaur National Monument, and they were also instrumental in passage of the Wilderness Act of 1964. However, they did not succeed in preventing all massive damming projects. Indeed, one of Sierra Club executive director David Brower's greatest regrets was that his organization had not stopped the damming of Glen Canyon in Arizona. Shortly thereafter, when the Grand Canyon was threatened with potential damming, Brower initiated a massive public relations campaign, using several full-page advertisements in the *New York Times*. While the damming was successfully thwarted, the Sierra Club's hard hitting public lobbying came with a price: the Internal Revenue Service revoked the Club's tax-exempt status. In 1969, due to conflicts over this loss, the Sierra Club ousted Brower from its leadership. Brower immediately went on to form Friends of the Earth (and, later, Earth Island Institute).

The passion that Brower showed and the lengths to which he went to protect the Grand Canyon signaled a growing interest in direct political engagement by the traditionally more staid organizations that began during the conservation era. In fact, some of the newer organizations that began in the 1970s, such as Greenpeace (and, later, its offshoot, Sea Shepherd Conservation Society), adopted a distinctly more radical, direct action approach to environmental activism. Even so, the activities of older groups such as the Sierra Club and Wilderness Society tended to remain focused on the classic nature-protection issues that were at the heart of the earlier Conservation Movement. When the Sierra Club lost its tax-exempt status after having taken a more activist stance on the Grand Canyon, the entire environmental movement had to face the question of how to function effectively in the growing legal and bureaucratic complexities of the postwar United States.

A third event typically used to demarcate the modern Environmental Movement is the formation of Environmental Defense Fund (EDF) in 1967. Along with development of the Natural Resources Defense Council (1970), this represented the beginning of a new breed of environmental organization. These organizations relied extensively on scientific and legal expertise, and they received considerable financial backing from corporations and foundations (e.g., Ford Foundation). They focused on issues that were qualitatively different from the earlier Conservation Movement's concerns of preserving land and managing natural resources: these new organizations devoted their time to issues such as pollution, chemicals, and waste. In fact, EDF arose out of the battle to ban DDT, the leading culprit in Carson's book.

The development of organizations such as EDF, and numerous others that followed shortly thereafter, represented a shift toward a more professionalized movement and one that had the resources to tackle the increasingly complex environmental issues of the late twentieth century. Organizations founded back during the Conservation Movement era, along with organizations from the numerous social movements of the 1960s, were important sources of encouragement, expertise, and activists for the new environmental movement of this period. Over time, both the older and the newer organizations of the modern Environmental Movement became more professionalized, adding the "newer" issues to their agendas (e.g., pollution), and adopting mechanisms for greater mobilization of monetary resources and membership such as direct mail.

Finally, the first nationwide celebration of Earth Day on April 22, 1970, was the most publicly visible event staged by environmental activists, and it clearly indicated that a new Environmental Movement had indeed come of age. This massive outpouring of public support for environmental awareness and activism—nearly 20 million Americans took part in some way—was initiated by Wisconsin Senator Gaylord Nelson and organized by students, including Denis Hayes, a Harvard law student at the time and now president of a prominent environmental philanthropy group, the Bullitt Foundation. One important environmental organization of this period, Environmental Action, was actually founded using mailing lists of Earth Day participants. Environmental Action emulated other student movements and groups of the time, tending to be more forceful in its critiques of business and political actors and focusing on a nonhierarchical leadership structure. Largely because of the massive mobilization of public concern represented by Earth Day, several new environmental laws were passed in the late 1960s and throughout the 1970s. Likewise, other legal changes, such as increased flexibility in rules governing organizations' tax-exempt status and changes in the definition of legal standing (which grants legitimacy to stake claims in court), significantly increased the ability of environmental organizations to turn the vast resource of positive public opinion into a powerful voice for environmental protection.

The successes of the Environmental Movement of the 1960s and early 1970s stemmed in part from the fact that, compared to other activists and movements of the era, its activists appeared to be well-mannered, less disruptive, and more modest in their demands. Although there were some more outspoken activists and organizations early on, many organizations were relatively mild in their critique of the status quo and generated very little opposition. Notably, social elites and politicians were highly predisposed to support the movement, whereas critics on the Left felt that environmental activists were diverting attention and resources from other more contentious, and fundamentally important, issues. However, the nonthreatening appearance of the movement and its elite support faded as various corporate and governmental interests found themselves increasingly at the receiving end of environmental condemnation. Simultaneously, public support for environmental issues began to decline somewhat and media coverage waned as the costs of environmental cleanup and protection became more apparent. Indeed, during the energy crisis in 1973–1974 the public grew increasingly concerned that environmental reforms could compromise national energy supplies and economic development.

Despite some slippage in public support, a majority of the public continued to support environmental protection throughout the 1970s. In fact, while many other activist movements of the period began to weaken or collapsed, the numbers of Environmental Movement organizations and the members they attracted continued to grow. Several events throughout the 1970s showed the continuing importance of environmental issues, both nationally and internationally. By the early 1970s, environmental activism and concern had clearly spread beyond the United States, as evidenced by the United Nations Conference on the Human Environment (1972); the celebration of World Environment Day (1977); and the beginning of environmental movements in India (Chipko), Brazil (rubber tappers), and Kenya (Greenbelt). In the United States, the Carter administration (1976–1980) legitimized movement concerns by supporting environmental causes and appointing leading activists to government positions. Public concern for environmental dangers did not wane in the 1970s in part because a number of serious environmental calamities occurred. In 1972, there was a disastrous flood at Buffalo Creek in West Virginia that resulted from unsafe storage of strip-mining waste. In the mid-1970s, scientists determined that chlorofluorocarbons (CFCs) were destroying Earth's protective ozone layer. In 1978, an investigation of health problems at Love Canal, New York, led residents to discover they were living on top of a toxic waste dump. And, finally, in 1979, a partial melt down at the Three Mile Island nuclear power plant in Pennsylvania scared Americans everywhere.

Environmental activism continues today, fed by the continual onslaught of environmental threats and informed by almost a century of experience dating back to the Conservation Movement. Contemporary activists and organizations are armed with increasingly sophisticated scientific, legal, and bureaucratic expertise and they have become increasingly diverse in tactics and concerns. Activism occurs in a variety of organizational forms, from relatively small, volunteer-based groups to large, national and international, highly professionalized organizations. Activists and organizations range from those who try to compromise and work within the system (such as EDF) to those such as Earth First! and Sea Shepherd that engage in more direct action and desire to subvert the system. Environmental activism has also grown to incorporate greater consideration of human rights and environmental justice. Since 1978, when residents of Love Canal discovered the government wasn't going to help them without a fight, grassroots organizations fighting local environmental threats have proliferated. These organizations are particularly likely to include women and minorities as leaders and core members. Their activism is motivated by concerns for the health of their families and communities. Environmentalism has grown into a truly broad-based movement, focusing on the protection of natural areas and wildlife (for their sake and humans') as well as the human right to a decent environment.

RACHEL CARSON, *The Obligation to Endure* (1962)

Rachel Carson (1907–1964) was a scientist, holding a master's degree in Zoology, who wrote publicly accessible books and articles on the natural world. This excerpt comes from her most famous work where she documented the harmful impacts of chemicals, particularly DDT, on the environment and wildlife, particularly birds. Chemical companies reacted negatively to Carson's research and engaged in extensive personal attacks on her character. Nevertheless, her work is seen as vitally important in establishing the groundwork of the modern environmental movement.

The history of life on earth has been a history of interaction between living things and their surroundings. To a large extent, the physical form and the habits of the earth's vegetation and its animal life have been molded by the environment. Considering the whole span of earthly time, the opposite effect, in which life actually modified its surroundings, has been relatively slight. Only within the moment of time represented by the present century has one species—man—acquired significant power to alter the nature of his world.

During the past quarter century this power has not only increased to one of disturbing magnitude but it has changed in character. The most alarming of all man's assaults upon the environment is the contamination of air, earth, rivers, and sea with dangerous and even lethal materials. This pollution is for the most part irrecoverable; the chain of evil it initiates not only in the world that must support life but in living tissues is for the most part irreversible. In this now universal contamination of the environment, chemicals are the sinister and little-recognized partners of radiation in changing the very nature of the world—the very nature of its life. . . .

It took hundreds of millions of years to produce the life that now inhabits the earth—eons of time in which that developing and evolving and diversifying life reached a state of adjustment and balance with its surroundings. The environment, rigorously shaping and directing the life it supported, contained elements that were hostile as well as supporting. Certain rocks gave out dangerous radiation; even within the light of the sun, from which all life draws its energy, there were short-wave radiations with power to injure. Given time—time not in years but in millennia—life adjusts, and a balance has been reached. For time is the essential ingredient; but in the modern world there is no time.

The rapidity of change and the speed with which new situations are created follow the impetuous and heedless pace of man rather than the deliberate pace of nature. Radiation is no longer merely the background radiation of rocks, the

---

Source: Excerpted from chapter 2 of Rachel Carson, *Silent Spring*, Greenwich, CT: Fawcett, 1962.

bombardment of cosmic rays, the ultraviolet of the sun that have existed before there was any life on earth; radiation is now the unnatural creation of man's tampering with the atom. The chemicals to which life is asked to make its adjustment are no longer merely the calcium and silica and copper and all the rest of the minerals washed out of the rocks and carried in rivers to the sea; they are the synthetic creations of man's inventive mind, brewed in his laboratories, and having no counterparts in nature.

. . . new chemicals come from our laboratories in an endless stream . . . These sprays, dusts, and aerosols are now applied almost universally to farms, gardens, forests, and homes—nonselective chemicals that have the power to kill every insect, the "good" and the "bad," to still the song of birds and the leaping of fish in the streams, to coat the leaves with a deadly film, and to linger on in soil—all this though the intended target may be only a few weeds or insects. Can anyone believe it is possible to lay down such a barrage of poisons on the surface of the earth without making it unfit for all life? They should not be called "insecticides," but "biocides."

. . . Along with the possibility of the extinction of mankind by nuclear war, the central problem of our age has therefore become the contamination of man's total environment with such substances of incredible potential for harm—substances that accumulate in the tissues of plants and animals and even penetrate the germ cells to shatter or alter the very material of heredity upon which the shape of the future depends. . . .

It is not my contention that chemical insecticides must never be used. I do contend that we have put poisonous and biologically potent chemicals indiscriminately into the hands of persons largely or wholly ignorant of their potentials for harm. We have subjected enormous numbers of people to contact with these poisons, without their consent and often without their knowledge. If the Bill of Rights contains no guarantee that a citizen shall be secure against lethal poisons distributed either by private individuals or by public officials, it is surely only because our forefathers, despite their considerable wisdom and foresight, could conceive of no such problem. . . .

The public must decide whether it wishes to continue on the present road, and it can do so only when in full possession of the facts. In the words of Jean Rostand, "The obligation to endure gives us the right to know."

SIERRA CLUB, *Should We Also Flood the Sistine Chapel So Tourists Can Get Nearer the Ceiling?* (1967)

In 1967, the Sierra Club placed this advertisement in the *New York Times* in order to fight the proposed damming of the Grand Canyon. David Brower (1912–2000) was the leader of the Sierra Club at the time; his

Source: Reprinted from David Brower, *For Earth's Sake*, Salt Lake City: Gibbs Smith, 1990, p. 368.

aggressive public lobbying, exemplified by this advertisement, cost the Sierra Club its tax-exempt status and cost him the position of executive director of the Sierra Club. Brower went on to form Friends of the Earth and, later, the Earth Island Institute.

SHOULD WE ALSO FLOOD THE SISTINE CHAPEL SO TOURISTS CAN GET NEARER THE CEILING?

EARTH began four billion years ago and Man two million. The Age of Technology, on the other hand, is hardly a hundred years old, and on our time chart we have been generous to give it even the little line we have.

It seems to us hasty, therefore, during this blip of time, for Man to think of directing his fascinating new tools toward altering irrevocably the forces which made him. Nonetheless, in these few brief years among four billion, wilderness has all but disappeared. And now these:

1) There are proposals before Congress to "improve" Grand Canyon. Two dams would back up artificial lakes into 148 miles of canyon gorge. This would benefit tourists in power boats, it is argued, who would enjoy viewing the canyon wall more closely. (See headline). Submerged underneath the tourists would be part of the most revealing single page of earth's history. The lakes would be as deep as 600 feet (deeper for example, than all but a handful of New York buildings are high) but in a century, silting would have replaced the water with that much mud, wall to wall.

There is no part of the wild Colorado River, the Grand Canyon's sculptor, that would not be maimed.

Tourist recreation, as a reason for the dams, is in fact an afterthought. The Bureau of Reclamation, which has backed them, has called the dams "cash registers." It expects the dams would make money by sale of commercial power.

They will not provide anyone with water.

2) In Northern California, four lumber companies have nearly completed logging the private virgin redwood forests, an operation which to give you an idea of its size, has taken fifty years.

Where nature's tallest living things have stood silently since the age of the dinosaurs, much further cutting could make creation of a redwood national park absurd.

The companies have said tourists want only enough roadside trees for the snapping of photos. They offered to spare trees for this purpose, and not much more. The result would remind you of the places on your face you missed while you were shaving.

3) And up the Hudson, there are plans for a power complex—a plant, transmission lines, and a reservoir near and on Storm King Mountain—effectively destroying one of the last wild and high and beautiful spots near New York City.

4) A proposal to flood a region in Alaska as large as Lake Erie would eliminate at once the breeding grounds of more wildlife than conservationists have preserved in history.

5) In San Francisco, real estate interests have for years been filling a bay that made the city famous, putting tract houses over the fill; and now there's a new idea—still more fill, enough for an air cargo terminal as big as Manhattan.

There exists today a mentality which can conceive such destruction, giving commerce as ample reason. For 74 years, the Sierra Club (now with 46,000 members) has opposed that mentality. But now, when even Grand Canyon is endangered, we are at a critical moment in time.

This generation will decide if something untrammelled and free remains, as testimony we had love for those who follow.

We have been taking ads, therefore, asking people to write their Congressmen and Senators; Secretary of the Interior Stewart Udall; The President; and to send us funds to continue the battle. Thousands *have* written, but meanwhile, Grand Canyon legislation still stands a chance of passage. More letters are needed and much more money, to help fight the notion that Man no longer needs nature.*

David Brower, Executive Director
Sierra Club
Mills Tower, San Francisco

☐ Please send me more details on how I may help.
☐ Here is a donation of $________ to continue your effort to keep the public informed.
☐ Send me "Time and the River Flowing," famous four color book which tells the complete story of Grand Canyon, and why T. Roosevelt said, "leave it as it is." ($25.00)
☐ Send me "The Last Redwoods" which tells the complete story of the opportunity as well as the destruction in the redwoods. ($17.50)
☐ I would like to be a member of the Sierra Club. Enclosed is $14.00 for entrance and first year's dues.

Name________________

Address________________

City________________ State________ Zip______

*The previous ads, urging that readers exercise a constitutional right of petition, to save Grand Canyon, produced an unprecedented reaction by the Internal Revenue Service threatening our tax deductible status. IRS says the ads may be a "substantial" effort to "influence legislation." Undefined these terms leave organizations like ours at the mercy of administrative whim. (The question has not been raised with any organizations that favor Grand Canyon dams.) So we cannot now promise that contributions you send us are deductible—pending results of what may be a long legal battle.

The Sierra Club, founded in 1892 by John Muir, is nonprofit, supported by people who, like Thoreau, believe "In wildness is the preservation of the world." The club's program is nationwide, includes wilderness trips, books and films—as well as such efforts as this to protect the remnant of wilderness in the Americas. There are now twenty chapters, branch offices in New York (Biltmore Hotel), Washington (Dupont Circle Building), Los Angeles (Auditorium Building), Albuquerque, Seattle, and main office in San Francisco.

DENNIS PULESTON, *Birth and Early Days: The Founding of EDF* (1990)

Dennis Puleston (1905–2001) studied the effects of chemicals like DDT on wild birds, particularly osprey, verifying Rachel Carson's work. Puleston and others used scientific findings to fight against the widespread use of DDT. Ultimately, DDT was banned in the United States. The Environmental Defense Fund (EDF) was founded in 1967 through the struggle to ban DDT with Dennis Puleston as its first chairman. Here he reflects upon the founding of EDF.

The conception, if not the birth, of EDF can be traced to the mid-sixties. The Brookhaven Town Natural Resources Committee (BTNRC), under the chairmanship of Art Cooley and with membership comprising local residents, was formed to address such matters as the protection of harbor seals and kingfishers in New York State, the control of dredging and spoil deposition in local harbors, the reduction of pollution by duck farms in the Great South Bay, and the preservation of the Carmans River ecosystem. I was a member of the committee, which also included scientists from Brookhaven National Laboratory and the State University of New York at Stony Brook, as well as students from Bellport High School, where Art taught in the Science Department. . . .

In 1966 BTNRC became involved in the litigation that was crucial to the birth of EDF—the famous DDT case. In June of that year Victor Yannacone, Jr., a Patchogue lawyer, had instituted legal action against the Suffolk County Mosquito Control Commission (SCMCC) in a class action suit on behalf of all the people in Suffolk County, to prevent the Commission from the further use of DDT. The plaintiff in the suit was Yannacone's wife, Carol.

Rachel Carson's book *Silent Spring*, published in 1962, had highlighted, clearly and eloquently, the environmental disasters caused by the spraying of broad-spectrum chlorinated hydrocarbon pesticides such as DDT. DDT is persistent and therefore travels up food chains and concentrates in non-target carnivores such as hawks, salmon, and crustaceans.

My own studies, which I began in 1948 on Gardiners Island (off eastern Long Island), showed that by the mid-1960's the fish-eating osprey were having very poor reproductive success, and eggs that had not hatched contained DDT and its metabolites in high concentrations . . . Moreover, since Carson's book was published, it had been shown that DDT interferes with the female bird's ability to produce sufficient calcium carbonate for a healthy eggshell. . . .

BTNRC, strongly disturbed by these developments, had appealed to the SCMCC to use a less environmentally-destructive substitute for DDT. The SCMCC

Source: Excerpted from M. L. Rogers, *Acorn Days: The Environmental Defense Fund and How It Grew*, New York: EDF, 1990.

stated flatly that DDT killed mosquitoes, it was cheap, easy to apply, and it would continue to be used. . . . Strong and irrefutable scientific testimony was needed to support the case against DDT. We set to work preparing affidavits and a voluminous collection of scientific papers to serve as a convincing technical appendix. Graphs, photographs, and charts were also prepared. I recall being asked by Yannacone to illustrate seven food-chain charts covering the main Long Island ecosystems . . . These would show how DDT was transmitted throughout a food chain, to be concentrated in the carnivores at the top of the chain. I had to spend an entire weekend preparing these illustrated charts, which were intended to make an ecologist out of the judge hearing the case. . . .

In late November, 1966, the action was heard. The six-day trial was taken up largely with the testimony of scientists and other expert witnesses. . . . Altogether, the evidence against DDT was overwhelming. It was not only an environmental poison, it was also of declining value in mosquito control. The Court-imposed ban held for about a year . . . Much of BTNRC's testimony was used in the imposition of a statewide ban by the governor of New York in July 1970. Extensive hearings, in which EDF's scientists and lawyers played a major role, brought about a nationwide ban in 1972.

Because it was the first of its kind, the case aroused national interest out of all proportion to the actual results achieved. Appeals for help came pouring in to BTNRC; most of the cases involved the unwise use of chemical pesticides. It was difficult to turn down these appeals, but BTNRC had other responsibilities and our jobs were demanding our full attention. Moreover, we had no secretarial or administrative help, and we realized we must either refuse to undertake any more litigation activities, or we must organize on a more formal basis and attempt to secure funds. We decided, albeit hesitantly, to follow the latter course, and in the fall of 1967 the Environmental Defense Fund was formed as a non-profit membership corporation under the laws of the State of New York, established for educational and scientific purposes.

We had no office and we sometimes referred to ourselves as the "Fundless Environmental Defenders." However, the National Audubon Society (NAS), in the person of its chief biologist, Roland Clement, indicated a willingness to help us. . . . EDF was beginning to receive financial support from an enthusiastic membership and there was the promise of more substantial help from some foundations, including the Ford Foundation, which was very interested in environmental problems. It was therefore possible for us to establish the first EDF office, in the attic above the Stony Brook post office. There was very little space, but at least it served as a center for EDF activities. We also hired an executive director . . . EDF was now, several years after its incorporation, well on its way. . . . EDF's staff of dedicated scientists, lawyers and economists expanded, and the Board of Trustees welcomed many prestigious national figures to its ranks. We opened offices in Washington, D.C., and Berkeley, California. Our nerve center, which since 1970 had operated out of a converted farmhouse in Setauket, Long Island, moved in 1977, to New York City.

As we entered the seventies we saw an end to those early struggles, when we had operated so often by a "seat-of-the-pants" type of intuition. We were no longer considered by some as a handful of wild-eyed, bomb-throwing radicals. Our child had grown into a mature, respected adult, a vitally-needed protector of an environment that was under every-growing pressures of many kinds. But we would never forget those early days. In spite of the long, weary hours of meetings, the frustrations and setbacks, we had learned to work and struggle together in an atmosphere of mutual regard and loyalty that bound us in a very special kind of love.

DENIS HAYES, *The Beginning: Earth Day* (1970)

Denis Hayes (1944–) was a Harvard law student and former anti-Vietnam war activist when he left law school to help Wisconsin Senator Gaylord Nelson organize the first Earth Day celebration in the United States (April 22, 1970). The now-disbanded group, Environmental Action, developed out of the mailing lists generated from organizing the first Earth Day, with Hayes as its national coordinator. The following is the speech given by Denis Hayes on the first national Earth Day, at the Sylvan Theater in Washington, D.C.

I suspect that the politicians and businessmen who are jumping on the environmental bandwagon don't have the slightest idea what they are getting into. They are talking about filters on smokestacks while we are challenging corporate irresponsibility. They are bursting with pride about plans for totally inadequate municipal sewage treatment plants; we are challenging the ethics of a society that, with only 6 percent of the world's population, accounts for more than half of the world's annual consumption of raw materials.

Our country is stealing from poorer nations and from generations yet unborn. We seem to have a reverse King Midas touch. Everything we touch turns to garbage—142 tons of smoke, 7 million junked cars, 30 million tons of paper, 28 billion bottles, 48 billion cans each year. We waste riches in planned obsolescence and invest the overwhelming bulk of our national budget in ABMs and MIRVs and other means of death. Russia can destroy every American twelve times; America can destroy every Russian forty times. I guess that is supposed to mean that we are ahead.

We're spending insanely large sums on military hardware instead of eliminating hunger and poverty. We squander our resources on moon dust while people live in wretched housing. We still waste lives and money on a war that we should never have entered and should get out of immediately.

We have made Vietnam an ecological catastrophe. Vietnam was once capable of producing a marketable surplus of grain. Now America must feed her. American bombs have pockmarked Vietnam with more than 2.6 million craters a year, some

---

Source: Reprinted from Environmental Action, *Earth Day—The Beginning*, New York: Bantam, 1970.

of them thirty feet deep. We spent $73 million on defoliation in Vietnam last year alone, much of it on 2,4,5-T, a herbicide we've now found causes birth defects. We dumped defoliants on Vietnam at the rate of 10,000 pounds a month, and in the last fiscal year alone we blackened 6,600 square miles. We cannot pretend to be concerned with the environment of this or any other country as long as we continue the war in Vietnam or wage war in Cambodia, Laos, or anywhere else.

But even if that war were over tomorrow, we would still be killing this planet. We are systematically destroying our land, our streams, and our seas. We foul our air, deaden our senses, and pollute our bodies. And it's getting worse.

America's political and business institutions don't seem yet to have realized that some of us want to live in this country thirty years from now. They had better come to recognize it soon. We don't have very much time. We cannot afford to give them very much time.

When it comes to salvaging the environment, the individual is almost powerless. You can pick up litter, and if you're diligent, you may be able to find some returnable bottles. But you are forced to breathe the lung-corroding poison which companies spew into the air. You cannot buy electricity from a power company which does not pollute. You cannot find products in biodegradable packages. You cannot even look to the manufacturer for reliable information on the ecological effects of a product.

You simply can't live an ecologically sound life in America. That is not one of the options open to you. Go shopping and you find dozens of laundry products; it seems like a tremendous array unless you know that most are made by three companies, and the differences in cleaning power are almost negligible. If you really want to be ecologically sound, you won't buy any detergents—just some old-fashioned laundry soap and a bit of soda. But there's nothing on those packages to tell you the phosphate content, and there's nothing in the supermarket to tell you, only meaningless advertising that keeps dunning you.

We are learning. In response, industry has turned the environmental problem over to its public relations men. We've been deluged with full-page ads about pollution problems and what's being done about them. It would appear from most of them that things are fine and will soon be perfect. But the people of America are still coughing. And our eyes are running, and our lungs are blackening, and our property is corroding, and we're getting angry. We're getting angry at half-truths, angry at semitruths, and angry at outright lies.

We are tired of being told that we are to blame for corporate depredations. Political and business leaders once hoped that they could turn the environmental movement into a massive antilitter campaign. They have failed. We have learned not to place our faith in regulatory agencies that are supposed to act in the public interest. We have learned not to believe the advertising that sells us presidents the way it sells us useless products.

We will not appeal any more to the conscience of institutions because institutions have no conscience. If we want them to do what is right, we must make them do what is right. We will use proxy fights, lawsuits, demonstrations, research, boycotts, ballots—whatever it takes. This may be our last chance. If environment is a fad, it's going to be our last fad.

Things as we know them are falling apart. There is an unease across this country today. People know that something is wrong. The war is part of it, but most critics of the war have, from the beginning, known that the war is only a symptom of something much deeper. Poor people have long known what is wrong. Now the alley garbage, the crowding and the unhappiness and the crime have spread beyond the ghetto and a whole society is coming to realize that it must drastically change course.

We are building a movement, a movement with a broad base, a movement which transcends traditional political boundaries. It is a movement that values people more than technology, people more than political boundaries and political ideologies, people more than profit. It will be a difficult fight. Earth Day is the beginning.

14

Gay and Lesbian Activism

—Craig A. Rimmerman

Like so many of the social movements that came of age during the 1960s and 1970s, the activism of gays and lesbians in this period was rooted in the events of previous eras. There was, for example, a vibrant gay culture already existed in the streets, apartments, saloons, and cafeterias of New York City by the late nineteenth and early twentieth centuries. When laws were enacted that prohibited them from gathering in any state-licensed public place, as a part of the virulent New York City crackdown of the 1930s, lesbians and gays fought back in courageous ways.

Even during World War II when lesbians and gays in the military experienced much harassment, they did not accept it passively. Although they did not yet forge an organized resistance movement per se, lesbians and gays began to build their own supportive communities within the military as well as in port cities such as New York and San Francisco once the war ended.

Notwithstanding the very important group identity developed by lesbians and gay men by the late 1940s, postwar society still refused to recognize them and demonized them as "perverts," "psychopaths," and "deviates." Still, lesbians and gays refused to accept such labels. Instead many gay men became active in something they called the Homophile Movement so that they might actually fight for greater recognition and equal rights. In 1951, Communist Party activist Harry Hay, then working at the Los Angeles People's Education Center as a music teacher, decided to form an organization called the Mattachine Society along with several of his Education Center colleagues—Rud (Rudi) Gernreich, Bob Hull, Dale Jennings, and Chuck Rowland. They intended the Mattachine Society to attract a large gay constituency, one that was capable of militant gay activity. In its early years, Mattachine devoted considerable energy to challenging and repealing repressive legislation and altering public opinion. It also published and publicly distributed the nation's first homophile magazine, *One.* By the mid-1950s, the Mattachine Society had emerged as the first effective gay political organization in the United States.

But the Mattachine Society was not immune to serious criticism. The fact that the group had little space for lesbians who also wanted to speak out, for example, led women such as Phyllis Lyon and Del Martin not only to criticize Mattachine but also to form their own organization called the Daughters of Bilitis (DOB) in 1955. While the DOB eschewed much of the Mattachine Society's ideology and tactics, they agreed that publishing a newspaper was important and began distributing their own, *The Ladder*, in 1956. This paper came out regularly between 1956 and 1971 and garnered the DOB national attention.

Lesbians were not the only ones critical of the Mattachine Society founded by Harry Hay. Since this was the height of the McCarthy era, Hays' connection to the Communist Party, in combination with the organization's militant political rhetoric and activist mission, generated particular controversy and led to serious disagreements over Mattachine's future. Those critical of Mattachine such as Hal Call, Marilyn Reiger, and David Finn argued that gays should try to work through the system to achieve gains and adopt a more legalistic strategy. Mattachine's defenders, on the other hand, felt that such a strategy was both naïve and limiting. The escalating fear of communism and militancy in this period ultimately worked in favor of the rebel members who actually expelled Hay from the Mattachine Society in 1953.

The split in the Mattachine Society was significant for the gay and lesbian rights because it foreshadowed divisions that would shape the movement as a whole from then on. One segment of that movement would gravitate toward a more assimilationist approach to activism and the other would advocate a more militant, liberationist strategy. The so-called "assimilationists" typically embraced a rights-based perspective and advocated working within the broader framework of existing institutions and fighting for a seat at the table. They were more likely to accept that change would have to be incremental, and many assumed that slow, gradual progress was built into the very structure of our framework of government.

The "liberationist" approach, on the other hand, tended to favor more radical, cultural change; change that was transformational in nature and that would most likely arise from outside the normal structures of the American political system. Liberationists argued that there was a considerable gap between access and power and that it was simply not enough to have a seat at the table. As the gay and lesbian movement evolved over time, it became clear that the political and cultural approaches to activism were not mutually exclusive, and indeed these strategies worked both in concert and in tension with one another as the gay and lesbian movements developed from one decade to the next.

Between the early 1950s when the Mattachine Society experienced its split, and the late 1960s, however, the assimilationist strategy clearly held sway. During that time the movement as a whole gained little ground and, in fact, experienced some significant setbacks. For example, a medical model of homosexuality gained currency in this period, one which equated homosexuality with mental illness, which made it even more difficult for gays and lesbians to stake a claim to mainstream society. But even in this more quiescent era, there were still those who challenged the assimilationist paradigm and sought the return to a more activist strategy.

This became particularly clear in 1965 when such activists as Barbara Gittings and Franklin Kameny began openly embracing unconventional politics and began picketing for basic rights and human dignity. Specifically, Franklin Kameny advocated for fair and equal treatment of lesbians and gays in the federal government. Working with Barbara Gittings and representatives of other gay and lesbian groups, he confronted prevailing federal government discriminatory policies by challenging employment restrictions and fighting security clearance denials.

Like Gittings, Franklin Kameny was willing to endorse unconventional politics (though not violence) in the form of picketing and demonstrations to convey challenges to traditional notions of heteronormativity. Kameny's endorsement of a more radical political strategy was inspired by the African American civil rights movement and Kameny wasn't the only one inspired by a rise in civil rights militancy. Indeed, as early as 1966, gay activists adopted a symbol of the civil rights movement—a black and white civil rights lapel button with an equals sign on a lavender background signaling their desire for more daring avenues to effect change.

One key event in 1969 not only escalated the call for a more activist posture within the gay and lesbian civil rights movement, but it also fractured the movement once again into two distinct ideological and strategic camps. On June 27, 1969, scores of gay men who frequented a bar, called the Stonewall Inn in New York City, found themselves in a dramatic confrontation with the police who had decided to raid the establishment that evening. The raid itself was not newsworthy, the police routinely harassed gay men wherever they gathered, but the fact was that these men fought back. The so-called "Stonewall Riot" quickly threw the more mainstream organizations associated with the homophile movement on the defensive.

Following Stonewall many lesbians and gays were newly energized. A noticeable number were veterans of the various social and political movements of the 1960s, and they began demanding that their organizations adopt a more confrontational, liberationist approach to change. It is within this broad context that the Gay Liberation Front (GLF) was founded in late 1969. Soon thereafter, similar militant organizations were created in other countries, including Australia, Belgium, Britain, Canada, France, and The Netherlands, which is a testimony to how the Stonewall Rebellion had consequences for the international lesbian and gay rights movement.

In America the GLF appealed to radicals and revolutionaries because it called for a complete transformation of society, and in doing so, attempted to unite all oppressed minorities into a broad-based movement for political and social change. As it attempted to build the coalitions necessary for this movement, the GLF championed a broad New Left platform. It attacked the consumer culture, militarism, racism, sexism, and homophobia. In challenging the latter, the GLF devoted considerable energy to how lesbians and gays were represented in the larger culture through language. With this in mind, the more widespread but clinical term "homosexual" was replaced by "gay," "pride" became an important feature of liberation consciousness, and "coming out" was a crucial element of the liberatory experience.

Within one year of the group's founding in New York, GLF organizations were born throughout the United States. College students organized many local groups on their campuses. Meetings were run according to participatory principles, and hierarchy was eschewed as much as possible. Yet there was considerable disagreement within the broader organization over its purpose (Should it focus only on gay liberation, or should it be part of a larger political movement for progressive change?), its organizational structure, and the role of women and minorities.

The euphoria and sense of unity that accompanied the birth of GLF were short-lived as the post-Stonewall lesbian and gay movements faced the internal conflicts that beset many political and social movements in the late 1960s and early 1970s. Disagreements over the treatment of women and other issues undermined the overall effectiveness of the GLF and ultimately led to its destruction. But the gay and lesbian rights movement as a whole did not die out. Even after the Stonewall Rebellion, the movement was always broader than just one group so, when the GLF fractured, another less radical organization called the Gay Activists Alliance (GAA) became more prominent in shaping movement strategy.

Founded by Jim Owles and Marty Robinson in New York City in December 1969, the GAA attempted to focus on the single issue of gay rights, without the issue fragmentation and anarchic organizational style that characterized the GLF. After initially joining the GLF, Owles and Robinson quickly became disenchanted with the GLF's inability to plan effectively and to temper revolutionary New Left doctrine in an effort to address the daily discrimination faced by lesbians and gays. The GAA membership thought that meaningful reform would occur only if lesbians and gays organized politically and exercised their political muscle to force positive legislative change.

In the aftermath of the 1969 Stonewall Rebellion, GAA-like groups sought laws that would protect lesbians and gays from discrimination. Within several years, they had succeeded in prompting the enactment of ordinances banning discrimination on the basis of sexual orientation in a number of localities throughout the United States. In addition, they were instrumental in getting the American Psychiatric Association to eliminate homosexuality from its list of recognized disorders in 1974 and, by the late 1970s, their activism had resulted in legalizing sodomy in 20 states.

But even the GAA's less militant strategies for change, and the basic civil rights of the gay and lesbian movement in this period generated a serious backlash. The Christian Right reacted to movement gains with hostility and a commitment to organizing their own grassroots constituency to undo such victories. During the 1970s, as a result of the Christian Right's effective mobilization, lesbian and gay rights suffered major setbacks both locally and nationally. Six anti-gay referenda appeared in 1977 and 1978 alone. It was a former Miss America, Anita Bryant, who helped to galvanize conservative opposition to lesbian and gay rights in 1977 with her "Save Our Children" campaign. On June 7 of that year, with her successful efforts to persuade voters to rescind a six-month-old Dade County, Florida, civil rights ordinance, the fight over lesbian and gay rights finally received considerable national attention in the mainstream press.

The 1970s also witnessed an increase in anti-lesbian and anti-gay violence as "fag bashings" became more commonplace throughout the United States. Anti-gay violence attracted considerable public attention in 1978 when Dan White, a member of the San Francisco Board of Supervisors, climbed into an open City Hall window and then shot and killed openly gay board member Harvey Milk and Mayor George Moscone, who had supported Milk and lesbian and gay rights more generally. This broader societal hostility that developed in the 1970s helped set the context for how many would react to gay men with the onset of AIDS in the summer of 1981 (and beyond), during conservative President Ronald Reagan's first year in office.

However, neither anti-gay violence and activism nor internal movement conflicts over ideology or strategy could take away from the most fundamental achievements of the gay and lesbian movement of the 1960s and 1970s. That movement pioneered the idea that "coming out" was a crucial, personal, and political statement and it made that process safer and more empowering today than it otherwise would have been. That movement also made it possible for gays and lesbians to challenge and redefine traditional notions of the family and gender roles in vitally important ways. Finally, the movement nurtured a lesbian and gay counterculture (one that included bisexuals and those who are transgendered), which not only helped to strengthen lesbian and gay identity nationwide, but also broadened that movement's power base in American society. Should the movements embrace a single-issue politics, or attempt to build coalitions with other aggrieved groups to foster more progressive social change? The question continues to be debated among various movement members especially given current battles over same-sex marriage and as they consider the relative strengths and weaknesses of pursuing assimilationist and liberationist strategies for political, social, and economic change.

Carl Wittman, *A Gay Manifesto* (1969)

Carl Wittman's famous manifesto was written as a more radical response to the mainstream homophile movement and organizations that were predominant as late as 1969. His statement is an excellent introduction and overview of central arguments offered by gay liberationists in their critique of the assimilationist, homophile strategy.

San Francisco is a refugee camp for homosexuals. We have fled here from every part of the nation, and like refugees elsewhere, we came not because it is so great here, but because it was so bad there. By the tens of thousands, we fled small towns where to be ourselves would endanger our jobs and any hope of a decent life; we have fled from blackmailing cops, from families who disowned or 'tolerated' us; we have been drummed out of the armed services, thrown out of schools, fired from jobs, beaten by punks and policemen.

And we have formed a ghetto, out of self-protection. It is a ghetto rather than a free territory because it is still theirs. Straight cops patrol us, straight legislators govern us. Straight employers keep us in line, straight money exploits us. We have pretended everything is OK, because we haven't been able to see how to change it—we've been afraid.

Source: Carl Wittman, "A Gay Manifesto," reprinted in *We Are Everywhere*, eds. Mark Blasius and Shane Phelan, New York: Routledge, 1997.

In the past year there has been an awakening of gay liberation ideas and energy. How it began we don't know; maybe we were inspired by black people and their freedom movement; we learned how to stop pretending from the hip revolution. Amerika in all its ugliness has surfaced with the war and our national leaders. And we are revulsed by the quality of our ghetto life.

Where once there was frustration, alienation, and cynicism, there are now new characteristics among us. We are full of love for each other and are showing it; we are full of anger at what has been done to us. And as we recall all the self-censorship and repression for so many years, a reservoir of tears pours out of our eyes. And we are euphoric, high, with the initial flourish of a movement.

We want to make ourselves clear: our first job is to free ourselves; that means clearing our heads of the garbage that's been poured into them. This article is an attempt at raising a number of issues and presenting some ideas to replace the old ones. It is primarily for ourselves, a starting point of discussion. If straight people of good will find it useful in understanding what liberation is about, so much the better.

It should also be clear that these are the views of one person, and are determined not only by my homosexuality, but my being white, male, middle class. It is my individual consciousness. Our group consciousness will evolve as we get ourselves together—we are only at the beginning.

I. **On Orientation**

1. *What homosexuality is:* Nature leaves undefined the object of sexual desire. The gender of that object is imposed socially. Humans originally made homosexuality taboo because they needed every bit of energy to produce and raise children: survival of species was a priority. With overpopulation and technological change, that taboo continued only to exploit us and enslave us.

   As kids we refused to capitulate to demands that we ignore our feelings toward each other. Somewhere we found the strength to resist being indoctrinated, and we should count that among our assets. We have to realize that our loving other is a good thing, not an unfortunate thing, and that we have a lot to teach straights about sex, love, strength, and resistance.
2. Homosexuality is *not* a lot of things. It is not a makeshift in the absence of the opposite sex; it is not hatred or rejection of the opposite sex; it is not genetic; it is not the result of broken homes except inasmuch as we could see the shame of American marriage. *Homosexuality is the capacity to love someone of the same sex. . . .*

II. **On Women**

1. *Lesbianism*: It's been a male-dominated society for too long, and that has warped both men and women. So gay women are going to see things differently from gay men; they are going to feel put down as women, too. Their liberation is tied up with both gay liberation and women's liberation.

This paper speaks from the gay male viewpoint. And although some of the ideas in it may be equally relevant to gay women, it would be arrogant to presume this to be a manifesto for lesbians.

We look forward to the emergence of a lesbian-liberation voice. The existence of a lesbian caucus within the New York Gay Liberation Front has been very helpful in challenging male chauvinism among gay guys, and anti-gay feelings among women's lib.

Problems and differences will become clearer when we begin to work together. One major problem is our own male chauvinism. Another is uptightness and hostility to homosexuality that many women have—that is the straight in them. A third problem is differing views on sex: sex for them has meant oppression, while for us it has been a symbol of our freedom. We must come to know and understand each other's style, jargon and humor . . .

III. **On Coalition**

Right now the bulk of our work has to be among ourselves—self educating, fending off attacks, and building free territory. Thus basically we have to have a gay/straight vision of the world until the oppression of gays is ended.

But not every straight is our enemy. Many of us have mixed identities, and have ties with other liberation movements: women, blacks, other minority groups: we may also have taken on an identity which is vital to us: ecology, dope, ideology. And face it: we can't change Amerika alone:

Who do we look to for coalition?

1. *Women's Liberation:* summarizing earlier statements, 1) they are our closest ally; we must try to get together with them; 2) a lesbian caucus is probably the best way to attack gay guys' male chauvinism, and challenge the straightness of women's liberation; 3) as males we must be sensitive to their developing identities as women, and respect that; if we know what our freedom is about they certainly know what's best for them.
2. *Black liberation:* This is tenuous right now because of the uptightness and supermasculinity of many black men (which is understandable) . . .
3. *Chicanos:* Basically, the same problem as with blacks: trying to overcome mutual animosity and fear, and finding ways to support them . . .
4. *White radicals and ideologues:* We're not, as a group, Marxist or communist. We haven't figured out what kind of political/economic system is good for us as gays . . .
5. *Hip and street people:* a major dynamic of rising gay lib sentiment is the hip revolution within the gay community. Emphasis on love, dropping out, being honest, expressing yourself through hair and clothes, and smoking dope are all attributes of this. The gays who are the least vulnerable to attack by the establishment have been the freest to express themselves on gay liberation.
6. *Homophile groups:* 1) reformist or pokey as they sometimes are, they are our brothers. They'll grow as we have grown and grow. Do not attack then in straight or mixed company; 2) ignore their attack on us; 3) cooperate where cooperation is possible without essential compromise of our identity . . .

SHIRLEY WILLER, *What Concrete Steps Can Be Taken to Further the Homophile Movement?* (1966)

Shirley Willer wrote the following essay when she was President of the Daughters of Bilitis, a most important lesbian organization in the 1950s, 1960s, and 1970s. It was printed in the organization's newspaper, *The Ladder,* which was a central vehicle for communicating the organization's platform and ideas from 1956 to 1971.

To an extent it is difficult for me to discuss what the homophile movement should be doing. I have some very clear ideas about what the Lesbian should be doing but the problems of the male homosexual and the female homosexual differ considerably.

Most perceptive authorities have stated that the basic problems in relations between the sexes arise from the completely artificial dichotomies of role and appearance ascribed to each sex by society. From the median beds wherein we lie, few persons, homosexual or heterosexual, arise whole and healthy individuals.

The social conformist is wracked by anxieties in his ambivalent clinging to the social artifacts which require the denunciation of his nature. The social non-conformist is driven to propound his personal revelation as being above reproach and beyond question. In such a society Lesbian interest is more closely linked with the women's civil rights movement than the homosexual civil liberties movement.

The particular problems of the male homosexual include police harassment, unequal law enforcement, legal proscription of sexual practices and for a relatively few the problem of disproportionate penalties for acts of questionable taste such as evolve from solicitations, wash-room sex acts and transsexual attire.

In contrast, few women are subject to police harassment and the instances of arrest of Lesbians for solicitation, wash-room sex or transsexual attire are so infrequent as to constitute little threat to the Lesbian community beyond the circle of the immediately involved. The rare occurrences serve to remind the Lesbian that such things are possible, but also that they rarely happen.

The problems of importance to the Lesbian are job security, career advancement and family relationships. The important difference between the male and female homosexual is that the Lesbian is discriminated against not only because she is a Lesbian, but because she is a woman. Although the Lesbian occupies a 'privileged' place among homosexuals, she occupies an under-privileged place in the world . . .

Lesbians have agreed (with reservations) to join in common cause with the male-homosexual—her role in society has been one of mediator between the male homosexual and society. The recent DOB convention was such a gesture. The reason we were able to get the public officials there was because we are women, because we offered no threat. However, they did not bargain for what they got. They did not

Source: The Ladder, November 1966.

expect to be challenged on the issues of male homosexuality. In these ways we show our willingness to assist the male homosexual in seeking to alleviate the problems our society has inflicted on him.

There has been little evidence however, that the male homosexual has any intention of making common cause with us. We suspect that should the male homosexual achieve his particular objectives in regard to his homosexuality he might possibly become a more adamant foe of women's rights than the heterosexual male has ever been. . . .

This background may help you understand why, although the Lesbian joins the male homosexual in areas of immediate and common concern, she is at the same time preparing for a longer struggle, waged on a broader base with the widest possible participation of the rank and file Lesbian. . . . its approaches must be as diverse as imagination will allow. . . . I can name a few dozen of the concrete steps your organizations should be taking. I do not doubt that you have tried them. Then, I say continue these and add more and more and more. . . .

Accordingly, proceeding from our statement of wish to offer a few constructive steps—steps we do not like to call concrete, but in full knowledge of the shifts of time and structure, we believe to be firm and tread-worthy.

1. To affirm as a goal of such a conference: to be as concerned about women's civil rights as male homosexuals' civil liberties.
2. To suggest that homosexual men attempt to appreciate the value of women as PEOPLE in the movement, respect abilities as individuals, not to seek them out as simple "show-pieces."
3. That those philosophical factors of homosexuality which engage both sexes be basic to our concepts of reform.
4. That the consideration of one sex not be a determinate factor in decisions of policy, but that a consideration of all arguments be heard and that CONSENSUS be the goal of the conference. Insofar as we do find trust and value in the male-oriented homophile organizations, we will find common ground upon which to work.

CHARLOTTE BUNCH, *Lesbians in Revolt* (1972)

Charlotte Bunch's essay, which appeared in the first issue of *The Furies* (1972), is a fine representation of the lesbian-feminist approach to political, social, and economic change. Bunch was a founding member of The Furies, a lesbian feminist separatist group that was created in 1971.

The development of lesbian-feminist politics as the basis for the liberation of women is our top priority; this article outlines our present ideas . . .

Source: Charlotte Bunch, "Lesbians in Revolt," *The Furies*, 1972.

Lesbianism is a Political Choice

Male society defines lesbianism as a sexual act, which reflects men's limited view of women: they think of us only in terms of sex. They also say lesbians are not real women, so a real woman is one who gets fucked by men. We say that a lesbian is a woman whose sense of self and energies, including sexual energies, center around women—she is woman-identified. . . . Woman-identified lesbianism is, then, more than a sexual preference; it is a political choice. It is political because relationships between men and women are essentially political: they involve power and dominance. Since the lesbian actively rejects that relationship and chooses women, she defies the established political system.

Lesbianism, by Itself, is Not Enough

Of course, not all lesbians are consciously woman-identified, nor are all committed to finding common solutions to the oppression they suffer as women and lesbians. Being a lesbian is part of the challenging male supremacy, but not the end. For the lesbian or heterosexual woman, there is no individual solution to oppression. . . .

Sexism is the Root of All Oppression

. . . Our war against male supremacy does, however, involve attacking the latter-day dominations based on class, race, and nation. As lesbians who are outcasts from every group, it would be suicidal to perpetuate these man-made divisions among ourselves. We have no heterosexual privileges, and when we publicly assert our Lesbianism, those of us who had them lose many of our class and race privileges. Most of our privileges as women are granted to us by our relationships to men (fathers, husbands, boyfriends) whom we now reject. This does not mean that there is no racism or class chauvinism within us [but r]ace, class, and national oppressions come from men, serve ruling-class white male interests, and have no place in a woman-identified revolution.

Lesbianism is the Basic Threat to Male Supremacy

Lesbianism is a threat to the ideological, political, personal, and economic basis of male supremacy. The lesbian threatens the ideology of male supremacy by destroying the lie about female inferiority, weakness, passivity, and by denying women's "innate" need for men. Lesbians literally do not need men, even for procreation. . . .

We offer the beginning of the end of collective and individual male supremacy. Since men of all races and classes depend on female support and submission for practical tasks and feeling superior, our refusal to submit will force some to examine their sexist behavior . . .

Lesbians Must Form Our Own Movement to Fight Male Supremacy

Feminist-lesbianism, as the most basic threat to male supremacy, picks up part of the women's liberation analysis of sexism and gives it force and direction. Women's liberation lacks direction now because it has failed to understand the importance of heterosexuality in maintaining male supremacy, and because it has failed to face class and race as real differences in women's behavior and political needs. As long as straight women see lesbianism as a bedroom issue, they hold back the development of politics and strategies that would put an end to male supremacy and they give men an excuse for not dealing with their sexism. . . .

Lesbians must form our own political movement in order to grow. Changes that will have more than token effects on our lives will be led by woman-identified lesbians who understand the nature of our oppression and are therefore in a position to end it.

CHICAGO GAY LIBERATION FRONT, *A Leaflet for the American Medical Association* (1970)

> Perhaps the greatest policy success of the early 1970s was the American Psychiatric Association's 1973–1974 decision to remove homosexuality from its official *Diagnostic and Statistical Manual* list of mental disorders. This decision did not come about because a group of doctors suddenly changed their views; it followed an aggressive and sustained campaign by lesbian and gay activists. The following pamphlet issued by the Chicago Gay Liberation Front captures the spirit underlining the organizing efforts well.

The establishment school of psychiatry is based on the premise that people who are hurting should solve their problems by 'adjusting' to the situation. For the homosexual, this means becoming adept at straight-fronting, learning how to survive in a hostile world, how to settle for housing in the gay ghetto, how to be satisfied with a profession in which homosexuals are tolerated., and how to live with low self-esteem.

This adjustment school places the burden on each individual homosexual to learn to bear his torment. But the 'problem' of homosexuality is never solved under this scheme; the anti-homosexualist attitude of society, which is the cause of the homosexual's trouble, goes unchallenged. And there's always another paying patient on the psychiatrist's couch.

Dr. Socarides claims, "A human being is sick when he fails to function in his appropriate gender identity, which is appropriate to his anatomy." Who determined "appropriateness"? The psychiatrist or moralist? Certainly there is no scientific basis for defining "appropriate to his anatomy." In a study of homosexuality in other species and other cultures, Ford and Beach in *Patterns of Sexual Behavior* conclude, "Human homosexuality is not a product of hormonal imbalance or 'perverted heredity.' It is the product of the fundamental mammalian heritage of general sexual responsiveness as modified under the impact of experience."

Other than invoking moral standards, Dr. Socarides claims that homosexuality is an emotional illness because of the guilt and anxieties in homosexual life. Would he also consider Judaism an emotional illness because of the paranoia which Jews experienced in Nazi Germany?

Source: Chicago Gay Liberation Front pamphlet, 1970.

We homosexuals of gay liberation believe that the adjustment school of therapy is not a valid approach to society.

We refuse to adjust to our oppression, and believe that the key to our mental health, and to the mental health of all oppressed peoples in a racist, sexist, capitalist society, is a radical change in the structure and accompanying attitudes of the entire social system.

Mental health for women does not mean therapy for women—it means the elimination of male supremacy. Not therapy for blacks, but an end to racism. The poor don't need psychiatrists (what a joke at 25 bucks a throw!)—they need democratic distribution of wealth. OFF THE COUCHES, INTO THE STREETS!

We see political organizing and collective action as the strategy for effecting this social change. We declare that we are healthy homosexuals in a sexist society, and that homosexuality is at least on a par with heterosexuality as a way for people to relate to each other (know any men that don't dominate women?).

Since the prevalent notion in society is that homosexuality is wrong, all those who recognize that this attitude is damaging to people, and that it must be corrected, have to raise their voices in opposition to anti-homosexualism. Not to do so is to permit the myth of homosexual pathology to continue and to comply in the homosexual's continued suffering from senseless stigmatization.

A psychiatrist who allows a homosexual patient—who has been subject to a barrage of anti-homosexual sentiments his whole life—to continue in the belief that heterosexuality is superior to homosexuality, is the greatest obstacle to his patient's health and well-being.

We furthermore urge psychiatrists to refer their homosexual patients to gay liberation (and other patients who are victims of oppression to relevant liberation movements). Once relieved of all patients whose guilt is not deserved but imposed, psychiatrists will be able to devote all their effort to the rich—who do earn their guilt but not their wealth, and can best afford to pay psychiatrists' fees.

We are convinced that a picket and a dance will do more for the vast majority of homosexuals than two years on the couch. We call on the medical profession to repudiate the adjustment approach as a solution to homosexual oppression and instead to further homosexual liberation by working in a variety of political ways (re-educating the public, supporting pickets, attending rallies, promoting social events, etc.) to change the situation of homosexuals in this society.

Join us in the struggle for a world in which all human beings are free to love without fear or shame.

15

Labor Activism

—JOSEPH A. MCCARTIN

The 1960s and 1970s gave birth to a wide range of social movements and turbulent protest politics, as African Americans, Chicanos, American Indians, feminists, environmentalists, anti-war activists, gays and lesbians formed organizations to advance their causes. Less well known, but no less significant, was the movement of government workers to organize and defend their interests on the job. During the 1960s and 1970s, a veritable social revolution took place in local, state, and federal workplaces as government workers organized unions. At the beginning of this period, civil servants lacked the right to bargain collectively with their employers. Nor did they enjoy the same minimum wage, maximum hours, or overtime pay protections that private sector workers had won through the New Deal-era Fair Labor Standards Act. As a result, many government employees, including postal workers, clerks, secretaries, sanitation workers, police officers, firefighters, and teachers, experienced a decidedly second-class form of citizenship in the workplace. In the early 1960s, however, public employees began to organize unions, inspired in many cases by the civil rights movement. Between 1955 and 1975, the number of unionized government employees grew by tenfold, from roughly 400,000 to over 4 million workers, a number which might even rival the combined membership of all the other protest organizations spawned in the 1960s. The public employees' union movement thus demands attention as the single most important aspect of class-based organization to emerge in this tumultuous period.

To understand the significance of the public employee union movement in these years, consider the general condition of 1960s and 1970s labor activism in private sector industries like auto, steel, textiles, and transportation. After demonstrating great militancy in the 1930s and 1940s, private sector unions entered a period of declining momentum after the mid-1950s. The merger of the American Federation of Labor and the Congress of Industrial Organizations to form the AFL-CIO in 1955 marked the apex of post–World War II American trade unionism. At that time, nearly 35 percent of all nonagricultural U.S. workers were organized in unions. By 1980, however, only 23 percent of workers were organized, as highly unionized manufacturing industries like steel and auto downsized and job growth increasingly shifted to the largely nonunion service and retail sectors. By the mid-1970s, large industrial unions like the United Steel Workers of America (USWA) and the United Automobile Workers (UAW) began to see their size and clout diminish. As service employment increasingly supplanted industrial employment, labor militancy as well as union organization declined. In the 1950s, the United States witnessed an average of more than 350 large-scale strikes or lockouts annually. But by the 1970s, this annual average had fallen by 18 percent.

This is not to say that private sector workers who were already in unions were quiet and contented in the 1960s and 1970s. Indeed, one of the myths of postwar American history is that once unionized industrial workers won improved wages, health care, vacation, and retirement benefits from their employers in the 1950s, they merged into a large and undifferentiated suburban middle class. To the contrary, class divisions remained, even if they became somewhat less visible during the era of postwar prosperity. Such divisions burst into view in 1969, for example, when the number of major strikes leapt up over 400, higher than at any point since the end of the Korean War in 1953, as workers fought back against an aggressive "take-it-or-leave it" bargaining stance adopted by General Electric and many other large employers. Pockets of militancy also emerged *within* unions by the end of the 1960s, especially as African Americans, women, and rank-and-file union members demanded fairer treatment from both their union leaders and employers. In 1968, black autoworkers challenged the white leadership of the UAW when they formed "Revolutionary Union Movements" within various locals of their union. In 1976, rank-and-file truck drivers also formed a dissident group within the International Brotherhood of Teamsters in an effort to democratize their union and rid it of corruption. But such rank-and-file movements were unable to mitigate the impact of larger economic trends on workers. By the mid-1970s, rising inflation, unemployment, and industrial plant closings were reminding many just how tenuous prosperity was for seemingly middle-class American workers.

Nonunion private sector workers not only endured more exploitation than their unionized counterparts, but they also were afforded few opportunities to organize and protest on their own behalf after 1960. Efforts to expand unionism among non-industrial private sector workers proceeded unevenly. A case in point was the United Farm Workers (UFW) union headed by César Chávez. Bursting on the scene with successful strikes and boycotts in the mid-1960s, the union seemed poised to organize millions of largely Hispanic farmworkers. However, the UFW never achieved a firm power base even its home state of California and by the 1980s it was struggling for survival. In fact, a variety of structural factors inhibited the organization of not only farmworkers, but nonindustrial workers in general after 1960. Jobs in the expanding service sector were more dispersed and less stable than manufacturing jobs, and service sector companies were smaller, faced more vigorous competition, and therefore tended to be less interested in concluding agreements with unions. As jobs shifted into this sector, the weaknesses in American labor law, which allowed employers great leeway to resist unionization, became more glaring and law firms that specialized in subverting union organizing drives proliferated. As a result, unionization rates in the private sector began to decline significantly by the early 1970s. It is in this context that the importance of the public employee union upsurge becomes clearer. While private sector workers began to encounter new and seemingly insurmountable barriers to their unionization by the 1960s, public employees saw new opportunities to organize.

Public employee unions had actually experienced their first important breakthroughs in the mid-1950s, when liberal Democratic mayors of New York and Philadelphia began bargaining with municipal workers represented by the American Federation of State, County, and Municipal Employees (AFSCME). In 1959, Democratic governor Gaylord Nelson of Wisconsin signed the first statewide law guaranteeing public sector workers the right to organize and bargain collectively. And in 1962, collective bargaining came to the federal sector when President John F. Kennedy signed Executive Order 10988, allowing federal workers to unionize and bargain collectively over some aspects of their working conditions. Following these important breakthroughs, a majority of states and most of the nation's largest municipalities opened the door to unionism and collective bargaining for their public employees. By the mid-1960s, a wide array of government workers were forming unions and protesting their working conditions.

A review of some major labor conflicts involving government workers in this period gives a sense of just how broad this union upsurge was. In 1960, New York City public school teachers affiliated with the American Federation of Teachers (AFT) struck, ultimately winning recognition and a collective bargaining contract. In 1965 social workers struck in New York City, and in 1966 its transit workers walked out. In 1968, the African American sanitation workers of Memphis, Tennessee, forced the city to recognize AFSCME as their representative after a long and bloody strike, during the course of which strike supporter Rev. Martin Luther King Jr. lost his life to sniper's bullet. In 1970, tens of thousands of postal workers staged an illegal walkout that pushed the federal government into reorganizing the postal service and bargaining with postal workers over their compensation. In 1969, firefighters struck the city of Gary, Indiana, and in 1974, a police strike hit Baltimore. In 1975, tens of thousands of clerks, secretaries, social workers, and others employed by the state of Pennsylvania walked off the job. In many of these cases, workers defied the law to stage their strikes; for even when governments did grant public workers the right to organize rarely did they also recognize the workers' right to strike. But such was the spirit of militancy among public sector workers in the 1960s and 1970s that those workers were often undeterred by laws they considered unjust and discriminatory, and public sector strikes grew tenfold between 1963 and 1973. That this militancy coincided with the emergence of the civil right and feminist movements is not surprising. The public sector had historically attracted high proportions of minority and women workers. In the 1960s, such workers began to reject the traditional conception of the "civil servant," which connoted servility to them and chafed at regulations that they felt denied their equal rights.

One of the singular characteristics of the public employee union movement was that it spanned a wide spectrum of workers, from the low-waged and unskilled to well-educated professionals. Indeed the two groups that most symbolized public employee unionism in the 1960s were sanitation workers and teachers. The 1968 Memphis strike provided a great impetus for the organization of sanitation workers nationwide. In the nation's largest municipalities, those workers tended to be African American or Hispanic men with little education. Their militancy brought strikes and union organization to New York, Atlanta, Detroit, Washington, D.C., and other large cities in the 1960s and 1970s. Meanwhile, public school teachers, most of whom were white, organized at a torrid pace in the 1960s. By the mid-1970s, teacher strikes (or threatened strikes) had become a commonplace feature of life in a growing number of American school districts as both the AFT and its rival organization, the National Education Association (NEA), competed to represent the interests of the nation's teachers. African American sanitation workers had rallied behind the slogan of the Memphis sanitation strikers: "I AM A MAN." Teachers embraced the chant of "Teacher Power." For these disparate groups, organizing was a way of achieving recognition from a society that took their work for granted.

More evidence of the broad appeal of unionization among public employees in this period can be found in the case of the nation's air traffic controllers. Employed by the Federal Aviation Administration (FAA), air traffic controllers, who guided planes into, out of, and between the nation's airports did not appear to be a group ripe to engage in protest politics. Most were white, male, military veterans, not prone to be swept up in the turbulent politics of the 1960s. However, they endured often harsh and difficult working conditions in their pressure-filled jobs, including mandatory uncompensated overtime. Thus in the aftermath of President Kennedy's Executive Order 10988, many controllers experimented with organization. When the FAA failed to respond to early controller organizations, controllers decided to form a more aggressive group, the Professional Air Traffic Controllers' Organization (PATCO), in 1968.

PATCO evolved into a militant organization in its first two years of life. In the summer of 1968, the organization staged a national work-to-rule action, a concerted slowdown that caused major delays in air travel in order to dramatize the need for the FAA to hire new controllers and update its equipment. In 1969, several hundred PATCO controllers staged a small "sick-out" to protest the slow pace of reforms in working conditions at the FAA. When the FAA responded by trying to intimidate PATCO leaders, the organization responded by staging a three-week sickout involving more than 3,000 controllers in 1970. The controllers claimed to be sick, but their action caused the same effect as a strike and thus violated federal law, causing unprecedented travel delays, and costing the nation's airlines tens of millions of dollars of lost revenue. And yet PATCO not only survived this confrontation, it got the government to drop its efforts to fire PATCO leaders, went on to win formal recognition from the federal government in 1973, and achieved the first union contract covering air traffic controllers one year later. In the 1970s, PATCO emerged as one of the most militant unions in the federal service. Throughout the decade, its leaders campaigned tirelessly for the liberalization of federal employee relations law, including a demand for the right to strike for federal workers. PATCO also experienced many of the internal tensions that affected other unions in this period as the predominantly white male controller workforce became more diverse racially and by gender in the 1970s.

If PATCO's rise illustrated the broad-based appeal of public employee unionism in the 1960s, its demise illustrated the shifting fortunes of the public employee union movement. Before the mid-1970s, most Americans sympathized with the plight of government workers and supported their efforts to organize. But the onset of a broad economic crisis in the mid-1970s eroded a good deal of that support. When inflation began to wipe away the wage gains of private sector workers and well-paying industrial jobs began to be lost to "de-industrialization" in the mid-1970s, even many unionized private sector workers began to fear that the demands of public sector unions were forcing their tax bills upward. An emerging "tax revolt" put public sector unions increasingly on the defensive. PATCO dug in to resist this shift. Undeterred by softening public support for public employee strikes, PATCO decided to challenge the administration of President Ronald Reagan by calling a walkout involving some 12,000 air traffic controllers on August 3, 1981, to win major changes in working conditions and pay. Instead of negotiating with the union, Reagan fired the controllers and replaced them. Public opinion tended to support Reagan's action. The 1981 crushing of PATCO amounted to the most significant instance of "union busting" since the New Deal era and it had a chilling effect on American unions in the 1980s. Although the public sector labor movement survived the PATCO debacle, it no longer had the expansive momentum it had enjoyed in the 1960s and 1970s.

As public sector unionism's growth slowed, the problems affecting the American union movement as a whole deepened after 1981. Just as the rise of conservative politics and policies after 1980 took an enormous toll on the other activist movements of the 1960s and 1970s the labor movement also began to wither. By the end of the twentieth century, less than 15 percent of all U.S. workers were in unions and labor militancy was diminishing sharply. The strike, once the chief expression of worker militancy in the United States, began to disappear. By 2002, the number of workers on strike in the United States was a mere one-sixtieth of the number that had struck a half-century earlier in 1952. As labor protest waned, the public sector labor movement that elicited such optimism in the 1960s assumed a defensive posture from which it did not to emerge as the century drew to a close.

MIKE ROCK, *Remembering Work as an Air Traffic Controller* (ca. 1960)

Speaking to a workshop of union leaders in 1979, PATCO co-founder Mike Rock recounts the conditions that led to the formation of the organization.

The equipment was obsolete. . . . There was no such thing as coordination. You went to work in an atmosphere of you arrived at work, you were in a hole, you worked for 8 hours or 10 hours without getting a leave. We did not have cafeterias or anything. . . . You ate on position if you were given the time. If you had a coffee break,

Source: Mike Rock Speech to PATCO Leadership Seminar, January 1979, transcription of videotape in the author's possession.

you had your coffee right at your position. The trainees' function was to take the coffee orders and the sandwich orders and to bring them to journeymen controllers. The trainees were not even allowed to talk to journeymen practically. . . . It was complete chaos throughout the system. There was no such thing as radar handoffs. . . . You would terminate the air craft if you had radar, and turn it over to another facility or another sector. Most of the sectors were not even radar. . . . And you can imagine the chaotic conditions with this type of operations. . . . It was like an insane asylum. You went to work as an air traffic controller, your whole thing was to survive that day. Fuck anybody in the other sectors as long as I didn't run anybody together today and get caught. And we had near mid-air collisions by the dozens, but nobody reported them. The bosses didn't report them, and the controllers certainly didn't report them because in those days, if it was written up you were suspended or fired. So everybody was protecting their own asses by not reporting. The only thing that was ever reported was when the pilot officially filed a complaint. Then we would have to file some type of paperwork. . . . The big FAA chiefs in Washington, they never went out into the field. They were never in the facilities. All they would get was the sweet, beautiful reports from their chiefs in their areas: everything was running smooth. Look at our track record. We have no incidents, no mid-air collisions, we are running a damn good system. . . . There was no overtime. The overtime we had in those days was after the 8th hour, when you worked the 9th and the 10th and your extra day on Saturday, the sixth day, you worked for less money. You worked for straight time. . . . The [control] centers were the pits. Nobody wanted to go into a center, because if you got into a center, you never got out. And they were dirty, stinking, old little buildings. Dust would be coming down. And because we were under the military concept, we had to wear white shirts with the skinny ties, right. You weren't allowed to wear a colored shirt. You had to wear a white shirt. And when you reported to work and you were a trainee, they might hand you a mop. They tell you to wear a tie and a white shirt, but they wanted you to mop the floors, clean out the ashtrays. . . . At the same time, they're telling you to come to work with a white shirt and tie. If you came with a colored shirt, they'd send you home and charge you 8 hours leave. And this was for the entire system. If you defied a boss, you were fired. There was no unions. There was no such thing as a grievance. . . . Everybody was terrified of losing their job when they came to work. If you were sick, you were afraid to tell a manager, because you'd lose your job.

RUSSELL SOMMER, *Controllers Experiment with Organization* (1967)

Following President Kennedy's Executive Order 10988 allowing federal workers to organize, air traffic controllers began to do so. But their initial efforts met with unreceptive responses from the government,

Source: [Russell Sommer], "Gathering Storm: A Study of the Impending Crisis in Federal Aviation Employee/Management Relations," NAGE Local R12-5, September 20, 1967, copy in possession of the author.

as air traffic controller Russell Sommer noted in this excerpt of a 1967 analysis of the FAA's growing labor relations crisis.

The Federal Aviation Agency is entering a critical period. . . . Our agency stands at a crossroad. One way leads to new levels of achievement through cooperation based on respect and a new maturity: the other leads to a stormy confrontation between agency management and its employees which would be a tragedy for the agency and for the public we serve. We are alarmed because many do not seem to realize that the clouds are gathering—accelerated by the growing sophistication of the controller workforce and the growing paralysis of middle management in dealing with the "new relationship." . . . Public employees have become cynical about exhortations to "dedication" and "loyalty" from those who forget that loyalty is not one-way and dedication must be earned. . . .

. . . A few years ago, the FAA controller was victim of his environment rather than master. Inadequate equipment, constant training, procedural change, location change, youth and newness of the "system" contributed to his insecurity. Partially out of necessity because of the very magnitude of agency growth, the FAA ruled its workforce crudely but effectively by the "carrot" and "stick" philosophy. . . . "Loyalty" was synonymous with agreement and, in the selection of supervisors, the ability to *lead* or inspire confidence in subordinates were weighed in terms of force rather than persuasion. The system worked for a time, shaping a professional workforce and bringing a high degree of standardization, but only at a cost. It shut off management from valuable input. Many talented employees stopped suggesting, or were ignored. We tended to tell management what *we thought it wanted to hear*, even when the manager desperately needed to be told the truth.

. . . A system based on blind faith and obedience must weaken when faith is shaken by revelation of error or when obedience no longer can be compelled. FAA management *practice*, as divorced from its oft-stated philosophy, has been described by a manager as a "father-son relationship." Like many fathers, the agency failed to prepare for the day when its sons would grow up.

. . . Forming an employee organization in government requires considerable reorientation of thought. It isn't an easy decision; it is almost an act of desperation. The employees must decide that they are going to speak out for their unit and, in the interim, forget about promotions and kudos. . . . The realization that those who *care* have united simply because they *do* care where the agency is going is gradually dawning on management—but it is a slow process. . . . Once the employee group is formed, its leaders find that, having taken their stand, fear is gone . . . We stand at a crossroad. Options remain, but we are rapidly losing them. . . .

NATIONAL DIRECTORS OF PATCO, *Challenging the Federal Government* (1970)

The Professional Air Traffic Controllers Organization (PATCO) was formed in 1968 with the goal of forcing the FAA to address controller issues, whether the agency wanted to or not. It pursued a series of confrontations with the government culminating in a nationwide "sickout" in 1970. This letter warns Transportation Secretary John Volpe that a sick-out will occur unless PATCO's demands are addressed.

January 25, 1970

Dear Mr. Secretary,

At a duly constituted meeting of the Board of Directors today, it has been resolved that as of February 15, 1970, all optional air traffic services rendered by our membership above and beyond those that they are required to perform by their contract and by regulations will be withdrawn, specifically including the services of the many controllers who are in a present condition of fatigue and who are medically entitled to a period of respite for the preservation of their own health.

This resolution is predicated upon two years of almost total inaction by the Department towards the solution of problems that have always been obvious and continue to be immediate. The Board requests that sometime no later than the first week in February a meeting be held between yourself and your staff with these directors in Washington, DC, for the purpose of attempting to resolve the problems and differences that have precipitated this resolution. . . . The Board has agreed that it would be amendable to some kind of realistic mediation to be handled by the various aviation associations who would be most directly concerned with the withdrawal of the described services provided that these representatives are fairly chosen and that the Department as well as this Organization agree to listen to any recommendations which may be forthcoming with a disposition to be convinced.

. . . We consider it to be most unfortunate that things have reached the current state of affairs and offer to you in good faith, meaningful discussion at any time which might permit the substitution of some solutions for confrontation.

Respectfully,

The National Directors of PATCO

Source: National Directors of PATCO to John A. Volpe, January 25, 1970, PATCO file, Box 322, Entry 14, Records of the Federal Aviation Administration, Record Group 237, National Archives II, College Park, Maryland.

RICHARD JONES, *Confronting Racial Discrimination in the Late 1960s* (2002)

After winning formal recognition from the federal government two years after the 1970 sick-out, PATCO began dealing with issues of racial discrimination. In an excerpt from a 2002 interview, Richard Jones recalls what it was like to be one of the first black controllers to work at the Washington Air Route Traffic Control Center in Leesburg, Virginia, where he faced discrimination that the union was slow to eliminate. Although he was eventually able to feel comfortable at this job, and even had some very positive experiences with some white supervisors, Jones found entry into this profession most difficult.

Very strange in that the first day I went there, of course they gave us a tour of the center and I saw not one black face. And I started to get a little worried. . . . I hung around there and didn't see any black faces but said, 'So what? We'll push on.' Actually I went through what they call the basic course . . . without a problem at all for the most part. As the days came and went, I ran into a few other blacks and I was pleasantly surprised in that they were all very supportive. And I asked one of the first to come up to me, how many blacks do they have here? He said ten. I thought, 'oh well that's pretty good.' And he said, 'Well don't look for many more around the country because we have a lot more than any other center. . . .'

To be perfectly frank, that was the most difficult phase of my career. . . . When they [white controllers] entered that center, they took on . . . the culture of the outside. The confederate flag was still hanging. . . . there was a tree, in fact that tree is still there in Leesburg, and they refused to cut that tree down because of history and the history is that there were any number of slaves hung from that tree, and the community refused to cut it down. That was the culture in Leesburg. So they just took on that flavor, unfortunately. . . .

CHERYL JENNI, *Confronting Sexual Harassment in the Mid-1970s* (2002)

As women began to enter air traffic controller workforce that in the mid-1960s was all-male, they faced resistance. In a 2002 interview, Cheryl Jenni recalls her experiences as one of the first women to work at the Denver Air Route Traffic Control Center.

Source: Richard Jones interviewed by author, June 24, 2002, tape in the author's possession.
Source: Cheryl Jenni interviewed by author, October 29, 2002, tape in the author's possession.

Yeah, there were a couple of instances of really minor sexual harassment. Which I'm grateful they were minor because the supervisors were absolutely no help. Oh, there was a fellow who used to just stare at me for the whole shift. And he never ever did anything, but it was pretty uncomfortable. And there was another guy who . . . walked up to me one day at the bulletin board and started massaging my shoulders. And it really hurt his feelings when I said "hands off."

. . . Well, you know all of that stuff was unfolding right about '75, '77. And I'm an avid reader of *Ms. Magazine*, and because of some things I've read I know what the timing was on some of those terms. Of course, they started on the east coast and took a long time to get to Denver [where I worked]. But I don't know whether I even called it sexual harassment at the time, I knew it wasn't supposed to be going on. . . . I'm trying to remember if . . . I might have called it flirting, guys coming on to me, which is a term I still would occasionally use.

PATCO Local Union Newsletter, *Preparing for Confrontation* (ca. December 1979)

As inflation raised the cost of living for all Americans in the second half of the 1970s, PATCO controllers grew restless and began to consider striking when their contract expired in 1981. This editorial appeared in a PATCO local union newsletter in Texas.

Unionism/Moral Obligations, Strikes/Legal ramifications! These are very emotional words and issues which bring out emotional responses by every air traffic controller in the FAA today. They are the issues which everyone has a strong view about. These are also the issues which are argued day after day in facilities around the country. . . .

. . . The real issue rests in a single word. . . . The word is POWER. Not usually associated with government employees, is it? Power is a word that has an almost ominous quality about it yet it is something that all people want, in one way or another. . . . The Rockefellers have power; [football player] Earl Campbell and [baseball player] Pete Rose have power; airline pilots have power and so do doctors. . . . [A]ll have taken skills, talents, and situations and parlayed them into taking control of their lives as well as their economic well being. Do we as air traffic controllers have the skills and situations to have power? Is it bad or wrong to desire power? . . . Do we have the power to control our environment? Do we have the tools?

The power formula has two factors. 1. How much economic impact do you have? 2. How replaceable are you?

Source: Editorial, *Dallas-Fort Worth Newsletter*, December 1979, Records of the Professional Air Traffic Controllers Organization, Southern Labor Archives, Pullen Library, Georgia State University, Atlanta, Georgia.

Medical school restricts the number of doctors available to the market place so the interests of doctors are protected. The FAA has done the same thing for us. The controller workforce is not replaceable! You know that! They know that!

. . . Remember, the exercise of power lies at your fingertips. Remember the laws involved. People who generate great income and who are not readily replaceable have power. . . .

If you agree that the power is there, then decide whether you will use it to control your own destiny or give it to your employer to use as he sees fit. The tools are here, will you use them? Think long and hard, but remember that once power is taken away, it is difficult, if not impossible to re-attain.

Charles Phillips

RONALD A. OBERHAUSER, *A Broken Union* (1981)

After Ronald Reagan fired the striking members of PATCO in 1981, he received many letters like this one from controllers who justified their strike in light of their patriotism and their past service to their country.

November 30th, 1981

Dear Mr. President,

My name is Ronald Oberhauser. I am, or I guess I should say, I was an Air Traffic Controller prior to [August] 5th, 1981. That, Mr. President, if you have forgotten was the day myself and my fellow controllers were fired by you.

I am writing to you Mr. President to let you know, contrary to what I feel you believe, myself and a vast majority of the fellow controllers you fired are not now or ever were liars, thiefs or subversives trying to destroy the United States Government. I'll challenge our records of government service against you or any of your staff. We've encouraged safety and have been more honest to the American people than you or any of your White House staff. I can only speak for myself when I say, after spending six (6) years in the Marine Corps, during which I spent a year in Viet Nam, and eleven (11) years as an air traffic controller, I never once endangered the lives of my fellow workers or the public which I was serving. My work always came first. That, I know now, was a mistake. It has cost me my family, my home and many years of dedicated public service.

I am about to turn 37 years old and because I took a stand on something I believed in, I must go out and try to find a job where I might build a new career. Sir may I remind you what I did was nothing more than what the founders of our great country did.

Source: Ronald A. Oberhauser to President Ronald Reagan, November 30, 1981, File 81-34, Entry 14, Box 163, Records of the Federal Aviation Administration, Record Group 237, National Archives II, College Park, Maryland.

The only difference is that they won the battle and I and my fellow controllers lost. There has been one other time in my short life that I have seen a group of people criticized, shamed and forgotten, as the striking controllers have been, and that sir is when I returned from Viet Nam.

I am not looking for sympathy, Mr. President. What I am looking for is justice and equality. I was tired of being a second class citizen. Not having the same rights and privileges as other citizens of this country just because I worked for the government. I hope and pray that someday government employees will have those rights. I don't feel Mr. President it will happen in your administration. You sir are cold and unconcerned about the "Common Man." . . .

I hope Mr. President that you get a chance to read this. I feel it is one of many voices trying to tell you that today's government is not for the working people. It is caught up in its own political rhetoric.

Ronald A. Oberhauser

16

Native American Activism

—Troy Johnson

"ALCATRAZ INVASION"—Wacky Indian Raid, Alcatraz "Invaded" read the March 9, 1964, headlines of the *San Francisco Chronicle.* Five Bay Area Sioux Indians, Garfield Spotted Elk, Walter Means, Richard McKenzie, Mark Martinez, and Allen Cottier, had laid claim to Alcatraz Island and struck the first blow in the battle for Indian self-determination. Like so many of the social movements that came of age in this period, the protest actions of American Indians grew more radical over the course of the 1960s. Also like those other movements, the militancy of the 1960s and 1970s had deep roots in earlier decades. Indeed, since at least the 1950s Indians had engaged in more than 20 major demonstrations and nonviolent protests aimed at ending further reductions of the Indian land base, stopping the termination of Indian tribes, and halting brutality and insensitivity toward Indian people.

Prior to the late 1960s, the Indians most at the forefront of the struggle for greater civil rights and legal protections were quite traditional. The protests of this period were typified by the participation of elders, medicine people, and entire communities. These early activists rarely sought to forge alliances outside of tribal boundaries as the younger generation of more radical Indian activists would in actions such as the occupation of Alcatraz. Still, even in the 1950s, Indians were quite militant. The Six Nations people, for example, used both passive resistance and militant protests to block various New York State projects.

The Tuscarora and Mohawk demonstrated in opposition to the building of power projects such as the Fort Randall Dam on the Missouri River and the Kinzua Dam. In April 1958, "Mad Bear" Anderson led a stand against a tide of land seizures; a move that ultimately brought armed troops onto Indian land. The New York power authority planned to expropriate 1,383 acres of Tuscarora land for the building of a reservoir and back flooding of Indian lands. Anderson and others blocked surveyors' transits and deflated vehicle tires as harassment tactics. When the Tuscarora refused to accept the state's offer to purchase the land, 100 armed state troopers and police invaded Tuscarora lands. The troops were met by a nonviolent front of 150 men, women, and children blocking the road by lying down or standing in front of government trucks. Seneca and Mohawk Indian people set up camps on the disputed land, challenging the state to remove them. Anderson and other leaders were arrested, but the media attention forced the power company to back down. The Federal Power Commission ruled that the Indians did not have to sell the land.

Following the Six Nations' success, the Miccosukee Indian Nation of Florida summoned Anderson to help them in their own militant fight against the federal government which was also attempting to take land from them as part of the Everglades Reclamation Project. In 1959, several hundred Indian people marched on BIA headquarters in Washington, D.C., protesting the government policy of termination of Indian tribes and attempted a citizen's arrest of the Indian commissioner.

The 1960s witnessed a continuation of localized Indian protest actions but a greater number of young people also started involving themselves in the protest actions. Not only did youth initiate the brief Indian occupation of Alcatraz Island in 1964 but even before this event they had participated in a number of "fish-ins" intended to protect the fishing rights guaranteed to the tribes of the Pacific Northwest, particularly along the Nisqually and Puyallup rivers. As more young people committed themselves to the cause of Native American rights, the entire movement grew more radical and new organizations burst onto the scene.

Out of the Pacific Northwest fish-ins, for example, grew a new group called the Survival of American Indians Association (SAIA) and, in urban Minneapolis, Minnesota young Indians founded an organization called the American Indian Movement (AIM) on July 28, 1968. Although AIM initially concentrated its efforts on eliminating the discriminatory practices of local city government in the areas of employment and housing, and more specifically on halting police brutality toward urban Indian people, eventually it became an organization working for greater Indian rights all over the country. In the summer of 1968, young Indians founded yet another militant organization called the United Native Americans (UNA) in the San Francisco Bay Area. UNA had a pan-Indian focus and sought to unify all persons of Indian blood throughout the Americas and to develop a grassroots organization. Its goal was to promote self-determination through Indian control of Indian affairs at every level.

Unlike other social movements of this period, the American Indians unique legal position as a group who had signed formal treaties with the U.S. government and other foreign governments meant that the Native American movement would involve itself in protests that had international as well as national implications. The year 1968 witnessed radical protests across the country but members of the Iroquois nation initiated a protest that involved Canada as well as the United States. Canada had restricted the free movement of Mohawk Indians between the United States and Canada, demanding that the Mohawk pay tolls to use the bridge and pay customs on goods brought back from the United States. Members of the Iroquois League felt that this was an infringement of rights granted to them under a treaty they had signed with Great Britain and, citing Canada's obligations under the Jay Treaty of 1794, members of the Mohawk tribe challenged the legality of tolls and customs collections on the Cornwall International Bridge.

Just as young Indians grew more militant over the course of the postwar period, do did specific Indian tribes. In addition to the rise in activism among the Mohawk, the Miccosukee, and the Bay Area Indians, the Taos Pueblo Indians of New Mexico also reasserted their claims to ancestral lands in the 1950s. On August 13, 1951, Taos Indians filed a suit before the Indian Claims Commission, seeking support for the validity of title to Taos Blue Lake. On September 8, 1965, the Indian Claims Commission affirmed that the U.S. government took the area unjustly from its rightful owners, the Taos Pueblo Indians. The return of Taos Blue Lake clearly indicated that activism could net Indians substantive victories, but it illuminated just how the complex relationship continued to be between the federal government and Native Americans in this period.

Notably, the federal government tried to use the Indian victory at Taos Blue Lake to its advantage just as the Pueblo Indians had. In fact, during the ceremony that returned the Taos Blue Lake to the Pueblo Indians, President Richard Nixon took the opportunity to sell his administration's new Indian policy. Specifically, he proposed a bold new plan for Indian self-determination that would officially bring the termination era to an end and transfer responsibility for tribal affairs from the federal government to Indian people.

But Nixon's policy of self-determination would soon be tested in California, particularly in the Bay Area, which had become the hotbed for the newly developing Indian activism. In 1969, young California Indians had formed the Native American Student Union to forge a new pan-Indian alliance between the newly emerging Native American studies programs on the various campuses. In San Francisco, members of the Native American Student Union prepared to test Nixon's commitment to self-determination before a national audience by once again occupying Alcatraz Island. With the battle cry "We Hold The Rock!" Richard Oakes would be identified as the leader of the occupation, LaNada Boyer would be the only person to participate for the entire 19 months, and Dennis Turner, another member of the union, would become a member of the Indian counsel on the island. With the occupation of Alcatraz Island, the social movement of the American Indian people had come to full maturity. For the first time in their history, Native American leadership came from within the ranks of the oppressed rather from outside organizations.

Of course American Indian activists had not come of age in a social vacuum. The 1960s were heady years in America as various racial and minority groups struggled to insure that they received the civil rights to which they were entitled. And the lessons of other social movements were not missed by Indian people. As civil rights issues and rhetoric dominated the headlines, Indian groups adopted the vocabulary and techniques of various social movements of this period in order to get Indian issues covered by the media and before the American public. The National Indian Youth Council (NIYC), a group of young college-educated Indians who had organized following the American Indian Charter Convention held in Chicago in 1961, was adopting some of the ideas of the civil rights movement when it decided to hold the numerous fish-ins in the Pacific Northwest. Likewise, borrowing from the student movement, Native Americans in the United Native American (UNA) located an unused bungalow at the University of California at Berkley, occupied it, and later received permission to develop a Native Cultural center on campus.

Indian people were also inspired by the activists in the anti-war movement. American Indians not only experienced the Vietnam War first hand, but they returned home from the war they faced some uniquely difficult choices. Those who attempted to return to life on the reservation returned to high unemployment, poor health facilities, and substandard housing conditions. Those who elected to relocate to urban areas encountered "double discrimination." First, they were faced with the continuing discrimination against Indian people that resulted in high unemployment, police brutality, alcoholism, and death. Secondly, the returning veterans experienced the discrimination being felt by other Vietnam veterans who were viewed as participants in an unpopular war. In an attempt to acquire skills for future employment, many of these Indian veterans utilized their GI bill and enrolled in colleges in the Bay Area. Indian students from these colleges, many of them Vietnam veterans, filled the ranks of the rising Indian activism movement now.

By the late 1960s, Indian activists also shared a great deal with the African Americans who had recently gravitated toward an ideology of Black Power. Following the Alcatraz occupation, the American Indian Movement became not only the primary voice of the American Indian protest movement but also the primary organization to embrace and articulate an ideology of "Red Power" that, like "Black Power" stressed self-determination as the foundation for a more militant approach to attaining rights. Reflecting the Indian movement's turn to Red Power militancy following the Alcatraz occupation, there were some 62 occupations; some were of private land and facilities, while others were of federal facilities such as the Washington, D.C., BIA headquarters building. The most dramatic, however, was the 1973 occupation of Wounded Knee village in South Dakota.

In February 1973, AIM leaders and about 200 activists from the Oglala Sioux Nation declared themselves independent from the United States and no longer subject to the dictatorial leadership of a man named Richard "Dickey" Wilson, who the Bureau of Indian Affairs had appointed Tribal Chairman of the Oglala Sioux Nation of South Dakota. Where the occupation of Alcatraz Island had been nonviolent, the Wounded Knee occupants were armed and considered dangerous. The government decided that it could not assume a waiting posture as it had at Alcatraz. Weapons, personnel, and equipment, some of which had been used in Vietnam were supplied by the Department of Defense. Ultimately gunfire was exchanged between government forces and AIM security resulting in a U.S. Marshal being paralyzed and two Indians being killed.

Following these injuries and deaths both sides agreed upon a tenuous cease-fire. But tensions between the occupiers and the federal authorities only grew and the situation worsened. Both groups established, violated, and reinstated cease-fires and eventually, on March 26 some 340 FBI agents decided to surround Wounded Knee and force a surrender. Covertly supported by the U.S. Army and bolstered by 130,000 rounds of M-16 ammunition, 4,000 rounds of M-1 ammunition, 24,000 flares, 12 M-79 grenade launchers, 600 cases of C-S gas, 100 rounds of M-40 high explosive rounds, as well as helicopters and Phantom jets, the FBI was willing to take Wounded Knee by force, but ultimately, on May 8, 1973, the occupation ended with no such assault. Hunger, lack of electricity, low morale, and the inability to bring new Indian blood onto the Wounded Knee compound ultimately doomed the occupation. AIM had lost this war of attrition. Nevertheless, the occupation at Wounded Knee indicated that the movement of American Indians that existed by the early 1970s meant business and, with both AIM and the government forces armed and more than willing to shoot to kill, the stakes in the movement's struggle had grown higher than ever.

There can be little doubt that American Indian activism has had a profound and positive impact on government policy toward the Indian Nations. The oft-spoken goal of the activists was one of self-determination for Indian people—the rights of Indians to handle their own affairs with as little government intervention as possible. Following on the heels of the Wounded Knee occupation, Congress passed Public Law 93-638, the Indian Self-Determination and Education Assistance Act, which expanded tribal control over tribal governments and education. The Act also encouraged the development of human resources and reservation programs and authorized federal funds to build needed public school facilities on or near Indian reservations. The Act was hailed by many as the most important piece of legislation passed in the twentieth century.

MANIFESTO OF THE AMERICAN INDIAN MOVEMENT GRAND GOVERNING COUNCIL, *The Trail of Broken Treaties* (1972)

The Trail of Broken Treaties and The Twenty Points Manifesto was the coming together of three separate movements: the battle for fishing rights (Fish-Ins) in the Pacific Northwest, the murder of the Alcatraz Occupation leader, Richard Oakes, and a movement to impress upon President Nixon and his administration the continuing failures in the administration of Indian Affairs. The twenty points included, among other things, the restoration of constitutional treaty-making authority and the creation of a commission to review treaty commitments and violations.

We need not give another recitation of past complaints nor engage in redundant dialogue of discontent. Our conditions and their cause for being should perhaps be best known by those who have written the record of America's action against Indian people. In 1832, Black Hawk correctly observed: *You know the cause of our making war. It is known to all white men. They ought to be ashamed of it.*

Source: American Indian Movement Grand Governing Council, aimggc@worldnet.att.net.

The government of the United States knows the reasons for our going to its capital city. Unfortunately, they don't know how to greet us. We go because America has been only too ready to express shame, and suffer none from the expression—while remaining wholly unwilling to change to allow life for Indian people.

We seek a new American majority—a majority that is not content merely to confirm itself by superiority in numbers, but which by conscience is committed toward prevailing upon the public will in ceasing wrongs and in doing right. For our part, in words and deeds of coming days, we propose to produce a rational, reasoned manifesto for construction of an Indian future in America. If America has maintained faith with its original spirit, or may recognize it now, we should not be denied. Press Statement issued: October 31, 1972

STATEMENT BY THE AMERICAN INDIAN MOVEMENT, *The American Indian Movement* (1968)

The American Indian Movement was founded in 1968 by Clyde Bellecourt, Eddie Benton Banai, Dennis Banks, and Mary Jane Wilson, Chippewa Indians from Minnesota. AIM arose out of concerns of Native Americans in Minneapolis, Minnesota, and focused on changing the life of Indians in the urban centers. AIM members coordinated a neighborhood patrol to monitor police activities in Indian neighborhoods and to prevent unjust arrests and police mistreatment of American Indian residents. AIM ultimately extended their area of concern to include the reform of Indian and federal government relations. Members of AIM participated in Native American activism across the United States from 1969 to 1975.

How? When? Where? Did AIM start?

The American Indian Movement was founded on July 28, 1968 in Minneapolis, Minn. to unify the more than 20 Indian organizations which were then felt to be doing little, if anything, to change life in the Indian ghetto. As it became clear that most of these organizations treated Indians paternalistically, with little incentive to manage their own affairs, AIM, first called the Concerned Indian American (CIA), redirected its attention away from the organizations and toward the Indian people as the means to Indian self determination.

A catalyst for AIM in 1968 in the city of Minneapolis was the pervasive police harassment of Indian people. While Indians represented only 10% of the city's population, 70% of the inmates in the city jails were Indian. To divert Indians from the jails, AIM formed a ghetto patrol, equipped with two-way radios which monitored the police radios. Whenever a call came over involving Indians, AIM was there first, and for 29 successive weekends prevented any undue arrests of Indian people. . . .

Source: Copyright © 1999 Michigan State University Library and Mike Wicks.

Who founded AIM?

The cofounders of AIM were Dennis Banks, Clyde Bellecourt, and George Mitchell, Chippewa's of Minnesota. Banks is from Leach Lake Reservation and Mitchell and Bellecourt from White Earth. Banks now serves as National Director, succeeding Verne Bellecourt also of White Earth.

How extensive an organization is AIM?

There are 79 chapters of AIM internationally, eight of which are in Canada. AIM has also developed ties with aboriginal organizations in Australia, and with natives in Micronesia and continues to grow on and off the reservation.

What is the structure of AIM?

Unlike other organizations dealing with Indian Affairs, uniquely begins with the people and pyramids to a national organization. It is the chapters which dictate and direct priorities to the national officers who, in turn, create and guide AIM in the long range strategy to meet those priorities. Each chapter is independent and autonomous. The national officers are Chairman, John Trudell; Treasurer, Larry Anderson; Secretary, Carol Stubbs; National Executive Director, Dennis Banks.

NEW YORK TIMES, *The BIA and the Plight of the American Indian* (1973)

This June 1973 article from the *New York Times* captures in a snapshot the situation that Native American people found themselves in in the twentieth century. They lagged behind in life expectancy, employment, education, and health care while leading all populations in suicide in school dropouts. Reservation Indians faired even worse. Unemployment was up, suicides were up, alcoholism was up: activism could not be far behind!

The problem is indeed not a lack of money. It is rather, where does the money go? The BIA's appropriations rose by more than $530 million in fiscal 1973, while overall federal expenditures for Indians, including funding for Indian programs in such agencies as the Office of Economic Opportunity and the Department of Health, Education, and Welfare, climbed to $925 million. Most of these moneys end up in the pockets of the BIA 15,000 employees, other government employees and their capitalist friends, including some tribal chairmen.

The government is spending almost $2,000 for each reservation Indian, yet the average annual income of each Indian *family* remains considerably below that figure, and the misery of the reservations is blatant.

The 500,000 Indians still on reservations (there are roughly an equal number in the cities) can find no escape from the BIA, which affects everything from the education of their children and the preservation of their natural resources to the

---

execution of their wills. 25–30 percent of all Indian children are removed from their families and placed in foster homes. One of the most frequently advanced grounds for separating Indian children from their parents is the abuse of alcohol. However this standard is very rarely applied against non-Indian parents in areas where rates of problem drinking are the same among Indians and non-Indians. . . .

STATEMENT BY THE AMERICAN INDIAN MOVEMENT, *Wounded Knee* (1973)

On February 28, 1973, several hundred Oglala Lakota people, supported by members of the American Indian Movement (AIM) occupied the village of Wounded Knee, South Dakota—the sight on the 1890 Wounded Knee Massacre. While the initial objective was to remove Oglala Sioux Nation President Richard (Dicky) Wilson, the occupation soon settled down into a stalemate that lasted 71 days. The frustration felt by residents of the Pine Ridge Reservation were captured in an anonymous note pasted to the door of the town's trading post, "It is better to die on your feet than to live on your knees."

The Indian peoples who have tried to function through the white man's system since the Indian Reorganization Act of 1934, who have seen their land taken away and their hopes destroyed, saw the first real effort in years to regain power over their lives in the liberation of Wounded Knee.

Hundreds of Indians representing more than 75 different tribes, supported the just demands of the Oglala Sioux people on Pine Ridge Reservation at the risk of their own lives and their freedom. The Sioux, like every Indian tribe in the country have ceded land to the US government; and in payment for that land the U.S. government is supposed to provide us with certain goods and services, they provide tyranny.

At Wounded Knee we finally said, "The hell with that. You are going to honor your treaty with us from now on and we are going to force you to do that because if you don't you will have to kill us." That was the point of Wounded Knee.

We have a treaty that is 105 years old and for 105 years it has been continually violated. It is time for the United States to live up to its pledges to the Indians. The United States has signed 371 treaties with Indian peoples and the result of these treaties is that our water has been stolen, our minerals have been stolen, and our land has been stolen. All of this must be paid for retroactively and in perpetuity.

We are the landlords of this country and at Wounded Knee we showed up to collect. These treaties supersede any state laws and, in fact, prevail over federal law. If the country is going to live up to its Constitution, then in fact it must live up to its treaty commitments. We still have to go to court to ascertain our treaty rights. Once again we have

---

to rely on the White Man and wait for him to give us the right we already have. If he goes against his Constitution and convicts us, we will prove to the world that this is really a police state instead of a free country. The Wounded Knee trials are the most important of the century. They will expose how American practices its founding philosophy.

INDIANS OF ALL TRIBES, *Alcatraz Is Not an Island* (1969)

Alcatraz Island was occupied in November 1969 by a group of young American Indian college students. These students came from tribal groups from across the United States and were truly "Indians of All Tribes." This group, later incorporated under California law became Indians of All Tribes, Inc. The student leader, Richard Oakes, Mohawk stated that "Alcatraz is not an Island," it is an idea, an idea that Indian people can be free again to self-determine their future and that of their children.

We came to Alcatraz with an idea. We would unite our people and show the world that the Indian spirit would live forever. There was little hate or anger in our hearts, for the very thought of a lasting unity kept us who are in harmony with life. From this island would grow a movement which must surely encompass the world. All men of this earth must hunger for peace and fellowship. . . .

Source: Richard Oakes, Mohawk, California, Alcatraz Island, November 1969.

Alcatraz, the idea, lives. We can only pray the Great Spirit that all brothers and sisters who can understand our song join us. Speak now your love of the Indian people. Dance with us the great unity. Chant with us the earth renewal. Let all men and women be proud. Let our children bathe in truth and never know the broken promises of the past. Let Indians of All Tribes be the pathway to People of one earth.

Source: Wilma Mankiller, Cherokee, Interview by author (Dr. Troy Johnson), December 1993.

RICHARD OAKS, *Indian Proclamation* (1969)

Various proclamations were issued by the occupiers of Alcatraz Island. These proclamations gave voice to the frustration felt by Native Americans after years of neglect and gave direction to those who supported the occupation. The proclamations invited the U.S. government to acknowledge the wrongs done and to allow Indian people the right of self-determination for their future.

Source: Indians of All Tribes, San Francisco, Alcatraz Island, 1969.

To the government of the United States from Alcatraz Island, Indian Territory.

We native peoples of North America have gathered here to claim our traditional and natural right to create a meaningful use for our Great Spirit's land. Therefore let it be known that our stand for self-determination is on Alcatraz. We invite the United States to acknowledge the justice of our claim. The choice now lies with the leaders of the American Government—to use violence upon us as before to remove us from our Great Spirit's land, or to institute a real change in its dealings with the American Indian. We do not fear your threat to charge is with crimes on our land. We and all other oppressed peoples would welcome this spectacle of proof before the world of your title by genocide. Nevertheless, we seek peace. . . .

INDIANS OF ALL TRIBES, *Proclamation to the Great White Father and All His People* (1969)

The occupiers of Alcatraz Island used the irony of "right of discovery" to claim title to the vacant land. The prison had been closed in 1963 and lay empty. The irony was that Christopher Columbus had claimed title to "The New World" by right of discovery when the New World to Columbus was the old world to millions of Native peoples.

The irony of offering trade good in payment for Alcatraz reflects the shameful price paid for Manhattan Island by the Dutch in 1626. It also referred to the shameful price being offered California's first people for lands stolen from them in the settling of the American West.

We, the Native Americans, reclaim the land known as Alcatraz Island in the name of all American Indians by right of discovery. We wish to be fair and honorable in our dealings with the Caucasian inhabitants of this land, and hereby offer the following treaty:

We will purchase said Alcatraz Island for twenty-four dollars ($24) in glass beads and red cloth, a precedent set by the white man's purchase of a similar island about 300 years ago. We know that $24 in trade goods for these 16 acres is more than was paid when Manhattan Island was sold, but we know that land values have risen over the years. Our offer of $1.24 per acre is greater than the 47 cents per acre the white men are now paying the California Indians for their land.

We will give to the inhabitants of this island a portion of the land for their own to be held in trust by the American Indian Affairs and by the bureau of Caucasian Affairs to hold in perpetuity—for as long as the sun shall rise and the rivers go down to the sea. We will further guide the inhabitants in the proper way of living. We will offer them our religion, our education, our life-ways, in order to help them achieve our level of civilization and thus raise them and all their white brothers up from their

Source: Indians of All Tribes, San Francisco, Alcatraz Island, 1969.

savage and unhappy state. We offer this treaty in good faith and wish to be fair and honorable in our dealings with all white men.

The US Government policy of termination of Indian reservations and relocation to urban areas was a thinly disguised attempt to gain title to additional Indian lands in the 1950s. Indian treaties would be abrogated. Indian reservations would be broken up and sold to the highest bidder and Indian people would be relocated to twelve major US cities. Posters such as these advertised good jobs, happy homes, and job training. The truth was far different. The unrest caused by the relocation program fed into the larger unrest that was beginning to give rise to the Red Power Movement.

Department of the Interior: Bureau of Indian Affairs, *The Bureau of Indian Affairs Relocation Program* (1952)

Poster

> The U.S. government policy of termination of Indian reservations and relocation to urban areas was a thinly disguised attempt to gain title to additional Indian lands in the 1950s. Indian treaties would be abrogated. Indian reservations would be broken up and sold to the highest bidder and Indian people would be relocated to 12 major U.S. cities. Posters such as these advertised good jobs, happy homes, and job training. The truth was far different. The unrest caused by the relocation program fed into the larger unrest that was beginning to give rise to the Red Power movement.

Come to Denver!

THE CHANCE OF YOUR LIFETIME!

Good Jobs

Retail Trade

Manufacturing

Government-Federal, State, Local

Wholesale Trade

Construction of Buildings, Etc.

Happy Homes

Beautiful Houses

Many Churches

Source: Department of the Interior, Bureau of Indian Affairs, Washington DC, 1952.

Exciting Community Life
Over Half of Homes Owned by Residents
Convenient Stores
Shopping Centers

Training

Vocational Training
Auto Mechanics
Beauty Shop
Drafting
Nursing
Office Work
Watch making
Adult Education
Evening High School
Arts and Crafts
Job Improvement
Homemaking

Beautiful Colorado

Tallest State, 48 Mt. Peaks Over 14,000 Ft
350 Days Sunshine
Mild Winters
Zoos
Museums
Mountain Parks
Drives
Picnic Areas
Lakes
Amusement Parks
Big Game Hunting
Trout Fishing
Camping!

17

Poverty Rights Activism

—FELICIA KORNBLUH

Throughout U.S. history, citizens with the fewest economic resources have had the least political power. This has not stopped parents from doing what they could to feed their children, from trying to access decently waged jobs, or demanding services from their government. Poor people have claimed first-class citizenship at the ballot box, in courtrooms, and in the consumer marketplace. At times their fights have met with notable success, as they did during the 1930s at the height of the Great Depression. Because the poor marched together and organized to demand relief from the government, the administration of President Franklin Delano Roosevelt enacted a series of "New Deal" programs that gave poor and working people direct financial aid—especially when they were unemployed, old, or raising parents without help from working spouses—as well as some protection for efforts they made to organize into labor unions at work.

In the 30 years between the launching of federal aid to the poor under the New Deal and the re-emergence of a mass movement of the poor in the 1960s and 1970s, poor women and men continued to engage in a variety of individual protests. However, in the middle 1960s, these individual protests were joined by many that were collective and openly political. To a large extent, the change occurred because poor people were inspired by the activism they saw in the African American civil rights movement, in the North as well as in the South. Urban civil rights campaigns over schools, housing, police brutality, and public benefits introduced many low-income and unemployed Americans to new activist strategies as well to the inner workings of urban political machines. The groundwork was laid for poor people to forge their own movement.

The poor also began to act collectively because, in the early 1960s, the government itself had begun to deal with poverty in new ways that both inspired and disappointed those most in need of aid. New government programs such as urban renewal, and a new federal commitment to achieving a "Great Society" for all, promised to make major changes, although they often served the middle class at least as much as they served poor people. Nevertheless, the promise of these programs, and the language of rights that accompanied them, generated hope. Once President Lyndon Johnson declared a "war on poverty," poor people themselves came to believe that they were entitled to participate actively in planning the war and that they deserved to benefit from it.

Although the Johnson administration focused most of its energy on issues such as education, employment training, and energizing communities to participate in politics, women and men who received public assistance benefits felt just as entitled to get involved as did other poor people. They claimed "welfare rights," which included their rights to participate in politics, to see that their children were adequately educated, to be treated decently by the employees of government programs, and to receive enough in benefits so that they and their families could live in dignity.

Activist groups devoted to the cause of welfare rights organized in virtually every part of the United States. The first groups emerged at the local level in 1963–1964. The first to use the term, "welfare rights," was the Alameda County Welfare Rights Organization in Northern California, which emerged in 1963. In New York City, neighborhood agencies, such as the Stryckers Bay Community Council and Mobilization for Youth, spurred organizing by welfare mothers and fathers. In Los Angeles, a public housing tenant named Johnnie Tillmon founded ANC (Aid to Needy Children, the leading California welfare program) Mothers Anonymous. The widening number of local groups joined with one another. On June 30, 1966, welfare recipients and their allies held a nationally coordinated protest action, a march on welfare departments across the country that leaders called "the birth of a movement." Local and national leaders met to create a National Welfare Rights Organization (NWRO) in August, 1967. Immediately thereafter, they conducted a precedent-setting march on the federal headquarters of the Department of Health, Education, and Welfare, the bureaucracy that managed public assistance programs.

From the founding of NWRO until its end, the movement made simultaneous advances and retreats. In 1968, the movement and its attorneys won their first case before the U.S. Supreme Court and helped restore benefits to thousands of women and children. They participated in the Poor People's Campaign organized by the Southern Christian Leadership Conference (SCLC). They also mourned the loss of SCLC leader Reverend Martin Luther King, Jr., and faced attempts to restrict benefits and raise barriers to their organizing. In 1969, welfare recipients and middle-class "Friends" coordinated a national boycott of the Sears retail chain and won thousands of dollars' worth of goods and credit for poor people. At the same time, they confronted benefit cuts and a "backlash" by white voters against the public benefit costs and urban riots of the late 1960s.

Welfare rights activists interacted most with national policy makers between 1969 and 1972, when the Nixon administration sponsored legislation in Congress to create a Family Assistance Plan that would have provided a minimum income to all U.S. families with children. NWRO helped apply the pressure that drove the White House to create its plan, and it created its own Guaranteed Adequate Income plan. NWRO lobbied and protested to improve the president's plan, negotiated about it with bureaucrats and members of Congress, and, when the negotiations failed, it was one group among many that worked to defeat it. Exasperated about the unwillingness of officials to recognize their concerns, they occupied the office of the Secretary of Health, Education, and Welfare on May 13, 1970, and refused to leave until they were arrested.

By the early 1970s, the balance between advances and retreats had definitely tipped toward retreats. In 1971, the NWRO newspaper recorded 31 states that had either implemented cutbacks in their welfare programs or were preparing to do so. NWRO expanded its reach in regions such as the South; through demonstrations such as the national Children's March for Survival in 1972, the organization attempted to build coalitions with other women's and civil rights groups. But they faced overwhelming obstacles in terms of political opposition, funding, and internal conflict. In 1974, the national headquarters office of NWRO shut its doors.

The most important people in the welfare rights movement were the welfare mothers and fathers who formed the membership of NWRO and served as its elected leaders. Beulah Sanders was a migrant from North Carolina to New York City. She entered activist politics when her family was displaced by an urban renewal scheme, and she began to organize other public assistance recipients while on the payroll of the federal War on Poverty. She led the New York Citywide Coordinating Committee of Welfare Groups and became the first vice chairman and, later, chairman of NWRO. Other key activists from New York were Jennette Washington, a Floridian by birth who believed that welfare activists should use confrontational tactics such as occupying government offices in order to keep them from implementing anti-welfare policies. Joyce Burson, a leader from the New York borough of Brooklyn, preferred more moderate tactics, such as negotiation with officials who had resources the welfare recipients wanted. In California, the leaders included Johnnie Tillmon from Los Angeles, a migrant from Arkansas who was active in a trade union and the Democratic Party before she helped found the welfare rights movement, and Catherine Jermany, who led the California Welfare Rights Organization after Tillmon became the first chairman of NWRO. In Washington, D.C., the key leader was Etta Horn, head of NWRO's Committee on Ways and Means, which coordinated the Sears boycott.

Working- and middle-class activists were also vitally important. Frank Espada, a Puerto Rican electrician from Brooklyn, helped organize the first welfare rights action groups in what became the strongest center of the movement in the country. Rhoda Linton, a white former student of social work, arrived after Espada and helped build the Brooklyn Welfare Action Council. Ezra Birnbaum and Richard Cloward, a staff member of and advisor to the anti-poverty center Mobilization for Youth, helped organize early welfare rights groups. Birnbaum helped the movement access welfare manuals, which contained information about "minimum standards" goods that the welfare department promised to distribute to clients, but which the clients almost never received. Demands for these goods became the center of many welfare rights demonstrations. Cloward, and coauthor Frances Fox Piven, developed a "crisis theory" of welfare, in which militancy at the grassroots could lead to major changes in national policy; their theory informed the thinking of NWRO leaders. Hulbert James, an African American activist who had received a law degree from Howard University, served as executive director of the Citywide Coordinating

Committee of Welfare Groups and, later, as a member of the NWRO staff. Tim Sampson, a California social worker, helped create the California Welfare Rights Organization and then became the Associate National Director of NWRO. George Wiley, an African American chemist and former leader of the civil rights group CORE, coordinated the 1966 demonstrations that gave "birth" to the movement and served as the first executive director of NWRO. Carl Rachlin, a labor and civil rights lawyer, served as general counsel to NWRO and represented hundreds of welfare recipients in their appeals of bureaucratic decisions. Attorney Edward Sparer headed the poverty law center, the Center on Social Welfare Policy and Law. He pursued litigation on welfare rights in the federal courts, and advised NWRO leaders on legal strategies.

Even though the poverty rights movement of the 1960s and 1970s had many powerful middle-class leaders and supporters, ultimately the movement's greatest strength was that ordinary low-income people played the most central role. This made it different from prior efforts at social welfare reform in U.S. history. It also made it quite unique among the social movements of the post–World War II period. Although leaders such as Beulah Sanders sometimes felt that their concerns were not taken seriously among NWRO staff, they had far greater opportunities for political speech, action, and leadership in the welfare rights movement than their predecessors had in the reform movements of the early twentieth century or the 1930s.

The poverty rights activism of this period also forged a remarkable series of important alliances across lines of class, race, and sex. Welfare mothers and fathers alone did not have all of the resources they needed to win battles with welfare departments or legislatures. Moreover, a range of working- and middle-class people were eager to participate in the movement, either because they saw it as an extension of the black freedom movement or because they had particular expertise about welfare that they wanted to share. These alliances were severely tested when the political climate became chillier for welfare clients early in the 1970s. Although the movement experienced relatively few internal tensions early on, when the country shifted in a more conservative direction, and the movement came under attack, serious conflicts developed between women and men, welfare recipients and professionals, and whites and African Americans.

Just as the poverty rights movement depended upon the strength of its alliances and the health of the coalitions it had built, so was it deeply dependent upon the resources that it received from the federal, state, and city governments as it sought to sustain organizing and improve the lives of poor women and men. Although this dependence was understandable and perhaps unavoidable, when the government grew dramatically more conservative, and many resources previously available to the poor disappeared, the movement suffered a major setback. Welfare rights campaigns for "minimum standards," for example, relied on state laws and municipal regulations that in theory provided each recipient of public aid with a wide array of goods. When welfare mothers and fathers began demanding these benefits, state and city governments withdrew the benefits by passing new state laws or administrative regulations. The welfare rights movement was left without one of its key tactics, and without the rhetorical advantage of being able to accuse its opponents of "illegal" benefit denials.

Although it faced enormous resistance and was unable to achieve its largest goals, the poverty rights movement was remarkably robust and successful relative to other movements in U.S. history for economic justice. Poor people and their allies built a large-scale national movement that at least temporarily changed the agenda in Congress, the White House, the federal courts, and statehouses and city halls across the country. The example NWRO provided of organizing among public assistance recipients had echoes in the late 1970s, in the formation of local groups such as the Downtown Welfare Action Center in New York City and a National Welfare Rights Union with headquarters in Detroit. In later years, the Center for Third World Organizing, headed by former NWRO staff member Gary Delgado, sponsored poverty rights organizing in Oakland, California, and the Kensington Welfare Rights Union in Philadelphia led hundreds in a protest demonstration at the Republic National Convention in 2000.

Beyond welfare organizing per se, the legacy of the poverty rights activism of the 1960s and 1970s may be seen in today's organized campaigns for living wages—city resolutions or state laws that forbid wages to drop below a decent level—by trade unions and nonprofit agencies such as the Center for Third World Organizing and the Industrial Areas Foundation. As the activists of the poverty rights movement saw it, the struggles for "civil rights" and "economic rights" were inseparable. They demonstrated that it was possible to persuade large numbers of people to take action on behalf of an ambitious agenda for both kinds of rights, even when the forces arrayed against such an agenda were formidable.

LOW INCOME MOTHERS IN NEW YORK CITY, *Letters to the Mayor* (1960s)

The seedbed for the poverty rights movement of the 1960s lay in the dissatisfaction of poor people with the way they were treated, and their willingness to express their grievances to the politically powerful. In New York, hundreds of mothers of young children wrote to the city's mayor to ask for material help and sympathy for their plight. In 1963, these women's personal campaigns for recognition and support grew into the first collective demands for "welfare rights" in low-income neighborhoods throughout the city.

a. Letter from Mrs. Rosemarie Williams and Mr. Russell Williams, 734 Melrose Ave., Bronx, NY, to Mayor Wagner, April 6, 1962

This letter is just to let you see for yourself the kind of help a tax-paying citizen gets from the Department of Welfare.

Source: New York City Municipal Archives, Robert F. Wagner, Jr., Papers Subject Files—Welfare, Box 157/ Folder 1800, Box 158/ Folder 1809.

About the last week in January I applied for public Assistance to only get help until my husband's job picked up because he was laid of[f] unexpectedly and we had no money for rent or food. I have two children and had no money coming in from anywhere. We were desperately in need of anything we could get our hands on and had to borrow food and a little change from friends and relatives . . .

My baby, who is only six months old, had to drink water for milk sometimes because I had not even a can of milk in the house. The Department of Welfare didn't write a letter or even phone to let us know anything. I only wanted help for a few weeks as I told them. I didn't want to be on permanently and they wouldn't even send one check to help us along.

. . . I am a citizen born and raised here in the United States and it's a shame that I must almost beg for help when it is being taken out of my pay check every week. I think something should be done to help people when in need. Now I'm not asking for any help and I hope I'll never have to apply again.

b. Letter from Mrs. Bernice Inge, New York City, New York, to Mayor Robert F. Wagner, Jr., April 3, 1962

My name is Mrs. Bernice Inge. I am on Welfare.

. . . I went to court every 3 months to renew a warrant that I have for my husband. Mayor I have been every where look[ing] for him but I can't seem to fine [find] him . . . My children are in the 6 & 7 grade in school. They don't have [b]ut a very few clothes to ware [wear]. The welfare will not give me any money for clothes or any thing for them. I don't want to keep my children out of school. They are very bright children & they love school.

Mayor I have been so worried I didn't know just where to turn & I was told by many people to write you and explain . . .

My son sleeps with me. My [d]aughter sleeps on a little couch in the kitchen. I have a one room apartment. I know that my son is to[o] old to be sleeping with me but there is no one to help us. So I am on my last hope. Mayor Wagner please help. I can't help me self. I need your aid very badly . . .

c. Letter from Evelyn Forbes, Bronx, NY, to Mayor Wanger [sic], no date

Dear Mayor Wanger

Thanks for everything you have done for me. I hate to ask you for another favor but its important. Would you please ask them how is sixty four dollars is going to buy four people a coat My children are not small they are big for their ages. I am sending you this note so you could see it yourself.

Thank you

Evelyn Forbes

P.S. Good luck on election [sic]

d. Letter from Mrs. Threresa Vasta, Brooklyn, NY, to Mayor Wagner, November 12, 1962

Dear Sir,

I am Mrs. Threresa Vasta I have three children one of them is 11 months old and the other two go to school. . . . Now what I want to tell u is because of this the welfare is giving me a hard time I called up my investigator to tell him that I can't get along on the money I am getting which is $29.00 a week all I get from him is insulting remarks . . . I ask him for money because I haven't any and I am in badly need of it. I have no money to give to my oldest girl so she can go to school also we have no money for food. My baby needs winter clothes I can't even take him to the doctors I don't know what to do or who to turn to. I'm not good at explaining things but I am trying to make you see how hard it is for me. I am by my self. I just got over being sick and so did my children. So please help me.

. . . I have no time for games. My children are hungry and my oldest one is missing school because I have no money to send her when I told them of this they told me to make her walk it and its seven long blocks away I have no lunch money for her to [take]. . . . I am an [A] merican born. I think I deserve the right treatment. Fair Treatment that is. In which I don't think they are giving me.

Sincerely Yours,

Mrs. Threresa Vasta

e. Letter from Gloria Arce (Gloria Arce Perez), Norfolk Street, NYC, to Whom It May Concern, Department of Welfare, Albany, NY, October 22, 1962 (forwarded to the Office of the Mayor, City of New York)

I want to inform your department, that I, GLORIA ARCE-PEREZ, of legal age, Citizen of the United States by birth in Puerto Rico, and actually residing at above mentioned address in the State of New York, City of New York very respectfully request and beg that your office start a prompt investigation, on regard to my case.

Sometime on [sic] early January, about the 19th of January 1962, I arrived from Puerto Rico, with my three minor children; during the first few months, I stayed among other relatives, suffering of a real hardship case; this was hurting myself and my children, so, I visited the Welfare Department, non-resident session, and they opened my case, on hardship basis and as emergency, for the past four months. An investigator named F. V. Romano, and my case docket is ADC 2185069. However, on three different occasions, this afore mentioned investigator, got fresh with me, and make improper advances; he threatened me, unaccount [sic] of this. . . .

. . . I believe that as a citizen, I must have the same rights and privileges of others; in my honest and humble opinion, I and my children, are victims of the discrimination and of a vindictive investigator, and that we are victimize[d] and my constitutional rights denied. However, I am in a democratic country, where these things, are investigated and corrected.

. . . So I sincerely hope, an investigation is performed, and my rights properly protected. Otherwise, against my will, I will be forced to bring this matter into the public opinion, and through the press media.

U.S. HOUSE OF REPRESENTATIVES, *Testimony by Welfare Rights Representatives and Representative Martha Griffiths at Hearings on Income Maintenance* (1969)

This excerpt of a congressional hearing transcript illustrates the differences in perspective between poverty rights advocates affiliated with the National Welfare Rights Organization (NWRO) and white, professional-class women affiliated with the feminist movement of the 1960s. While feminists such as Representative Martha Griffiths of Michigan believed that the greatest danger women faced in government employment programs was the possibility that they would not be placed in jobs, NWRO members such as Beulah Sanders of New York City believed that a greater danger lay in the possibility that mothers would be forced into jobs when they were needed at home to care for their children. The hearing transcript also shows that some men in the NWRO, such as executive director George Wiley, thought that government agencies should find jobs for men before they considered employing women.

Mr. WILEY: Our feeling is that a good number, in fact the vast majority, of the welfare recipients and many of the other people who need income support legitimately should not be in the labor force, because they have other important responsibilities at home, to take care of their families . . . [T]he important thing is that the men, that the people who are able to be heads of households or ought to be legitimate heads of households be the ones that get those jobs.

. . .

Representative GRIFFITHS: You say that this work incentive program [will] be used to force mothers to work. Well, [the Department of Labor] will have a choice as to which mothers work and which do not. But if you do not say anything about mothers working, then they are going to see to it that none work. They are not going to be given any chance to work. And in my opinion, this is wrong . . . I am a woman, Mr. Wiley, and I know the kinds of discriminations that have been used against women.

. . .

Mrs. SANDERS: Could I say one thing before you go, woman to woman?

Source: U.S. Congress, Joint Economic Committee, Subcommittee on Fiscal Policy, *Income Maintenance Programs—Hearings*, Ninetieth Congress, Second Session, June 11, 12, 13, 18, 19, 25, 26, and 27, 1968, vol. 1, 76–79.

Representative GRIFFITHS: Yes.

Mrs. SANDERS: . . . One of the things we are concerned about is being forced into these nonexisting positions which might be going out and cleaning Mrs. A's kitchen. I am not going to do that because I feel I am more valuable and can do something else. This is one of the things these people are worrying about, that they are going to be pushed into doing housework . . . But they do not have the training, they do not have the experience, they do not have the college degree [to get better jobs].

WELFARE FIGHTER, *Poems by Welfare Rights Activists* (1969–1970)

Low-income women were not only advocates and activists on their own behalf in the 1960s; they were also writers and thinkers who contributed regularly to the publications of NWRO and local welfare rights groups such as the New York Citywide Coordinating Committee of Welfare Groups. The poems that follow were all written by low-income women who participated actively in the welfare rights movement. Authors Nancy Gooding and Eliza Williams were active on the city and state levels.

Poem

How can a rich man know the needs of the Poor?
It's an experience he never had a chance to explore.
He has never fought the hard pains of hunger
Or the cramps that doesn't make life seem much longer
What does he know about being cold and freezing in wintery states?
He hops on a plane and go to summery places to vacate.
. . . He wouldn't dare pick up a mop, or a broom, to do a floor
He wants the poor people to be his slave forever more.
He don't care what form, fashion, or color they come
As long as they keep him comfortable, and supply him with a clean home.

Source: Nancy Gooding, "Poem," *Welfare Fighter*, vol. 1, no. 2 (March 28, 1969): 3; Tim Sampson papers, Center for Third World Organizing, Oakland, CA.

My Living Will Not Be In Vain

. . . We'd like to dress as you do,
We like to eat good food.
We like to wear hairdo's,

And dress our children decent to go to school.
We are not tramps nor are we lazy,
Nor are we stupid or crazy.
This is the regular welfare image.
That's why we're out on a pilgrimage.

Source: Eliza Williams, "My Living Will Not Be In Vain," *Welfare Fighter*, vol. 1, no. 9 (May, 1970): 12; Periodicals division, Wisconsin Historical Society, Madison, WI.

BEULAH SANDERS, *NWRO Leader on Work and Welfare* (1974)

Beulah Sanders was first vice-president, and later chairwoman, of the National Welfare Rights Organization. She was also the longtime elected leader of New York's Citywide Coordinating Committee of Welfare Groups. She believed strongly that women who received public assistance needed support and options as they sought to combine parenting with waged work, but that they did not need rules that forced them to leave the public aid rolls for the low-wage job market.

[A]nother thing that [the National Welfare Rights Organization] was all. . . . about [was] the training programs in [welfare], and see [Health, Education, and Welfare Secretary Robert] Finch didn't want to deal with that. You see they had all this money, but they hadn't come down with no training program that could really get welfare recipients on . . . [T]here is no federal program that comes down, set up to train and get people off welfare by training them and putting them into jobs. That's a lot of crap. It doesn't work. That is just something to keep your mouth closed . . .

[T]hey were trying to force women into slave labor jobs . . . [T]hey wanted women to go out there and take training as a housekeeper so that they could go out there and do housework. Who needs to be trained to keep house? . . . [H]ell, that's all I do when I came up as a kid. Kept house for my mother to go out and work. You know. So I really don't, don't need to be trained for it. But I don't feel that I should have to go out and do slave labor work for no pay, which I'm not going to get an adequate salary for . . .

[I]f they want us off the welfare rolls, come up with the training program and the jobs. You know, the women would be glad to take it. You put the mothers into

---

Source: Beulah Sanders Oral History Interview with Nick Kotz (1974) Transcript in Kotz Papers, Box 26/File titled "Beulah Sanders," pp. 8, 13, Wisconsin Historical Society, Madison, WI, Manuscripts Division.

the training program and you go the job waiting for 'em once they come out of it, they won't want to be bothered with welfare . . . If they had some other place to go, they'd do just that.

JOHNNIE TILLMON, *NWRO President Speaks on President Richard Nixon's* (1970)

In the fall of 1970, it appeared increasingly likely that President Nixon's major proposal for welfare reform would be defeated in the U.S. Congress. NWRO leaders joined with the office of U.S. Senator Eugene McCarthy to convene unofficial policy hearings on the president's plan. Unlike the official policy hearings convened by committees of the Senate and House of Representatives, the main testimony came from NWRO leaders such as Johnnie Tillmon and other women and men who received public benefits. They argued that they should have a more active role in the debate over changing the welfare system, because the well-being of their families depended in part on the fate of the Nixon plan.

We . . . understand that every Administration that comes has to have his own thing. So what we have come up with in the last 35 years is a lot of administrative ideas, a lot of reforms, and we stay in the same position that we are in now. Most of us were poor in 1935 and there are more of us poor now than there was in 1935.

We always have a lot of programs . . . and they all are geared around the poor. But nothing is actually filtered down to the poor. There are a lot of jobs created for other people, and when we do have an opportunity to participate in the jobs, we have the lowest paying jobs. Most of the jobs throughout our program are no larger than a welfare check. . . . We see ourselves as being some form of a political football.

. . . We don't see ourselves being lifted out of poverty through [President's Nixon's proposed] Family Assistance Plan . . . We just don't care to be kicked around any more. . . . We have always had some people who had expertise on being poor but who had never been poor. We feel that we want to participate in anything that concerns us. We feel that we have some expertise.

Source: Hearings on Family Assistance Plan, H.R. 16311, Wednesday, November 18, 1970, Washington, D.C., pp. 8–9. Transcription courtesy of Ward & Paul, Washington, D.C. From Kotz Papers, Box 17, File titled "NWRO—FAP Testimony Before Clean Gene," Manuscripts Division, Wisconsin Historical Society, Madison, WI.

WASHINGTON POST, *Newspaper Profile of Johnnie Tillmon, and Irate Letters from Readers* (1968)

Shortly after the assassination of Dr. Martin Luther King, Jr., NWRO and other organizations marked the beginning of the national Poor People's Campaign with a Mother's Day march through riot-torn neighborhoods in Washington, D.C. Coretta Scott King and Johnnie Tillmon were the two headline speakers of the event, which called for a repeal of restrictive national legislation on public aid. One sign of the increasingly fractious and divisive politics that surrounded welfare benefits in the late 1960s was the response of readers to a profile of Tillmon that ran in the women's section of the *Washington Post* newspaper.

Letter from "A Disgusted Reader" to *The Washington Post* [post-marked May 14, 1968]

This marching story is silly—not by you but by the marcher.

1. She receives more money from Welfare than I do or many more people do on retirement, also what has happened to support help from her Husband.

Also its a fact that a lot of women have children to receive more welfare money. I have been told that by some.

Also if she can work & make as much as her Welfare, why don't she? I can't go to Calif. on my retirement how could she afford to come to DC.

. . . [O]ur family never had or will have money to go to college. What do the negroes expect? that all the white should help them—why not the rich colored people help the colored. They don't want to work.

Source: Carolyn Lewis, "She Marched to Change Children's Future," *Washington Post*—For and about Women, May 13, 1968, p. C1, and Response Letters sent to NWRO by Carolyn Lewis, June 4, 1968. From: George Wiley Papers, Box 21/Folder 4, Wisconsin Historical Society, Madison, WI.

18

Prison Rights Activism

—Heather McCarty

The United States erupted in protest during the 1960s and 1970s and, like other Americans who became activists in this period, those who were locked away in prisons also found themselves seeking greater rights and trying to improve their living conditions. In particular, the civil rights and Black Power movements of this era inspired prisoners to become activists and they came to adopt much of the ideology as well as the tactics embraced by these movements. Mirroring the evolution of the civil rights movement on the outside, the prisoner rights movement began with convicts attempting to effect change by working through the system. Over time, as some prisoners and their supporters grew frustrated with the limited and slow nature of change, a segment of the movement grew more militant and more willing to engage in direct action to achieve their goals.

A variety of factors both internal and external to the penal system itself also inspired prisoner rights activism in the 1960s and 1970s. Changes in penological practice, prisoner demographics, and the social and racial climate of society in general, to name a few, contributed to prisoners becoming better organized and demanding increased rights and input in prison policies. Throughout this period, the prisoner rights movement attempted to address a wide range of issues including prison conditions, religious freedom for prisoners, capital punishment, censorship, parity for women prisoners, and prison and parole sentencing. While convicts and their supporters employed a mix of tactics to achieve their goals, the prison rights movement in this period largely focused their efforts on legal and direct action tactics.

Prisoners had been protesting the conditions under which they lived long before the 1960s. Convicts have a long history of trying to draw attention to the inhuman treatment and the brutal conditions they endured. Whether rendering themselves crippled to avoid forced labor under the brutal whip on Southern prison farms, or initiating hunger strikes to highlight the practices embraced by Northern penal institutions, prisoners have tried to improve their lot for centuries. Efforts to improve the U.S. prison system, however, achieved limited success because the 1871 ruling in *Ruffin v. Commonwealth* defined prisoners as "slaves of the state"—individuals without constitutional rights. This status left prisoners little power to legally challenge the prison system.

Little changed in the legal landscape for prisoners until 1964, when a group of Black Muslim prisoners—African American prisoners who practiced the Muslim faith—went to court arguing that prison officials denied them their rights to worship. In their now famous case, *Cooper v. Pate,* the court not only ruled that convicts had a right to religious freedom but, by extension, that prisoners had rights under the constitution more generally. Many penal scholars attribute the emergence of the modern prisoner rights movement to *Cooper v. Pate* because it permitted prisoners to file lawsuits on their own behalf and to legal efforts by Black Muslims in general. Between 1961 and 1978, federal courts ruled on 66 cases related to Black Muslims alone.

Throughout the 1960s and 1970s, many prisoners relied heavily on jailhouse lawyers to help them navigate the legal system. Jailhouse lawyers were convicts who taught themselves rudimentary legal skills while imprisoned and helped other prisoners prepare post-conviction petitions. Fearing the power that jailhouse lawyers could exert over their fellow convicts, many prisons forbade them from providing legal assistance. Ironically, this only led to more legal challenges to prison authority. In 1969, the U.S. Supreme Court ruled in *Johnson v. Avery* that jailhouse lawyers were indeed permitted to provide legal assistance when prison officials failed to provide adequate legal services for convicts. This victory expanded the practice of jailhouse lawyering, and many jailhouse lawyers proved to be worthy adversaries winning legal victories for convicts around the country.

While jailhouse lawyers helped prisoners bring legal challenges, the large number of prison litigation cases that took place during the 1960s and 1970s would have been impossible without support from outside activists, especially lawyers and law students who offered both their time and expertise to convicts. With this additional support, prisoners' rights petitions filed in federal courts more than quadrupled between 1970 and 1979. Many lawyers involved in earlier civil rights work, such as those in the National Lawyers Guild, brought their experience to the prisoner rights movement. The American Civil Liberties Union (ACLU) established the Prison Project in 1972; it was and remains the most successful prison litigation group in the United States. Even the American Bar Association committed itself to advancing correctional reform in 1970. By the close of the 1970s, prisoners and their advocates had improved convicts' access to due process rights through cases such as *Wolff v. McDonnell,* which guaranteed procedural protections to prisoners facing disciplinary action. They also successfully challenged censorship of prisoner mail, limits on communication with lawyers, and poor conditions of confinement. Their success filing Eighth Amendment cases not only helped to protect prisoners from cruel and unusual punishment but it also provided them with access to medical care, soap, water, clothing, and limited the length of time prisoners could spend in isolation.

As successful as many of their forays into the legal system were, legal tactics took time and change often came slowly. By the late 1960s, some prisoners began to grow frustrated at the slow nature of legal pursuits. Just as other activists in this period became more militant so did some prisoners, and they started engaging in direct actions. Prisoners and their supporters continued to use legal avenues, but direct action tactics proved successful in garnering attention for convict grievances. Prisoners began to enjoy greater support from white college students who had become more militant in the free speech and anti-war movements, and other militant groups such as the Black Panther Party took up their cause. A number of the activists in these outside movements became convicts themselves and they began encouraging the prisoners already there to launch their own struggle for increased rights. They argued that all prisoners were victims of an unjust system and advocated that prisoners unite together as a convict class. Prisoners periodically used this unity to transcend racial divisions and work together against the prison system. They organized large-scale protests to lobby legislators and the public to support changes in the prison system.

California's prisoners were some of the first to utilize more militant tactics. They organized some of the first large-scale prisoner work stoppages in the early 1960s and by the late 1960s, they were shutting down prison operations around the state with support from outside activists. In 1968, California prisoners organized the Unity Day Strikes that closed down prison operations at San Quentin State Prison, while prisoners at Folsom State Prison organized a sympathy strike. Outside activists helped to publish prisoner concerns in local newspapers and held rallies outside of San Quentin's gates to publicize the weeklong strike at San Quentin. As a result of the protests, officials agreed to allow an interracial group of prisoners to undertake a comprehensive study of prisoner grievances at San Quentin, and they promised to forward the findings to the head of the California Department of Corrections and the state legislature. These prisoners prepared a 78-page report entitled the *Convict Report on the Major Grievances of the Prison Population with Suggested Solutions* that addressed poor prison conditions and analyzed the failings of the California Department of Corrections. The administration initially attempted to prevent the convicts from delivering their report, but in the end they successfully forwarded their findings to the state legislature.

Inspired by the outcome of protests such as the Unity Day Strikes at San Quentin, prisoners across California decided to strike in order to draw attention to prison conditions across the state. The longest nonviolent strike took place at Folsom Prison in November of 1970 when almost all 2,400 prisoners refused to work or leave their cells for 19 days. The prisoners issued a manifesto with 31 demands, ranging from calls for improved living conditions to the release of all political prisoners. The Folsom work stoppage and other prisoner strikes inspired prisoners across the country to organize their own protests for greater convict power and better prison conditions.

Like their counterparts in California, prisoners at the Attica State Correctional Facility in upstate New York sought to improve prison conditions there. In 1970, a group calling itself the Attica Liberation Faction—comprised of Black Panthers, Black Muslims, radical whites, and Puerto Rican Young Lords—wrote several letters to the commissioner of corrections enumerating a list of 29 grievances and requesting that he to address them. Notably, these grievances mirrored many of the demands that Folsom prisoners had drafted in their recent manifesto. The response to the 1970 letters consisted of little more than vague promises of future discussions that never materialized. The disappointments of approaching officials in a peaceful manner, in combination with the long-standing tensions between prison officers and prisoners at Attica, eventually led to the largest prison riot of this era on September 9, 1971. After 1,281 prisoners seized control of the prison, taking scores of guards hostage, once again they asked officials to address their grievances. This time, however, they had the chance to directly tell all Americans what they felt needed change in the prison system—prison administrators agreed to let television cameras inside. By September 8, 1971, prisoner speeches had been broadcast to the entire nation. Although observers recommended that the State of New York continue negotiating with the prisoners so that this riot might end peacefully, after four days Governor Nelson Rockefeller ordered that the armed state troopers retake the prison by force. Trooper bullets killed 29 prisoners and 10 guards and severely wounded 89 others.

Prisoners engaged in numerous direct actions similar to Attica and Folsom on a smaller scale around the country during this period. Direct actions, regardless of size, were typically organized by a relatively small group of more radical prisoners and supported by outside activists. These convicts often self-identified as political prisoners. Some convicts believed that police had targeted, framed, and imprisoned them in order to neutralize their efforts as political agitators. Others argued that all crimes committed by racial minorities and the poor were responses to their oppressed status and therefore political in nature. Soon numerous activists in social movements outside of prison also adopted this perspective and rallied around famous political prisoners such as George Jackson, Eldridge Cleaver, and Ruchell McGee. When California prison officials charged black prisoners George Jackson, Fleeta Drumgo, and John Clutchette on January 27, 1970, with the murder of a white prison officer, outside activists formed the Soledad Brothers Defense fund to help fight the charges. Activists maintained that prison officials framed these men. Seven months later when a guard shot and killed Jackson alleging that he had tried to escape, prisoners and prisoner rights activists on the outside grew even more radical.

In addition to organizing support for political prisoners and aiding prisoners' direct actions inside of prison, outside activists tried other tactics to bring about reform in the prison system. Groups studied prison conditions and lobbied prison officials and legislators for change. The American Friends Service Committee (AFSC), a Quaker group active in the civil rights movement, the anti-war movement, and the prisoner rights movement, studied prison conditions in the United States and issued *Struggle for Justice* in 1971, a scathing critique of prisons and sentencing guidelines. Chief among the problems they identified were class-based criminal laws, forced treatment, and lengthy periods of inhumane incarceration.

As the 1970s came to a close, all radical political activism declined and prison activism was no different. Politicians from the Nixon administration ushered in a more conservative era, one in which voters fearful of recent increases in crime supported stronger law and order policies. By the 1980s, the public no longer viewed prisoners as reformable and worthy of rehabilitation; instead they perceived criminals as dangerous degenerates. As the nation turned to tough-on-crime policies, outside activists began to abandon the prisoner rights movement in favor of other causes and the activism within prisons began to wither. Ultimately, the diverse nature of the prisoner rights movement led to its downfall because it was not strong enough, nor ideologically coherent enough, to weather the funding cuts and a lack of public support that it faced in the late 1970s and thereafter.

Nevertheless, the prisoner rights movement of the 1960s and 1970s had a lasting impact on prison systems in the United States. Prison rights activists both inside and outside of prison brought about improvements in living conditions, extended due process protections, secured religious freedom, guaranteed access to legal materials, ended censorship, and even briefly limited capital punishment in many states. The movement extended constitutional rights and protections to prisoners and raised public awareness of prison conditions and problems with the judicial system. Prison systems have moved toward legal due process, extending increased protections to prisoners, and prisoners' constitutional rights have been recognized. Today's activists are using the tools made possible by early prison activism to continue to fight long-standing prison issues such as overcrowding, poor living conditions, inadequate health care, and mismanagement.

SAN QUENTIN PRISON, *The Outlaw* (1968)

Prisoners at San Quentin State Prison produced an underground newspaper called *The Outlaw.* The paper was produced anonymously without approval of prison officials. Prisoners used this newspaper as an organizing tool to bring convicts together across racial and ethnic lines to demand more say in prison operations.

The Outlaw

San Quentin Prison, July 1, 1968

The red-necked Bushbeater is Beat Again

At last the muckrakers who publish the OUTLAW have been apprehended and sent away. Never again will that subversive rag disturb the stagnant placidity of San Quentin. But what's this?? THE OUTLAW!!! Better luck next time Red [Convicts' nickname for San Quentin warden Louis Nelson.]. How many bum beefs does that make now??? About 27. Give it up Red, or tell us where it's at. Don't you realize you've got *4,000 of us?!!!!!*

... Some of us cons don't seem to know what side we're on. We're obsessed with near-sighted disputes based on race, ideology, group identity, and so on. We expend our energies despising and distrusting each other. All of this is helping the CDC. We permit them to keep us at each others throats. A handful of us are calling for

Source: The Outlaw, reprinted in Robert Minton, Jr., ed., *Inside: Prison American Style*, New York: Random House, 1971, pp. 13–17.

UNITY. This is for a purpose. We want to crush this empire that has been erected on our suffering. We call for *4,000 united convicts.* Wake up!!! put your prejudices, biases, and class distinctions aside for the purposes of our fight with the CDC. . . . UNITY that will rally to us support from the outside that will carry our plea to the proper places. . . .

We will lose everything if we play into the CDC's hands and let them move us into a riot situation. . . . DON'T let a riot or fire or any disturbance allow his [the warden's] bully hand to fall. . . . Don't let the pigs harass you into a bad move. Let's Get It Together for a while . . . UNITY, BLACK, BROWN, WHITE, UNITY!!!

SAN QUENTIN PRISON, *"Bill of Particulars," A Convict Report on the Major Grievances of the Prison Population with Suggested Solutions* (1969)

Prisoners conducted independent surveys with fellow convicts to identify the major grievances with operations at San Quentin State Prison in 1969. They compiled their findings into an 85- page report, including suggestions for remediation, and presented it to prison administrators in February. The "Bill of Particulars" summarizes the issues prisoners raised.

Bill of Particular

I. Objection to Adult Authority Resolution #171, primarily the refixing of the term of imprisonment at a length greater than originally fixed;
II. Objection to the method of effecting parole violations;
III. Objection to the long terms served by parole violators;
IV. Objection to the Adult Authority speculating about the degree of criminal involvement greater than the facts warrant;
V. Objection to the inordinate amount of time being served by first termers in certain offense categories;
VI. Objection to apparent lack of consideration given to time served in the deliberations that pertain to the determination of the term of imprisonment;
VII. Objection to allowing criminal acts of recent offenders to aggravate the standards used in fixing the term of imprisonment of inmates who have already served x-number of years for similar offenses;
VIII. Objection to basing denial upon the so-called "voice of the public" or the "public mood", when in fact the public hasn't said a word or otherwise manifested its mood;

Source: Bill of Particulars, *A Convict Report: On the Major Grievances of the Prison Population with Suggested Solutions*, San Quentin Prison, February 1969, 3, in the possession of the American Friends Service Committee, Oakland, CA.

IX. Objection to the constantly changing structure and policies of the Adult Authority and the failure to give the inmate population any indication of the reasons for, or the ramifications of, the changes;

X. Objection to the inadequate record kept of the Adult Authority hearings, and the lack of meaningful comment therein;

XI. Objection to the lack of continuity in Adult Authority expectations, demands, and policies from hearing to hearing and from member to member;

XII. Objection to the fact that the inmate body has no organized voice or other means calling for mitigation, while forces demanding aggravation have full and free access to the communications media.

GEORGE JACKSON, *Soledad Brother* (1970)

The excerpt below is from a letter written by famed political prisoner George Jackson to his lawyer and friend Faye Stender of the National Lawyers Guild Prison Project written in April of 1970.

Dear Fay . . .

Nothing has improved, nothing has changed in the weeks since your team was here. We're on the same course, the blacks are fast losing the last of their restraints. Growing numbers of blacks are openly passed over when paroles are considered. They have become aware that their only hope lies in resistance. . . . Up until now, the prospect of parole has kept us from confronting our captors with any real determination. But now . . . we have been transformed into an implacable army of liberation.

. . . the last ten years have brought an increase in the percentage of blacks for crimes that can *clearly* be traced to political-economic causes. There are still some blacks here who consider themselves criminals—but not many. Believe me, my friend, with the time and incentive that these brothers have to read, study, and think, you will find no class or category more aware, more embittered, desperate, or dedicated to the ultimate remedy—revolution. The most dedicated, the best of our kind—you'll find them in the Folsoms, San Quentins, and Soledads. They live like there was no tomorrow. And for most of them there isn't. Somewhere along the line they sensed this. Life on the installment plan, three years of prison, three months on parole; then back to start all over again, sometimes in the same cell. Parole officers have sent brothers back to the joint for selling newspapers (the Black Panther paper). Their official reason is "Failure to Maintain Gainful Employment," etc.

. . . The holds are fast being broken. Men who read Lenin, Fanon, and Che don't riot, "they mass," "they rage," they dig graves.

Source: George Jackson, *Soledad Brother: The Prison Letters of George Jackson*, New York: Bantam Books, 1970, pp. 30–31.

FOLSOM PRISON, *The Folsom Prisoners Manifesto of Demands and Anti-Oppression Platform* (1970)

Prisoners at Folsom State Prison drafted these demands during their 19-day work stoppage in November of 1970.

1. *We demand* the constitutional rights of legal representation at the time of all Adult Authority hearings, and the protection from the procedures of the Adult Authority whereby they permit no procedural safeguards such as an attorney for cross-examination of witnesses, witnesses in behalf of the parolee, at parole revocation hearings.
2. *We demand* a change in medical staff and medical policy and procedure. The Folsom Prison Hospital is totally inadequate, understaffed, prejudicial in the treatment of inmates. There are numerous "mistakes" made many times, improper and erroneous medication is given by untrained personnel. The emergency procedures for serious injury are totally absent . . .
3. *We demand* adequate visiting conditions and facilities for the inmates and families of Folsom prisoners. . . .
4. *We demand* that each man presently held in the Adjustment Center be given a written notice with the Warden of Custody signature on it explaining the exact reason for his placement in the severely restrictive confines of the Adjustment Center.
5. *We demand* an immediate end to indeterminate adjustment center terms to be replaced by fixed terms with the length of time served being terminated by good conduct and according to the nature of the charges, for which men are presently being warehoused indefinitely without explanation.
6. *We demand* an end to the segregation of prisoners from the mainline population because of their political beliefs. Some of the men in the Adjustment Center are confined there solely for political reasons and their segregation from other inmates is indefinite.
7. *We demand* an end to political persecution, racial persecution, and the denial of prisoners to subscribe to political papers, books, or any other educational and current media chronicles that are forwarded through the United States Mail.
8. *We demand* an end to the persecution and punishment of prisoners who practice the constitutional right of peaceful dissent. . . .
9. *We demand* an end to the tear-gassing of prisoners who are locked in their cells, such action led to the death of Willie Powell in Soledad Prison in 1968 and of Fred Billingslea on February 25, 1970 at San Quentin Prison. It is cruel and unnecessary.

Source: Folsom Manifesto, reprinted in Eve Pell, ed., *Maximum Security: Letters From California's Prisons*, New York: E.P. Dutton & Co., Inc., 1972, pp. 191–201.

10. *We demand* the passing of a minimum and maximum term bill which calls for an end to indeterminate sentences whereby a man can be warehoused indefinitely, rehabilitated or not. . . .
11. *We demand* that industries be allowed to enter the institutions and employ inmates to work eight hours a day and fit into the category of workers for scale wages. . . .
12. *We demand* that inmates be allowed to form or join Labor Unions.
13. *We demand* that inmates be granted the right to support their own families, at present thousands of welfare recipients have to divide their checks to support their imprisoned relatives who without the outside support could not even buy toilet articles or food. Men working on scale wages could support themselves and families while in prison.
14. *We demand* that correctional officers be prosecuted as a matter of law for shooting inmates, around inmates, or any act of cruel and unusual punishment where it is not a matter of life or death.
15. *We demand* that all institutions who use inmate labor be made to conform with the state and federal minimum wage laws.
16. *We demand* that all condemned prisoners, avowed revolutionaries and prisoners of war be granted political asylum in the countries under the Free World Revolutionary Solidarity Pact, such as Algeria, Russia, Cuba, Latin America, North Korea, North Vietnam, etc. . . .
17. *We demand* an end to trials being held on the premises of San Quentin Prison, or any other prison without the jury as stated in the U.S. Constitution as being picked from the country of the trial proceedings and of the peers of the accused; that being in this case, other prisoners as the selected jurors.
18. *We demand* an end to the escalating practice of physical brutality being perpetrated upon the inmates of California State prisons at San Quentin, Folsom, and Soledad Prison in particular.
19. *We demand* that such celebrated and prominent political prisoners as Reis Tijerina, Ahmad Evans, Bobby Seale, Chip Fitzgerald, Los Siete, David Harris, and the Soledad Brothers, be given political asylum outside this country . . .
20. *We demand* appointment of three lawyers from the California Bar Association for full-time positions to provide legal assistance for inmates seeking post-conviction relief, and to act as liaison between the Administration and inmates for bringing inmate complaints to the attention of the administration.
21. *We demand* update of industry working conditions to standards as provided for under California law.
22. *We demand* establishment of inmate workers insurance plan to provide compensation for work related accidents.
23. *We demand* establishment of unionized vocational training program comparable to that of the Federal Prison System which provides for union instructors, union pay scale, and union membership upon completion of the vocational training course.
24. *We demand* annual accounting of the Inmate Welfare Fund and formulation of inmate committee to give inmates a voice as to how such funds are used.

25. *We demand* that the Adult AUTHORITY Board appointed by the Governor, be eradicated and replaced by a parole board elected by popular vote of the people. . . . where authority acts within secrecy and within vast discretion, and gives heavy weight to accusations by prison employees against inmates, inmates feel trapped . . .
26. *We strongly demand* that the State and Prison Authorities conform to recommendation #1 of the "Soledad Caucus Report," to wit,

    "That the State Legislature create a full-time salaried board of overseers for the State prisons." . . .
27. *We demand* that prison authorities conform to the conditional requirements and needs as described in the recent released Manifesto from the Folsom Adjustment Center.
28. *We demand* an immediate end to the agitation of race relations by the prison administrations of this state.
29. *We demand* that the California Prison System furnish Folsom Prison with the services of Ethnic Counselors for the needed special services of Brown and Black population of this prison.
30. *We demand* an end to the discrimination in the judgment and quota of parole for Black and Brown people.
31. *We demand* that all prisoners be present at the time that their cells and property are being searched by the correctional officers of state prisons.

AMERICAN FRIENDS SERVICE COMMITTEE, *The Struggle for Justice: A Report on Crime and Punishment in America* (1971)

The American Friends Service Committee issued *The Struggle for Justice* in 1971 to critique the prison system and sentencing guidelines. The excerpt below is from "A Bill of Rights for Prisoners."

A BILL OF RIGHTS FOR PRISONERS

. . . the Bill of Rights for Prisoners includes the following:

1. Unrestricted access to the courts and to confidential legal counsel from an attorney of the individual's choosing or from a public defender. Adequate opportunity to prepare legal writs.
2. Freedom from the actuality or threat of physical abuse whether by custodial personnel or other prisoners.

Source: American Friends Service Committee, *The Struggle for Justice: A Report on Crime and Punishment in America*, New York: Hill & Wang, 1971, pp. 167–169.

3. Adequate diet and sanitation, fresh air, exercise, prompt medical and dental treatment, and prescription drugs.
4. Maintenance of relationships by frequent meetings and uncensored correspondence with members of the immediate family, personal friends, public officials, and representatives of the community. Regular opportunity for conjugal visitation by granting home furloughs.
5. Reasonable access to the press, through both interviews and written articles.
6. Freedom of voluntary religious worship and freedom to change religious affiliation.
7. Established rules of conduct available to prisoners in written form. Prohibition of excessive or disproportionate punishments. Procedural due process in any disciplinary hearing that might result in loss of good time, punitive (involuntary) transfer, or an adverse affect on parole decisions. . . .
8. Opportunity for the prisoner voluntarily to avail himself or herself of uncensored reading material and facilities especially for vocational training, counseling, and continuing education.
9. Opportunity in prison through work-release for work at prevailing wages. Eligibility for Social Security, unemployment compensation, and public assistance benefits upon release. . . .
10. A judicial proceeding for the determination of parole that incorporates full due process in the determination of sentence and parole date, including established rules of parole-board conduct. . . .
11. Full restoration of all civil rights and privileges upon release from prison. The right to vote in any election in which a prisoner would be entitled to vote if he had not been confined.
12. Unrestricted ability to petition for a redress of grievances. A separate authority with the power to correct instances of maladministration, abuse, or discrimination. Freedom from reprisals for making complaints. . . .

ELLIOT BARKLEY, *We Are Men* (1971)

This speech was given by a 21-year-old inmate by the name of Elliot Barkley, known by his friends as L.D. He articulates his views on why he and over 1,200 fellow inmates took over the Attica State Correctional Facility in upstate New York on September 9, 1971. This speech was recorded by television cameras that had been allowed into the prison yard to film the rebels.

To the people of America

. . . WE are MEN! We are not beasts and do not intend to be beaten or driven as such. The entire prison populace has set forth to change forever the ruthless

---

Source: The Tom Wicker Papers. The Southern Historical Collection. Davis Memorial Library. The University of North Carolina Chapel Hill. Chapel Hill, NC.

brutalization and disregard for the lives of the prisoners here and throughout the United States. What has happened here is but the sound before the fury of those who are oppressed. . . . We will not compromise on any terms except those that are agreeable to us. We call upon all the conscientious citizens of America to assist us in putting an end to this situation that threatens the lives of not only us, but each and everyone of us as well . . . We have set forth demands that will bring closer to reality the demise of these prisons institutions that serve no useful purpose to the People of America, but to those who would enslave and exploit the people of America.

. . . We invite *all the people* to come here and witness this degradation, so that they can better know how to bring this degradation to an end. . . .

19

Puerto Rican Activism

—Carmen Teresa Whalen

The Puerto Rican movement was one of the radical social movements that came of age in the 1960s and 1970s. Broadly defined, these were movements that sought civil rights, economic justice, and an end to U.S. imperialism and the war in Vietnam, as well as the elimination of bias and second-class citizenship based on race, ethnicity, gender, and sexuality. Addressing the multiple and overlapping structures of inequality, these social movements also crafted identity politics based on pride, thereby challenging social constructions of inferiority. The tactics of the era were confrontational, as people took to the streets, took over buildings, and made demands of local and federal government authorities, of the military-industrial complex, and of society at large. The goals were ambitious, as "radical" refers not only to the tactics, but also to the "radical" nature of the transformations that activists sought. Satisfied with neither reform nor incremental change, radical social movements, including the Puerto Rican movement, promoted the fundamental restructuring of U.S. politics, the economy, society, and indeed power relations in their everyday manifestations.

Along with the activist energy of the social movements of the 1960s and 1970s, the Puerto Rican movement drew inspiration from the historical legacies of Puerto Rican activism in Puerto Rico and in the United States. Puerto Rico had its own history of struggles against colonization, first against Spain and then, since 1898, against the United States. The movement to make Puerto Rico independent of the United States became particularly active in the 1950s when Pedro Albizu Campos and the Puerto Rican Nationalist Party stepped up the fight to end U.S. colonialism with a rebellion in Puerto Rico and with actions in the United States itself. Although the government seriously clamped down on the activists, these radicals served as role models for many young Puerto Ricans living on the U.S. mainland.

The Puerto Rican movement also grew from the earlier activism of Puerto Ricans living in communities throughout the United States. During the 19th century, early Puerto Rican communities like Tampa, Florida, Philadelphia, Pennsylvania, and New York City, were shaped by cigar makers and socialists, many of whom were struggling against Spanish colonial rule in Puerto Rico and Cuba. Thus began a historical legacy of political and labor activism. In New York City, Puerto Ricans were ardent supporters of radical Congressman Vito Marcantonio. By the 1950s, in communities throughout the Puerto Rican diaspora, activists had started a variety of community-based organizations to meet the needs of the rapidly growing Puerto Rican population of the post-World War II era. One especially important group was Aspira, founded in 1961 by Antonia Pantoja, to foster and support the educational achievement of Puerto Rican youth. Forming high school Aspira Clubs, youth met to learn about Puerto Rican history and to embrace their Puerto Rican culture. Some "Aspirantes" became the radical activists of the late 1960s and 1970s. Even as Puerto Rican youth challenged the more moderate political stances of the leaders of these community organizations, these important community-based organizations were instrumental in birthing a broader Puerto Rican social movement.

The Puerto Rican movement was comprised of a broad spectrum of diverse groups working on a variety of issues, many of them intersecting. Throughout the communities of the Puerto Rican diaspora, political groups addressed local issues through grassroots, community-based activism, often seeing these local issues as part of larger struggles. The Puerto Rican movement confronted issues such as poverty, housing discrimination, residential displacement stemming from urban renewal programs, police brutality, inadequate health care, inferior and biased education; in short, economic exploitation and racism in their many guises. Puerto Rican activists sought to politicize, organize, and mobilize people in their communities and in their daily lives. Many young Puerto Ricans living in the United States had begun to draw connections between the challenges that their communities faced here and the colonial status of Puerto Rico. As a result, the Puerto Rican movement that came of age in the 1960s and 1970s in the United States often bridged "homeland and barrio politics."

Two important activist groups that exemplify this bridging of "homeland and barrio politics" were the Young Lords and the Puerto Rican Socialist Party. With branches in several communities throughout the Puerto Rican diaspora, both groups called for independence for Puerto Rico, while addressing the issues confronting Puerto Ricans in the United States. The Young Lords, comprised primarily of second generation, Puerto Rican youth, sought dramatic change in the United States, as well as in Puerto Rico. The Young Lords originated in Chicago in 1967, out of a street gang that became politicized in response to local issues, especially the "urban renewal" programs that were destroying Puerto Rican neighborhoods. Emblematic of the postwar diaspora, by 1971 there were branches in New York City; Philadelphia; Newark, New Jersey; Bridgeport, Connecticut; and Heywood, California; and later in Puerto Rico. The Young Lords lasted until 1972 and illustrated the extent to which some portions of the Puerto Rican movement drew inspiration from other U.S. social movements, as well as from political struggles in Puerto Rico.

With the cry of "All Power to the People," the Young Lords advocated a socialist society based on meeting the needs of the people, grassroots community controlled services, and independence for Puerto Rico. In New York City, the Young Lords' major "offensives" included cleaning up their neighborhoods and piling the garbage in the streets when the city refused to provide basic services and collect the trash; taking over a church and offering the community services like childcare, breakfast programs, and free clothing that they criticized the church for failing to provide; and taking over Lincoln Hospital to call attention to inadequate health care. Identifying themselves as "a revolutionary political party fighting for the liberation of all oppressed people," the "Young Lords Party 13 Point Program and Platform," articulated their political analysis and their goals. While branches emerged in several communities out of shared conditions and shared concerns, each branch retained its own distinctive stamp, as revealed in the article, "The Philadelphia Young Lords," which appeared in the Young Lords' newspaper, *Pa'lante*. In Philadelphia, the Young Lords worked with the Black Panthers to run free breakfast programs so children would not have to go to school hungry and to address the issue of police brutality that plagued these activists and their communities.

Like the Young Lords, the Puerto Rican Socialist Party (PSP) had branches in many communities, including New York City, Philadelphia, and Boston. Prior to 1971, the PSP had been the Movement for Independence (MPI), an island-based group working for Puerto Rico's independence. With the shift to the PSP, this political organization retained its focus on Puerto Rico's independence while simultaneously addressing the issues confronting Puerto Ricans in the United States. Striving to be a "scientifically based, disciplined, and efficient" party, the First Congress of the U.S. branch of the PSP issued their political declaration "on the Puerto Rican revolution in the belly of the beast," or "Desde las Entranas." PSP chapters remained active in the late 1970s.

In addition to daily activism in their local communities, Puerto Rican activists organized large marches, calling for Puerto Rico's independence from the United States. Commemorating the Nationalist insurrection in Puerto Rico 20 years earlier, the Young Lords organized a march to the United Nations on October 30, 1970. Calling for independence for Puerto Rico, 10,000 people marched. Six years later, the PSP, mobilized over 50,000 people in Philadelphia and San Francisco. On July 4, 1976, protesters called for "A Bicentennial Without Colonization" and challenged the official versions of the United States' bicentennial (1776–1976). These large marches brought the Puerto Rican movement to the attention of mainstream society and were emblematic of another strategy of the social movements of the era, as movements brought together large numbers of people and had them march as a group to express their views. For many Puerto Rican activists, calling for independence for Puerto Rico and opposing the war in Vietnam were part of global decolonization struggles linked to those taking place in the Third World. Puerto Rican activists opposed the war in Vietnam as another example of U.S. imperialism and as the thwarting of socialist revolutions, while also condemning the disproportionate casualties among the poor and people of color.

As in other movements, Puerto Rican women activists encountered contradictions between the language of liberation and their roles within the movement, their communities, and the larger society. In the Young Lords, women began meeting as a caucus and insisted that the men do the same. Iris Morales, Denise Oliver, and others demanded that women hold leadership positions and that the party revise its platform. Pablo "Yoruba" Guzman pointed to the Gay Liberation Movement as providing alternatives to rigid gender roles for men and women and insisted that there be a place for gay people in the party. The PSP described Puerto Rican women as "triply oppressed as Puerto Rican, woman, and worker," and asserted, "The task of integrating the Puerto Rican woman into the revolutionary struggle is complex, but her total incorporation into the revolutionary process is indispensable." In 1975, Esperanza Martell and others organized the Latin Women's Collective to address the needs of working-class women of color, which they felt were being ignored by the Women's Liberation Movement.

Student activists were key leaders and participants in the Puerto Rican movement. In addition to addressing community issues and independence for Puerto Rico, they demanded fundamental changes in academic institutions. Student activism opened doors to educational institutions and then insisted that those educational institutions meet their needs. High school and college students acted based on a renewed sense of racial and ethnic pride. Established on campuses throughout the Northeast, the Puerto Rican Student Union (PRSU) expressed their "culture of survival" in "Somos Puertorriqueños y Estamos Despertando." Student activists pushed for admissions and retention programs for Puerto Ricans and other Latinas/os, and demanded culturally inclusive curriculums, including the founding of Puerto Rican studies departments. They organized the first national conference of Puerto Rican students in 1970. The PRSU played a role in the birth of the Centro de Estudios Puertorriqueños/ the Center for Puerto Rican Studies as a research center at the City University of New York in 1973. Through Centro and the writings of others, the field of Puerto Rican studies emerged with several significant publications by the end of the 1970s. Poetry, music, theater, creative writings, and other art forms were also a central component of the movement, as politics found artistic expression and as the art world was politicized. For many, poet Pedro Pietri's "Puerto Rican Obituary" became an anthem for the movement.

The demise of the Puerto Rican movement as a mass movement coincided with the decline of other movements, suggesting the impact of external factors. Along with a broad shift to a more conservative era, police repression took its toll on individuals, their families, political groups, and the movement as a whole. The U.S. government's covert COINTELPRO program sought to undermine the Puerto Rican movement through divisiveness, suspicion, and outright repression. While making the connections between colonialism in Puerto Rico and the plight of Puerto Ricans in the United States was crucial, trying to foment radical change on both fronts created strategic and logistical challenges that overwhelmed even the most experienced groups and activists, and sometimes caused irreparable rifts within groups. Internal factors played a role, as some groups lost touch with their original objectives and became rigidly dogmatic; some became enmeshed in bickering or competition, instead of coalition building. Although many groups tried to confront issues such as internalized racism, classism, sexism, and homophobia, tensions persisted as these remained ongoing struggles.

The movement's strengths were in its vision, its optimism, its activism, and its accomplishments. In bridging "homeland and barrio politics," activists explored the deep, underlying issues that created economic and social hardships for Puerto Ricans in Puerto Rico and in the United States. Political and cultural activism challenged the prevailing racism and the plethora of popular and academic discourses that depicted Puerto Ricans as inferior, along with other negative stereotypes. Racial and ethnic pride, bilingualism and biculturalism, have persisted despite backlashes. Though problems persist, the impact on higher education in terms of student and faculty recruitment and retention, and curriculums that include Puerto Rican and Latina/o Studies have been lasting. New generations of activists continue to look to their predecessors for inspiration and to their cultural production, as well.

THE YOUNG LORDS PARTY, *13 Point Program and Platform* (1971)

The Young Lords were one of the radical political groups that comprised the Puerto Rican movement. Their 13 Point Program and Platform articulated their political perspective and became the basis for their activism. By 1971, the Young Lords had revised the fifth point at the insistence of women activists who criticized the previous statement that "machismo must be revolutionary," insisting that there could be no such thing.

1. WE WANT SELF-DETERMINATION FOR PUERTO RICANS. LIBERATION ON THE ISLAND AND INSIDE THE UNITED STATES. For 500 years, first spain and then the united states have colonized our country. Billions of dollars in profits leave our country for the united states every year. In every way we are slaves of the gringo . . . QUE VIVA PUERTO RICO LIBRE!
2. WE WANT SELF-DETERMINATION FOR ALL LATINOS. Our Latin Brothers and Sisters, inside and outside the united states, are oppressed by amerikkkan business. The Chicano people built the Southwest, and we support their right to control their lives and their land. The people of Santo Domingo continue to fight against gringo domination and its puppet generals. The armed liberation struggles in Latin America are part of the war of Latinos against imperialism. QUE VIVA LA RAZA!
3. WE WANT LIBERATION OF ALL THIRD WORLD PEOPLE. Just as Latins first slaved under spain and the yanquis, Black people, Indians, and Asians slaved to build the wealth of this country. For 400 years they have fought for freedom and dignity against racist Babylon. Third World people have led the fight for freedom. . . . NO PUERTO RICAN IS FREE UNTIL ALL PEOPLE ARE FREE!
4. WE ARE REVOLUTIONARY NATIONALISTS AND OPPOSE RACISM. The Latin, Black, Indian and Asian people inside the u.s. are colonies fighting for liberation. We know that washington, wall street, and city hall will try to

---

Source: Pa'lante, Young Lords Party, ed. Young Lords Party and Michael Abramson, New York: McGraw Hill, 1971, p. 150.

make our nationalism into racism; but Puerto Ricans are of all colors and we resist racism. Millions of poor white people are rising up to demand freedom and we support them. . . . POWER TO ALL OPPRESSED PEOPLE!

5. WE WANT EQUALITY FOR WOMEN. DOWN WITH MACHISMO AND MALE CHAUVANISM. Under capitalism, women have been oppressed by both society and our men. The doctrine of machismo has been used by men to take out their frustrations on wives, sisters, mothers, and children. Men must fight along with sisters in the struggle for economic and social equality . . . FORWARD SISTERS IN THE STRUGGLE!
6. WE WANT COMMUNITY CONTROL OF OUR INSTITUTIONS AND LAND. We want control of our communities by our people and programs to guarantee that all institutions serve the needs of our people. People's control of police, health services, churches, schools, housing, transportation and welfare are needed. We want an end to attacks on our land by urban renewal, highway destruction, and university corporations. LAND BELONGS TO ALL THE PEOPLE!
7. WE WANT A TRUE EDUCATION OF OUR AFRO-INDIO CULTURE AND SPANISH LANGUAGE. We must learn our long history of fighting against cultural, as well as economic genocide by the spaniards and now the yanquis. Revolutionary culture, culture of our people, is the only true teaching. JIBARO SI, YANQUI NO!
8. WE OPPOSE CAPITALISTS AND ALLIANCES WITH TRAITORS. Puerto Rican rulers, or puppets of the oppressor, do not help our people. They are paid by the system to lead our people down blind alleys, just like the thousands of poverty pimps who keep our communities peaceful for business, or the street workers who keep gangs divided and blowing each other away. We want a society where the people socialistically control their labor. VENCEREMOS!
9. WE OPPOSE THE AMERIKKKAN MILITARY. We demand immediate withdrawal of all u.s. military forces and bases from Puerto Rico, VietNam, and all oppressed communities inside and outside the u.s. No Puerto Rican should serve in the u.s. army against his Brothers and Sisters . . . U.S. OUT OF VIETNAM, FREE PUERTO RICO NOW!
10. WE WANT FREEDOM FOR ALL POLITICAL PRISONERS AND PRISONERS OF WAR. No Puerto Rican should be in jail or prison, first because we are a nation, and amerikkka has no claims on us; second because we have not been tried by our own people (peers). . . . FREE ALL POLITICAL PRISONERS AND PRISONERS OF WAR!
11. WE ARE INTERNATIONALISTS. Our people are brainwashed by television, radio, newspapers, schools, and books to oppose people in other countries fighting for their freedom. No longer will we believe these lies, because we have learned who the real enemy is and who our real friends are. We will defend our sisters and brothers around the world who fight for justice and are against the rulers of this country. QUE VIVA CHE GUEVARA!
12. WE BELIEVE ARMED SELF-DEFENSE AND ARMED STRUGGLE ARE THE ONLY MEANS TO LIBERATION. We are oppose to violence—the violence of hungry children, illiterate adults, diseased old people, and the violence of poverty and profit. We have asked, petitioned, gone to courts,

demonstrated peacefully, and voted for politicians full of empty promises. But we still ain't free. The time has come to defend the lives of our people against repression and for revolutionary war against the businessmen, politicians, and police. When a government oppresses the people, we have the right to abolish it and create a new one. ARM OURSELVES TO DEFEND OURSELVES!

13. WE WANT A SOCIALIST SOCIETY. We want liberation, clothing, free food, education, health care, transportation, full employment and peace. We want a society where the needs of the people come first, and where we give solidarity and aid to the people of the world, not oppression and racism. HASTA LA VICTORIA SIEMPRE!

JUAN RAMOS, *The Philadelphia Young Lords* (1970)

The Philadelphia Young Lords grew out of an earlier political group and then became one of the branches of the Young Lords. In this article, which appeared in *Pa'lante,* the Young Lords' bilingual newspaper on November 20, 1970, Philadelphia Young Lord Juan Ramos reveals the challenges confronted in Philadelphia and the Young Lords collaboration with the Black Panthers.

On Friday, November 5th, 1970, the Philadelphia Branch of the YOUNG LORDS PARTY took over the Kingsway Lutheran Church. This takeover came two weeks after the First Spanish Methodist Church was taken over by the YOUNG LORDS in New York City. . . .

Some people may think that church takeovers are becoming a game and that the Philly LORDS are just trying to copy the LORDS in New York. These people must realize that the oppression of Puerto Ricans in Philly is the same as the oppression in New York. The conditions in both of these colonies are the same. The same sufferings of drugs, inadequate health care, racist police, and the jails exist in Philly just like in New York or any other colony in amerikkka. The struggle is the same. . . .

During the month of November, the racist police of Philly launched a major wave of attacks and harassment at the Black and Puerto Rican community. Their excuse was that they wanted to stop 'drug traffic' in the area . . .

The people of the community and the LORDS organized a rally and march to protest against the injustices that were going on. After the rally, the march proceeded through the community to the steps of the church. LORDS and 400 people, later joined by Panthers, took over the Kingsway Lutheran Church. It is becoming apparent that the church, like all other institutions in our community, is not there to serve the people and that the only way they can be made to serve the people is if the people start doing it themselves . . .

Source: Article in *Pa'lante* on November 20, 1970, Collection of articles housed at Center for Puerto Rican Studies, Hunter College.

A day after the occupation of the church, the YOUNG LORDS PARTY Information Center was bombed in an attempt to scare the people and cause confusion. This didn't work—the people once divided and misguided, have united and once again shown what the power of the people is. They have turned the church, once a cold, empty building, into a center for all the community. They have made the church meet their needs. They have made the church theirs . . .

PUERTO RICAN SOCIALIST PARTY, *Declaration* (1973)

The Puerto Rican Socialist Party had been the Puerto Rico-based Movement for Independence until 1971. During their First Congress on April 1, 1973, the "United States Branch of the Puerto Rican Socialist Party" articulated the Party's analysis of the situation confronting Puerto Ricans in the United States and approved this "Political Declaration," entitled, "Desde las Entranas" or "in the belly of the beast."

Two million Puerto Ricans live in the United States where we are one of the most oppressed, discriminated against and trampled sectors of capitalist exploitation imposed by the bourgeois class. Unlike other immigrants, we came here driven by the genocidal politics practiced by yankee imperialism in Puerto Rico, because of the colonialism imposed on us, and as a result of its use of Puerto Rico as a base for its world-wide system of imperialist domination. This fact must be the basis of an understanding of our situation. It must also be a basis for our political action. . . .

The conditions under which the life of the Puerto Ricans in the U.S. develop are linked to the colonial exploitation of all our people. The discrimination that we suffer in all walks of life, unemployment, low wages, inferior, racist education, neglect within the trade unions, poor housing, the absence of public sanitation as well as the lack of adequate medical and hospital services, the humiliation of welfare, police brutality, the rampant rises in the cost of living—are all manifestations of the same problem: the oppression of our people by the United States ruling class. . . .

Undoubtedly, because we reside in the U.S., we are confronted with problems common to all sectors of the working class of this country; however, we are also confronted with our country's particular position before North American imperialist domination. There is, therefore, a direct relation between our struggle for national liberation and the struggle for social change waged by Puerto Ricans in the United States . . .

We believe that Puerto Ricans in the United States and those on the island form one nation, the Puerto Rican nation . . . [they] have to establish for themselves the objective of obtaining the independence of Puerto Rico.

Source: "Desde las Entranas" April 1, 1973, Center for Puerto Rican Studies.

. . . we must also seek revolutionary alliances with other sectors of the working classes of this country in order to achieve revolutionary change here in this country.

PUERTO RICAN STUDENT UNION, *Somos Puertorriquenos y Estamos Despertando* (c. 1971)

Student activists were a critical component of the Puerto Rican movement, addressing the broader issues of the movement, as well as those specific to educational institutions. Here, in an organizing pamphlet, the Puerto Rican Student Union (PRSU) describes their "Culture of Survival," revealing the racial and ethnic pride that inspired students and others to activism.

Riding the subway, taking the bus, or walking into another culture (white, middle class) every day of our lives, and then coming home to our own way of life has created in us Puerto Ricans here in the United States, a double psychology. At the job, in schools, in all of the institutions that we come across each day, we are told that our culture is no good, that it is old, inferior and irrelevant; that it will not enable us to deal with the "realities" of adopting and making it in "The American Way." We fight this by adopting black culture and becoming pure soul brothers, or by changing our names and moving into white neighborhoods where we can pass for white (if the whites don't hear our accents). But in each case, we come home again, to be confronted with ourselves, our Puerto Rican selves. These selves and that reality are unique. Our multiracial black, white and brown skins make us an integrated people in a white racist society. Our music, our slang, our customs all derive from an Afro-antillean culture that has been developed over the centuries and that continues to grow wherever it finds worthy roots. . . .

PEDRO PIETRI, *Puerto Rican Obituary* (1973)

Artistic and cultural expression were a key component of the Puerto Rican movement, as artists were activists and as activists drew on artists to inspire and shape the movement. A leader among these artist activists was Pedro Pietri, who read his "Puerto Rican Obituary" at the New York City Young Lords church takeover and elsewhere.

Source: Reprinted in the Center for Puerto Rican Studies' journal, Centro de Estudios Puertorriquenos Bulletin, Spring 1988: 60–63.
Source: Pedro Pietri, *Puerto Rican Obituary* (1973).

They worked
They were always on time
They were never late
They never spoke back
when they were insulted
They worked
They never took days off
that were not on the calendar
They never went on strike
without permission
They worked
ten days a week
and were only paid for five
They worked
They worked
They worked
and they died
They died broke
They died owing
They died never knowing
what the front entrance of the first national bank looks like

Juan
Miguel
Milagros
Olga
Manuel
All died yesterday today
and will die again tomorrow
passing their bill collectors
on to the next of kin
All died
waiting for the garden of eden
to open up again
under a new management
All died
dreaming about america
waking them up in the middle of the night
screaming: Mira Mira
your name is on the winning lottery ticket
for one hundred thousand dollars
All died
hating the grocery stores
that sold them make-believe steak
and bullet-proof rice and beans
All died waiting dreaming and hating

Dead Puerto Ricans
Who never knew they were Puerto Ricans
Who never took a coffee break
from the ten commandments
to **KILL KILL KILL**
the landlords of their cracked skulls
and communicate with their latino souls
. . . .
Here lies Juan
Here lies Miguel
Here lies Milagros
Here lies Olga
Here lies Manuel
who died yesterday today
and will die again tomorrow
Always broke
Always owing
Never knowing
that they are beautiful people
Never knowing
the geography of their complexion

PUERTO RICO IS A BEAUTIFUL PLACE
PUERTORRIQUENOS ARE A BEAUTIFUL RACE

If only they
had turned off the television
and tune into their own imaginations
If only they
had used the white supremacy bibles
for toilet paper purpose
and make their latino souls
the only religion of their race
If only they
had return to the definition of the sun
after the first mental snowstorm
on the summer of their senses
If only they
had kept their eyes open
at the funeral of their fellow employees
who came to this country to make a fortune
and were buried without underwears

Juan
Miguel

Milagros
Olga
Manuel
will right now be doing their own thing
where beautiful people sing
and dance and work together
where the wind is a stranger
to miserable weather conditions
where you do not need a dictionary
to communicate with your people
Aqui Se Habla Espanol all the time
Aqui you salute your flag first
Aqui there are no dial soap commercials
Aqui everybody smells good
Aqui tv dinners do not have a future
Aqui the men and women admire desire
and never get tired of each other
Aqui Que Pasa Power is what's happening
Aqui to be called negrito
means to be called **LOVE**

20

Student Activism

—Rusty Monhollon

Student activism in the 1960s and 1970s left a profound mark on American society, politics, and culture, transforming higher education and playing a crucial role in the civil rights, anti-nuclear, feminist, and anti-war movements. Students are most associated with their own distinct movement known as the "New Left" or simply "the Movement." Student activists did not reform American society as they had envisioned but nonetheless left a profound legacy: increased participation among women, and ethnic and racial minorities in political and social life; a greater awareness of the environment; a lasting impact on popular culture; and a general questioning of the limits of American power. As the student movement pursued its agenda, it made the university itself as a battleground for reform. Perhaps the most enduring consequence of student activism is that it was a key element in the decade's "cultural wars," battles that today still rage.

Student activism did not arise in a vacuum. World War II allowed marginalized groups to challenge traditional structures of power. The spectacular growth of the U.S. economy, spurred on by liberal government programs, permitted millions to join the middle class. An unprecedented "baby boom" (75 million births between 1946 and 1964) further increased consumer spending, shaped popular culture, and put new demands on the nation's educational system. The Cold War affected not only foreign policy but also domestic politics. It stimulated the economy with massive defense budgets, which helped fashion a moderate yet dominant political philosophy known as the liberal consensus. Cold War liberals—Democrats and Republicans alike—rejected radicalism, were committed to defeating communism at home and abroad, and remained fervent in their faith that the political system would bring inequality to an end. Yet beneath the placid surface, American life was rife with incongruities and uncertainty—grinding poverty, social and political inequality, and the threat of nuclear annihilation—that led many Americans, students foremost among them, to question American democracy.

Sheer numbers alone assured that this generation's impact would be great; when concentrated on college campuses its revolutionary potential was real. College enrollments doubled between 1946 and 1960, and doubled again by 1970. Student activism occurred at institutions of every size and kind, and in every corner of the nation. Activists came from a range of sociopolitical backgrounds but shared some common traits. Among early activists, many were from the urban middle class, including the so-called "red-diaper babies," the children of communists or socialists persecuted during the McCarthy era. Later, activists also came from working-class families and from smaller communities in the Midwest and elsewhere. Although contemporaries often depicted student activism as a rejection of the older generation, recent studies have found that activists—from both the left and the right—shared to a very large degree their parents' values.

Scholars often characterize this generation of students as idealistic, confident that they could change the world. Liberals like John F. Kennedy and Lyndon Johnson challenged them to conquer "the common enemies of man: tyranny, poverty, disease, and war itself," and thousands heeded the call. Some joined the Peace Corps, which channeled youthful energy into the United States' Cold War struggle in the so-called "Third World." Others joined Volunteers in Service to America (VISTA), which sought to eradicate poverty in Appalachia, on Indian Reservations, urban ghettos, and other economically depressed areas of the nation. VISTA workers sought to strengthen communities by establishing health clinics, day care centers, educational programs such as Head Start, and vocational training. While liberalisms' vision inspired many students, not all of them embraced its solutions. Indeed, many students were deeply suspicious of liberalism, and sought alternative paths to reform.

The struggle for racial equality was vital to student activism. The New Left shared the civil rights movement's democratic vision but was equally inspired by African Americans' use of nonviolent direct action to confront oppression publicly. The sit-in movement, begun in Greensboro in February 1960, sparked a wave of protests across the nation and led to the founding of the Student Nonviolent Coordinating Committee (SNCC), a dynamic organization that pushed the movement forward and produced many of its leading voices, including Robert Moses, Stokely Carmichael, Diane Nash, and John Lewis. In 1964, SNCC organized Freedom Summer, a voter registration drive in the South that included hundreds of white student volunteers. The students witnessed the pervasive poverty and violence (which included the murder of three civil rights workers, one a white student), that Southern blacks encountered daily. The experience left a deep impression on the white students.

Thus inspired, students at the University of Michigan in 1960 founded Students for a Democratic Society (SDS), which became the foremost white student organization in the New Left. Its 1962 Port Huron Statement, written principally by Tom Hayden, decried the complacency and impersonalization of the modern world, which had left people dehumanized and devoid of community. SDS believed students, by reclaiming the university from the "dull pedantic cant" of bureaucratic inertia, could radically reconstruct American society. SDS's first project was the Economic Research and Action Program (ERAP), a community-building and anti-poverty project in Northern ghettos, similar to SNCC's organizing in the South. Ironically, ERAP repudiated the Port Huron Statement, as it regarded students as a privileged rather than an oppressed group, and an "interracial movement of the poor," rather than university reform, as the principal means of reform. Nevertheless, ERAP illustrated the democratic idealism that stimulated many students. While it fell short of its goals, it did draw supporters to SDS's agenda.

The New Left was a significant—but not exclusive—part of the era's contested political terrain. Conservative student activism gave rise to the New Right. The Young Americans for Freedom (YAF), founded in 1960, was the leading student organization on the right. Although the New Left became a target for many conservatives, the issues that motivated them initially were unrelated to leftists: the Cold War, the growth of the welfare state, the perceived loss of individual rights, and the perceived growth of socialism.

The full impact of YAF's activism would not be felt for years, but SDS's was apparent by mid-decade. Students increasingly were attracted to its radical agenda and the struggle against what it called "the system." Events in 1964—Freedom Summer, the Free Speech Movement (FSM) at the University of California-Berkeley, and the Vietnam War—formed the crucible in which a distinct mass student movement was forged.

The FSM illustrated the overlap between student activism and other movements and demonstrated the political power students could wield. The movement flared when a nonstudent was arrested for handing out political literature in a place the university previously had permitted. While free speech was the immediate issue, the real target was the "multiversity," a euphemism for the modern university. To many, the multiversity was merely an impersonal education factory, funded by government and military research, which made students little more than cogs in a massive machine. Mario Savio, a student leader of the movement just returned from Freedom Summer, passionately told the crowd: "There is a time when the operation of the machine becomes so odious, that . . . you've got to put your bodies upon the gears and upon the wheels . . . and make it stop." When the administration allowed the police to restore "order," it pushed moderate and previously unreceptive students into the movement. What began as a flap over campus regulations became a referendum on the modern university and a host of other off-campus issues, one that quickly stirred thousands of students on campuses across the nation. The FSM also marked the beginning of a political "backlash" against student activism, as conservatives accused administrators' of "giving in" to student radicalism.

The FSM was a classic case of using nonviolent civil disobedience, tactics typical of early student activism. The Vietnam War, however, changed that, as it aroused and radicalized students. The movement grew from a small core of pacifists long opposed to nuclear proliferation and militarism, but by 1968, perhaps as many as 40,000 students from more than 100 campuses joined in anti-war demonstrations, many directed at symbols of the military on campus, such as the Reserve Officers Training Corps (ROTC). Anti-war activism profoundly affected national politics, too. Minnesota Senator Eugene McCarthy challenged President Lyndon Johnson's Vietnam policy by seeking the Democratic presidential nomination in 1968. Many students went "Clean for Gene," cutting their hair and shaving their beards before campaigning door-to-door.

In April 1970, the United States invaded Cambodia, and students from across the political spectrum responded with widespread condemnation and demonstrations.

At Kent State University in Ohio, confrontations between students and police convinced the governor to mobilize the National Guard to campus, a move that only elevated the tension. On May 4, several troops, believing protestors had thrown stones at them, fired into the crowd. Four students fell, mortally wounded; nine more were injured. Ten days later, police killed two students at Jackson State College in Mississippi, where students had been protesting the Kent State deaths, the war, and racial inequality. Students were mortified by the shootings and shut down completely more than one hundred campuses. President Richard Nixon defended the guardsmen, blaming instead "campus bums," and a broad segment of the public agreed. That many Americans approved of the use of state-sanctioned violence against demonstrators explains in part why Kent State was the turning point—some have called it the "death knell"—for both the anti-war and student movements. By the falling fall, the mood had changed noticeably on campus. Students now had to consider the sober possibility that the state could again use lethal force against protestors.

Even before Kent State, however, student activism was in decline, abetted by attacks from the government. The most notorious of these was the Federal Bureau of Investigation's Counter Intelligence Program, or COINTELPRO, which used a variety of questionable means to discredit student, civil rights, and anti-war organizations. COINTELPRO exacted a heavy toll, targeting not merely radicals but dissidents of every stripe. Vietnam had weakened public confidence in government; the disclosure of COINTELPRO's activities contributed further to its decline.

Student activism intersected with other movements, in particular struggles for equality. African Americans demanded that institutions of higher education recruit more black students and faculty and create black studies programs and cultural centers. The feminist movement derived much of its vitality from female students who, in struggling for racial equality, came to understand more fully their own subjugation as women. Feminists on campus helped establish women's studies programs across the country, but they altered expectations—among women and men—regarding traditional employment patterns and gender roles. Native American students in 1969 helped plan and execute the 19-month occupation of Alcatraz Island, from which the nascent American Indian Movement (AIM) flowered. Students similarly strengthened the Chicano movement, whether it was through campus support groups, working in the field alongside César Chávez and the United Farm Workers, or forming political organizations that promoted the creation of Chicano Studies programs, such as the Movimiento Estudiantil Chicano de Aztlán. Gay students drew strength from the civil rights movement, as the fight for basic human dignity was one with which homosexuals easily identified. Not until 1967 did universities recognize and provide gay student organizations equal access to campus facilities, which the courts affirmed in 1974. By the late 1960s, high school student activism, too, was commonplace, no doubt encouraged by swirling currents of cultural and political dissent. Students—teenagers and younger—had had struggled for racial equality, dating back to the 1950s. By the late 1960s, many high school students publicly demonstrated against the Vietnam War; the Supreme Court, in *Tinker v. Des Moines Independent School District* (1969), affirmed their right to free speech. Black high school students protested the lack of black teachers, the absence of black history and culture in the curriculum, and limited academic and social opportunities. Chicano students protested the lack of Hispanic teachers and administrators, and a Eurocentric curriculum that ignored their culture. High school students challenged rules governing permissible clothing and hairstyles and, by the mid-1970s, many public school dress codes had been modified or discarded.

Student protest was not limited to the United States. In 1968, major student protests took place in Czechoslovakia, Mexico, Germany, Japan, Canada, and England; in France, student strikes nearly toppled the government. The issues that motivated students around the world were broadly similar to those that drove American students—nuclear proliferation, racism, free speech, or political repression—but grew in response to problems specific to their own country. Students universally seemed to challenge authority, often university rules governing their personal behavior, but German students, for example, also opposed American involvement in Vietnam.

Since the mid-1970s, critics have bemoaned student apathy. The depth of student unrest in the 1960s was exceptional and, by comparison, succeeding generations of students may indeed appear to be dormant. Yet student activism never really went away. The best known episode of student protest since the 1960s came between 1984 and 1986, when thousands of American students joined their voices with thousands from around the world to protest apartheid in South Africa. They demanded that their universities divest themselves of corporations that did business with the white South African government. Since then, students have continued to struggle for equality, against racism, sexism, and violence toward women, gays, and lesbians, joined in the anti-globalization movement, and protested the use of sweatshop labor to manufacture university clothing and apparel, to name a few examples. While subsequent generations have not garnered the headlines as did the sixties' generation, neither that generation's legacy nor the revolutionary potential of students cannot be ignored.

THE REPORT OF THE PRESIDENT'S COMMISSION ON CAMPUS UNREST, *Jackson State* (1970)

The deaths of six students—four at Kent State University and two at Jackson State College—at the hands of law officers in 1970 signaled the end of student activism. In the aftermath, President Richard Nixon appointed a presidential commission to investigate the causes of campus unrest. An excerpt of that report describes the events at Jackson State University, which was—and continues to be—overshadowed by the tragedy at Kent State.

Two nights of campus demonstrations at Jackson State College in May 1970 ended in violent confrontation and tragedy. After 28 seconds of gunfire by Mississippi Highway Safety Patrolmen and Jackson city policemen, two black youths lay dying and 12 others were wounded. . . .

Source: President's Commission on Campus Unrest, *The Report of the President's Commission on Campus Unrest*, New York: Arno Press, 1970, pp. 411–459.

There had been no campus disturbances during the 1969–70 school year prior to the events of May 13. On May 7, three days after the shooting at Kent State, roughly 500 students attended a peaceful campus rally organized by student leaders to protest policies in Cambodia and Vietnam. In response to a call for one-day boycott, a smaller number of students refused to attend class the next day. . . .

There was some apprehension at Jackson State College on Thursday, May 14, but the campus was quiet and class attendance was normal. . . . At a 2.30 p.m. meeting with student leaders, [Jackson State President] Dr. [John A.] Peoples stressed the seriousness of what had happened the night before and told them the National Guard had been activated and was being mobilized. They reported to him that the general feeling among students was that there would be no disturbance on Thursday night. . . .

Around 9:30 p.m., a small group in the vicinity of Stewart Hall [a men's dormitory] began throwing rocks at passing white motorists. Lynch Street soon was sealed off as it had been the night before. The crowd swelled to between 100 and 200 persons, most of them onlookers who cheered the rock-throwers. . . . Students from the dormitory joined the demonstrators in jeering and yelling insults and obscenities. . . . Rocks and pieces of brick were thrown, but there were no serious injuries to firemen or police officers. . . . There were conflicting reports of small caliber gunfire from the area of Stewart Hall. . . . The gunfire from the highway patrol disturbed [authorities, who] decided the National Guard should move onto the campus and relieve the highway patrol and city police. . . .

[The police ordered the crowd] to disperse several times, but many students claimed that his words had been drowned out by the noise. Two officers staggered when struck on their helmets by thrown objects; one of them stated he was knocked to the ground. Inside the tank, an officer was loading a short-range tear gas shell, anticipating an order to fire gas. . . . Someone threw a bottle from the lawn behind the fence in front of Alexander Hall [a women's dormitory]. Almost simultaneously, another bottle was lobbed from behind the retaining wall across the street, to the rear of the police line. . . . Almost instantaneously, a general barrage of shotgun, carbine, rifle, and submachine gun fire began. . . . Bert Case [a reporter] made a tape recording of the gunfire. The fusillade lasted 28 seconds. Many of the officers emptied shot guns containing four rounds of buckshot. One patrolman, who fired four rounds, reloaded and fired four more, and reloaded and fired again. . . . In all, more than 150 rounds were fired. Most were fired into the air, but FBI investigation showed that nearly 400 bullets or pieces of buckshot struck Alexander Hall. The area of the South end of the west wing alone contained 301 separate bullet marks. The upper floor level was hardest hit, with 105 marks or bullet holes in the windows, panels, and wall. There were 83 separate buckshot or bullet marks counted in the fourth-floor area. There were 64 marks counted on the third floor, 36 on the second floor, and 13 separate bullet or buckshot marks in the windows, doors, and frames at ground level. . . . the Commission concludes that a significant cause of the deaths and injuries at Jackson State College is the confidence of white officers that if they fire weapons during a black campus disturbance they will face neither stern departmental discipline nor criminal prosecution or conviction. . . . The commission categorically rejects rhetorical statements that students must "expect" injury or death during civil disorders. Such statements make no distinction between legitimate dissent and violent protest. It is the duty of public officials to protect human life and to safeguard peaceful, orderly, and lawful protest. When disorderly protest exists, it is their duty to deal with it firmly, justly, and with the minimum force necessary; lethal force should be used only to protect the lives of officers or citizens and only when the danger to innocent persons is not increased by the use of such force.

THE FREE SPEECH MOVEMENT, *A Declaration of Independence* (1965)

The Free Speech Movement was central to the creation of a mass student movement in the 1960s. Although free speech on campus was the issue that first galvanized students, the university itself was the real target. As the document below illustrates, students demanded a greater voice in their own education and fewer rules and restrictions on their private behavior and conduct.

The Free Speech Movement at Berkeley was formed to defend the rights of free speech and political activity. Through negotiations, petitions, sit-ins, and a strike, we finally established the principle that the University may not regulate the content of speech. At the same time, the FSM has given students a new and well-deserved sense of dignity and self-respect.

Throughout this semester, however, the Regents have harassed the Berkeley campus in many ways. They are now preparing to impose new regulations that would destroy everything we fought for. In the last few months, we have become increasingly aware that it is not merely free speech and political activity to which the Regents object. They insist upon their right to govern every facet of University life—student conduct, student government, educational policy, political rights, and other areas of no proper concern to them.

The FSM, born in crisis, has never paused to organize a permanent membership nor to develop the close and continuous contacts between leaders and constituency necessary to a democratic movement. We never before believed that it would be necessary to form a permanent organization which would institutionalize the struggle; we never believed it would be necessary to plan on a long-term basis. The events of the past few weeks have proved us wrong. Now is the time for students to join together to form a permanent, democratic membership organization to carry on the fight to free this university from outside control. The successor to the FSM shall be the Free Student Union, based upon the following declaration:

As students, we have certain rights which no agency can legitimately grant or deny; among these the right to govern our own internal affairs, to set our own standards of conduct, and jointly with the faculty to determine the form and nature of our education.

Source: A Declaration of Independence. The Online Archive of California (OAC). An initiative of the California Digital Library © 2007 by The Regents of The University of California. Available at http://content.cdlib.org/xtf/view?docId=kt6g5004r8&chunk.id=&brand=oac&doc.view=entire_text.

Our University exists for the extension and transmission of human knowledge. It is a community consisting of students and faculty and those who are employed to serve our needs. Final authority in this community must therefore rest with us, the students and faculty.

Yet a body external to the life of the University—the Board of Regents—claims full power to govern the University in every detail, either directly or through its agent, the administration. No rights are reserved to the University community; neither the students nor faculty deliberative bodies have any powers save at the pleasure of the Regents.

Therefore, we the students of Berkeley now establish a Union which will fight to secure our rights and to end continual outside interference.

The FSM executive committee has voted to serve as an organizing committee for the union and to assume only interim responsibilities until such time as the union is functioning; the FSM will then officially dissolve. The FSM urges all students to join the Union. Membership cards shall be available for a 25 cents joining fee. The only requirement of membership is basic agreement with the above declaration and a commitment to fight for those principles.

One of the main reasons for the establishment of the Union is to form an organization in which every student is able to take part as a member. We shall hold our first general union meeting on May 5th, at which time proposals for internal organizational structure will be debated and voted upon. We hope that organizational forms will be developed which will encourage responsibility of every elected union official to a definite constituency, will maximize the amount of influence the individual member will be able to have on the union's policies, and will guarantee representation of minority views within the union. We also hope that the constitution will contain provisions for referenda, by the membership, on crucial policy decisions. Time, place, and manner of the first general union election will also be established at this meeting. We expect that well before the May 21st Regents' meeting, at which the Meyer Committee proposals may be adopted, the Union will be well organized and leading the struggle.

PERRYVILLE, ARKANSAS SCHOOL DISTRICT, *Dress Code* (1971–1972)

High school students not only participated in the civil rights and anti-war movements, but also were part of the broader cultural changes that helped define the era. Dress codes help to illustrate a cultural divide and also suggest the broad challenges to authority that underlay many of the era's reform movements.

Source: Wallace v. Ford, 346 F. Supp. 156 (1972). Available at http://www.lexisnexis.com/us/lnacademic/results/docview/docview.do?docLinkInd=true&risb=21_T5661621904&format=GNBFI&sort=BOOLEAN&startDocNo=1&resultsUrlKey=29_T5661621907&cisb=22_T5661621906&treeMax=true&treeWidth=0&csi=6443&docNo=1.

GIRLS: Dresses, skirts and blouses, dress slacks and blouses or pant suits may be worn. No divided skirts or dresses; no jeans or shorts may be worn. Blouses that are straight around the bottom may be worn outside the skirt or slacks. The length of the skirts or dresses will be no more than six (6) inches above or six (6) inches below the knee. Excessively tight skirts or pants will not be allowed. Girls are expected to be neatly dressed and well groomed at all times. Girls will not come to school with hair in rollers.

BOYS: Boys may wear dress or sport pants, including jeans. No frayed trousers or jeans will be allowed. Shirt tails, unless the tail is straight and hemmed, will be worn inside the pants. Socks are required at all times. Boys will be expected to be neat and well groomed at all times. This means that their hair will be trimmed; it will not be down over the ears, in the eyes or down over the shirt collar. The face will be clean shaven—no mustaches, beards or sideburns below the ear lobes.

GENERAL: No tie-dyed clothing will be worn. Shirt or clothing having slogans, pictures, or emblems, etc. will not be worn except school approved emblems. As amended (by memo to parents) at the beginning of the 1971–72 school year: After checking in some stores and talking with parents concerning the girls' dress, we have decided to relax the code. We will allow jeans that are made for girls to be worn providing: If the jeans open in front, a tunic or square-tailed blouse must be worn to conceal the opening. If the jeans open on the side, then an ordinary length blouse may be worn. In either case, the jeans will not be allowed if they fit too tightly.

COURT RULING FROM U.S. COURT OF APPEALS (1ST. CIR.), *Gay Students Organization of the University of New Hampshire v. Bonner* (1974)

Student activists continued organizing on campus even after the demise of the New Left. Gay students have been among the most vigilant of activists, in part because discrimination and violence against homosexuals has persisted or even increased since the 1970s. In 1974, the federal courts affirmed the right of gay student organizations to equal access to campus facilities.

In 1973, the University of New Hampshire officially recognized the Gay Students Organization (GSO). That fall, the GSO held a dance

---

Source: 367 F. Supp. 1088; 1974. Available at http://www.lexisnexis.com/us/lnacademic/results/docview/docview.do?docLinkInd=true&risb=21_T5594760387&format=GNBFI&sort=RELEVANCE&startDocNo=1&resultsUrlKey=29_T5594760398&cisb=22_T5594760397&treeMax=true&treeWidth=0&selRCNodeID=2&nodeStateId=411en_US,1&docsInCategory=11&csi=6323&docNo=3.

without incident on campus but the governor criticized the University for permitting such a "spectacle." The Board of Trustees directed the administration to suspend any GSO-sponsored social function. In December, when the GSO requested permission to sponsor a play on campus and have a social function afterward, the University permitted the play but denied permission for the social function. The play itself was innocuous, but several people complained that "Fag Rag Five" and "Fag Rag VI," two "extremist homosexual" publications, were handed out at the play. The governor then threatened to withhold state funding for the University unless the administration put a stop to what he called "indecency and moral filth." The administration launched an investigation to determine who had distributed the Fag Rag literature and warned GSO that any further such incidents would result in the suspension of its official recognition. The GSO sued the University, claiming the University had violated GSO's rights under the First and Fourteenth Amendments.

. . . In essence, this case is quite simple. The First Amendment guarantees all individuals, including university students, the right to organize and associate "to further their personal beliefs." . . . Absent the attendance of well-defined circumstances, a university must recognize any bona fide student organization and grant to that organization the rights and privileges which normally flow from such recognition—those rights and privileges which are necessary to the maintenance and growth of the organization. Moreover, although a university may reasonably regulate the activities of student organizations, once it grants a particular privilege to one or more organizations, the Fourteenth Amendment requires that that privilege be available to all organizations on an equal basis. From this, it follows that the GSO has the same right to be recognized, to use campus facilities, and to hold functions, social or otherwise, as every other organization on the University of New Hampshire campus. University officials must understand that "mere disagreement . . . with the group's philosophy affords no reason to deny it recognition. . . . The [University], acting here as the instrumentality of the State, may not restrict speech or association simply because it finds the views expressed by any group to be abhorrent." . . . Minority groups, as well as majority groups, must be given an opportunity to express themselves; for only in this way can our system of peaceful social change be maintained. . . . As the University must respect the rights of the GSO, so must the GSO respect the rights of the rest of the University community. This, in essence, is what the Constitution requires. For the foregoing reasons, the defendants are herewith enjoined from prohibiting or restricting the sponsorship of social functions or use of University facilities for such functions by the Gay Students Organization. Defendants are further enjoined from treating the Gay Students Organization differently than other University student organizations. So ordered.

SHULAMITH FIRESTONE, *Women and the Radical Movement* (1968)

Canadian-born Shulamith Firestone was a leading voice of radical feminism; her 1970 book, *The Dialectic of Sex: A Case for Feminist Revolution,* remains a critical work of feminist thought. As Firestone explains below, the emergence of radical feminism resulted from women's marginalization in other movements of the sixties, most notably the black freedom struggle.

Within the last year many radical women's groups have sprung up throughout the country. This was caused by the fact that movement women found themselves playing secondary roles on every level . . . be it in terms of leadership, or simply in terms of being listened to. They found themselves (and others) afraid to speak up because of self-doubts when in the presence of men. Their roles ended up concentrating on food-making, typing, mimeographing, general assistance work, and as a sexual supply for their male comrades after hours.

As these problems began being discussed, it became clear that what had at first been assailed so be a personal problem was in fact a social and political one. We found strong parallels between the liberation of women and the black power struggle, being oppressed by similar psychological/economic dynamic [forces]. . . . And the deeper we analyzed the problem, and realized that all women suffer from this kind of oppression, the more we realized that the problem was not just isolated to movement women.

It became necessary to go to the root of the problem, rather than to become engaged in solving secondary problems arising *out* of that condition. Thus, rather than storming the Pentagon as women, or protest the Democratic Convention as women, we must begin to expose and eliminate the causes of our oppression as women. Our job is not *only* to improve the conditions of the movement any more that it is to only improve the condition of professional working woman. Both are reformist if thought of only as ends in themselves; and it ignores the broader concept that one cannot achieve equality for sore members of one's group while the rest are not free.

In choosing to fight for women's liberation it is not enough, either, to explain it only in general terms of "the system." For the system oppresses many groups in many ways. Women must learn that the *specific methods* used to keep her oppressed is to convince her that she is at all times secondary to man, and that her life is defined in terms of him. We cannot speak of liberating ourselves until we free ourselves from this myth and accept ourselves as primary.

Source: From Notes from the First Year, New York: The New York Radical Women, 1968. Documents from the Women's Liberation Movement, Special Collections Library, Duke University. http://scriptorium.lib.duke.edu/wlm/notes/#newview.

In our role as radical women we are confronted with the problem of assuring a female revolution within the general revolution. And we must begin to distinguish the real from the apparent freedom.

Radical men may advocate certain freedoms for women when they overlap their own interest, but these are not true freedoms unless they spring out of the concept of male and female equality and confront the issue of male supremacy.

For example, man may want women to fight in the revolution because they need every able bodied person they can get. And they may need women to join the work force under a socialist economic system because they cannot afford, like capitalism, to have an unemployed (surplus) labor force not contributing work, being supported by the state. And man may therefore advocate state nurseries so that mothers are not kept from work.

21

Women's Rights Activism

—KATHLEEN C. BERKELEY

When American women "rediscovered" their feminism in the 1960s and 1970s, they were responding to both long-standing frustrations about their continuing "second-class" status in society and to specific concerns which arose out of the political and social unrest that characterized these decades. The feminist activism of their foremothers in the late nineteenth and early twentieth centuries had accomplished a great deal, such as the right to vote, but by the mid- to late twentieth century there was still much to be done.

Notably, feminism had not "died" when groups such as the National American Woman's Suffrage Association (NAWSA) accomplished their major goal in 1920. Indeed, the feminist movement only grew more diverse as important ideological debates arose regarding how best to improve women's lives now that they had access to the ballot box.

Women such as Alice Paul, president of the National Woman's Party (NWP), believed that women needed an Equal Rights Amendment (ERA) added to the U.S. Constitution and the NWP made this its primary goal in 1923. Many immigrant working-class women and native-born white middle-class women, however, did not agree with Paul's "rights-based" perspective and did not support the NWP's strategy. These social feminists (also described as "difference feminists") continued to advocate for social and labor reforms that benefited women because of their unique sociobiological function as mothers. Social feminists worried that passage of the ERA would undermine their rationale for viewing women as a special class in dire need of protective labor legislation.

African American women also stood a world apart from the feminism espoused by the equal rights advocates of the NWP and the social feminists associated with the Women's Bureau. The double jeopardy of racism and sexism complicated their relationship with a feminist movement dominated by white middle- and upper-class women as well as with the predominately black male leadership of the emerging civil rights movement. In response, African American women founded their own organization, the National Association of Colored Women (NACW) while continuing to be active in the National Association for the Advancement of Colored People (NAACP) despite its overarching race goals.

Feminist activity entered a quieter period from the onset of the Great Depression in 1929 to the election of John F. Kennedy to the presidency in 1960. Social feminists continued to make their presence felt at the federal level when Franklin D. Roosevelt won the White House in 1932. A strong network of activist women propelled a cadre of women into leadership positions in a number of New Deal social agencies and departments (Frances Perkins' historic appointment as Secretary of Labor is one example). Not to be outdone by the social feminists' influence on the Democratic Party, political feminists led by Alice Paul sought alliances with the Republican Party and were rewarded when the party endorsed the ERA at the 1940 national convention.

The U.S. entry into World War II and the Cold War that followed on the heels of an allied victory refocused the nation's attention and resources away from social reform. As feminism fell out of favor after 1946, a number of women's organizations, like the League of Women Voters, rejected the term "feminism." Nevertheless, women continued to make their presence felt and their issues count during this time, albeit with less fanfare.

Feminism's revitalization in the 1960s, which scholars dubbed second-wave feminism, developed from two distinct ideological fault lines: liberal feminism (also described as women's rights or equal rights feminism) and radical feminism (which the media popularized as the women's lib movement). Liberal feminism's pragmatic focus on "equal rights before the law" drew its inspiration from the unfinished business of first-wave feminism and the new opportunity for activism that came when President John F. Kennedy established a Presidential Commission on the Status of Women in 1961 and signed the Equal Pay Act in 1963.

Although women made only few measurable gains during the Kennedy administration, an executive order issued shortly before Kennedy's death would lay the foundation for the formation of a national feminist organization, similar to the NAACP. All that this resurgent feminist movement lacked was an emotional reference point and an easily identifiable leader. Such arrived when Betty Friedan's best seller, *The Feminine Mystique*, was published in 1963. This book inspired countless women to demand more from their society and led to the creation of several organizations such as the National Organization for Women (NOW) in 1966, the Women's Equity Action League (WEAL) in 1968, and the National Women's Political Caucus (NWPC) in 1971. These organizations advocated for a "gender blind" society and focused on removing legal barriers to women's full equality.

In stark contrast stood radical feminism's espousal of "liberation ideology" which developed out of the personal experiences of young, predominately white and middle class, college-age women who had joined the Civil Rights and Student Left/Anti-War movements of the 1960s. Their feminist awakening grew directly out of their personal experiences with being excluded from policy and strategy sessions, consigned to kitchen and clerical detail, and objectified as sex objects by the men in those activist movements. Between 1964 and 1967 individually and in small groups, women like Mary King, Casey Hayden, Jo Freman, Shulamith Firestone, and Robin

Morgan attempted to raise the issue of women's liberation with their "brothers" only to be criticized, shouted down, and belittled.

Beginning in 1967, many of these female activists came together in localized, decentralized women's liberation groups across the country. The liberation ideology espoused by these radical feminists varied from group to group, as did their groups' names. *Marxist feminists* remained committed to the theory that a class-based revolution would eradicate sexism and therefore did not form independent women's groups within the New Left. *Socialist-feminist* groups such as the Chicago Women's Liberation Union and Boston's Bread and Roses focused on the interplay among systems of race, class, and gender as the root cause of female oppression. *Radical feminists* such as the New York Radical Feminists and Redstockings subordinated issues of race and class and identified all women as belonging to the same class/caste.

As disparate as these ideological stances were, Consciousness-Raising (CR) provided a common link and rationale for action: "The personal is political." CR groups were small gatherings in which women divulged their innermost thoughts and experiences with male oppression. Sharing stories about the intimate details of their private lives (especially their domestic relationships as daughters, wives, and mothers) revealed and clarified the power (patriarchy) men exerted over women. Such revelations politicized women.

In ways that were similar to their foremothers' experiences during first-wave feminism, women of color in the 1960s and 1970s also confronted the indifference, bordering on racism, of their white sisters. Their issues—forced sterilization, unemployment, hunger, poverty, crime—which grew out of the double bind of racism and sexism, also set them apart from their brothers who tended to dominate the radical movements for social justice such as the Student Non Violent Coordinating Committee, the Black Panthers, the United Farm Workers, La Raza Unida, and the American Indian Movement. Frustrated by their second-class status in both movements, second-wave feminist women of color followed in the footsteps of their foremothers and founded separatist organizations such as the National Black Feminist Organization, the Mexican-American Women's National Association, the Organization of Pan Asian Women, and the Third World Women's Alliance.

Lesbian feminists also had difficulty gaining acceptance for their concerns and initially were not welcomed by mainstream feminists. Whether they were forced out or fled NOW chapters, lesbian feminists looked first for support among their more radical straight sisters in the grassroots women's liberation groups. When these groups' support also proved to be lukewarm, many lesbian feminists, touting the concept of "woman-identified-woman," formed separatist groups such as Radicalesbians and The Furies.

Although they were clearly not as democratic and inclusive as women of color and lesbians needed them to be, throughout the 1970s liberal feminists lobbied public officials for a number of reforms: equal access to state and federal job-training programs, enforcement of Title VII, maternity leave, federal funding for child care centers, the prohibition of sex discrimination in federally funded educational programs and institutions, and for a woman's right to control her reproductive life.

By 1976, they had made significant headway with their agenda and could point with pride to a number of stunning achievements: the 1969 ruling by the EEOC, which strengthened federal anti-discrimination laws; the passage of Title IX as part of the 1972 Education Act, which prohibited sex discrimination in educational institutions receiving federal assistance for any program or activity; the ERA, which was voted out of Congress in 1972 and appeared headed for ratification; *Roe v. Wade*, the Supreme Court's 1973 landmark ruling on abortion; and the Women's Rights Project, supported by the American Civil Liberties Union and headed by Ruth Bader Ginsberg (who in 1993 became the second woman to sit on the Supreme Court).

In keeping with their liberation ideology and their grassroots development, radical feminists stressed revolutionary socioeconomic and cultural changes and directed their efforts at the communities in which they lived. Radical feminists' bold insistence on a woman's right to control her body challenged prevailing cultural assumptions about femininity and male prerogative. In 1971, when New York Radical Feminists organized the first "speak-out" against rape, they challenged the "blame the victim" syndrome and redefined rape as a violent act of male power. The Boston Women's Health Collective challenged the control the male-dominated medical profession exerted over women's bodies (especially their reproductive lives). Their critique and the book they published in 1973, *Our Bodies, Ourselves,* pioneered the self-help health movement which in turn revolutionized the health-care system. Armed with knowledge about their bodies, women challenged heretofore routine decisions about drug regimes, medical tests, and surgical procedures and they advocated for research dollars to be allocated to women's diseases (breast and ovarian cancers). Always two steps ahead of their liberal sisters, radical feminists were the first to shine a spotlight on wife-beating (domestic violence), incest, pornography, and sexual harassment (which differs significantly from sex discrimination), and they lived up to their activist claims by founding "Take Back the Night" rallies (especially popular on college campuses), women's self-help health clinics, rape crisis centers, and shelters for battered women and children.

Even as feminists celebrated their legal, judicial, and cultural victories, a serious backlash was underway. At the height of feminist efforts to finally ratify the ERA, a powerful conservative voice among Republican Party women, Phyllis Schlafly, took aim at the proposed amendment in her monthly independent newsletter, *The Phyllis Schlafly Report* and in her newly formed organization, STOP-ERA. Hostility to the ERA grew exponentially when Schlafly zeroed in on the alleged "dangers" a gender-blind society posed to the American family. Thanks to such anti-feminist efforts, the amendment died on June 30, 1982.

Anti-abortion rights activists were also on the move almost from the moment the Supreme Court rendered its decision in *Roe v. Wade*. Leading the "Pro-Life" charge were members of the Catholic Church's hierarchy and lay community; by the end of 1973, anti-abortion activists had founded the National Right to Life Committee which worked with a broad coalition of conservative religious organizations bent on overturning the *Roe* decision. Although that goal has not yet been achieved, a series of Supreme Court decisions between 1980 and 1992 banned federal funding of abortions for poor women and placed serious limitations on all women's right to reproductive freedom.

Despite the rise of such conservative opposition, second-wave feminism clearly had a transformative effect on American culture and its institutions. New gender-neutral words such as firefighter, police officer, and airline steward replaced gender-specific words such as fireman, policeman, and stewardess. Rape Crisis Centers,

Domestic Violence Shelters, and Women's Health Clinics are as much a part of the urban landscape as schools and churches. Women serve as CEO's, college and university presidents, supreme court justices, senators, governors, mayors, high school and college coaches, and construction workers; men have made inroads into heretofore "traditional" women's occupations such as nursing, clerical, and elementary education and have laid claim to a new role: "househusband."

Still, the lofty agenda of second-wave feminists is not yet complete. Many women with the same training, education, and skills continue to earn less than men for the same work while the availability and cost of child care remain a concern for working families. Small businesses and the service industry, where most women find employment, rarely offer flexible work schedules or health-care benefits. At the opposite end of the occupational spectrum, the "mommy track" and the "glass-ceiling" continue to hamper many women's efforts to compete with men for elite positions in the business and professional worlds.

When political pundits began trumpeting the eminent "death" of feminism as the 1970s came to a close, their error was to mistake the ebbing of the second-wave for its demise. Instead, reaching back to the historic first Woman's Rights Convention held in Seneca Falls in 1848, feminism has exhibited a remarkable staying power in American society. Indeed, today, a third wave of feminists from generations X and Y are in the process of reinvigorating and redefining feminism for themselves. Chiding their second-wave mothers for "putting the concerns of First World white women first and framing them as universal," third-wave feminists envision "a new movement evolving from one in which there is a dialogue *about* feminism and race to a feminist movement whose conversation *is* race, gender, and globalization."

NATIONAL ORGANIZATION FOR WOMEN, *A Bill of Rights for Women* (1968)

At the National Organization for Women's Second National Conference, held in Washington, D.C. on November 18–19, 1967, the membership adopted the following Bill of Rights as its national policy for 1968.

WE DEMAND:

I. That the U.S. Congress immediately pass the Equal Rights Amendment to the Constitution to provide that "Equality of rights under the law shall not be denied or abridged by the United States or by any State on account of sex," and that such then be immediately ratified by the several States.

Source: Robin Morgan, ed., *Sisterhood is Powerful: An Anthology of Writings from the Women's Liberation Movement*, New York: Vintage Books, 1970, pp. 512–514.

II. That equal employment opportunity be guaranteed to all women, as well as men, by insisting that the Equal Employment Opportunity Commission enforces the prohibitions against racial discrimination.
III. That women be protected by law to ensure their rights to return to their jobs within a reasonable time after childbirth without loss of seniority or other accrued benefits, and be paid maternity leave as a form of social security and/or employee benefit.
IV. Immediate revision of tax laws to permit the deduction of home and child-care expenses for working parents.
V. That child-care facilities be established by law on the same basis as parks, libraries, and public schools [.]
VI. That the right of women to be educated to their full potential equally with men be secured by Federal and State legislation [.]
VII. The right of women in poverty to secure job training, housing, and family allowances on equal terms with men, but without prejudice to a parent's right to remain at home to care for his or her children; revision of welfare legislation and poverty programs which deny women dignity, privacy, and self-respect.
VIII. The right of women to control their own reproductive lives by removing from the penal code laws limiting access to contraceptive information and devices, and by repealing penal laws governing abortion.

BLACK WOMEN'S LIBERATION GROUP, MOUNT VERNON, NEW YORK, *Letter to the Brothers* (1968)

The first excerpt is a response to a statement issued in September 1968 by "the brothers" of the Black Unity Party from Peekskill, New York, calling on their "sisters" to reject the use of birth control pills by equating its use to the practice of forced sterilization and genocide. The second excerpt is from Elma Barrera's address at a national abortion conference held in New York in July 1971. Barrera had organized the first National Chicana Conference, which has held in Houston, Texas, two months prior to her New York appearance.

September 11, 1968

Dear Brothers,

Poor black sisters decide for themselves whether to have a baby or not to have a baby. If we take the pills or practice birth control in other ways, it is because of poor black men.

Source: Documents from the Women's Liberation Movement. An Online Archival Collection, Special Collections Library, Duke University, http://scriptorium.lib.duke.edu/wlm/poor/.

. . . Poor black men won't support their families, won't stick by their women—all they think about is the street, dope and liquor . . . a piece of ass, and their cars. That's all that counts. Poor black women would be fools to sit up in a house with a whole lot of children and eventually go crazy. . . . Middle-class white men have always done this to their women—only more sophisticated-like.

So when whitey put out the pill and poor black sisters spread the word, we saw how simple it was not to be a fool for men anymore (politically we would say that men could no longer exploit us sexually or for money and leave the babies for us to bring up). That was the first step in our waking up!

Black women have always been told by black men that we were black, ugly, evil bitches and whores—in other words, we were the real niggers in this society—oppressed by whites, male and female, and the black man, too.

Now a lot of black brothers are into a new bag. Black women are asked by militant black brothers not to practice birth control because it is a form of whitey committing genocide on black people. Well, true enough, but it takes two to practice genocide and black women are able to decide for themselves. . . . For us, birth control is freedom to fight genocide of black women and children.

. . . Poor black women in the U.S. have to fight back out of our own experience of oppression. Having too many babies stops us from supporting our children, teaching them the truth or stopping the brainwashing. . . .

But we don't think you are going to understand us because. . . . you want to use poor black women's children to gain power for yourself. You'll run the black community with your kind of black power—you on top.

Mt. Vernon, NY

Patricia Harden, welfare recipient; Rita Van Lew, welfare recipient; Sue Rudolph, housewife; Catherine Hoyt, grandmother; Joyce Hoyt, domestic; Patricia Robinson, housewife and psychotherapist.

ELMA BARRERA, *Statement* (1971)

I have been told that the Chicana's struggle is not the same as the white woman's struggle. I've been told that the problems are different and that . . . the Chicana's energies are needed in the barrio and that being a feminist and fighting for our rights as women, as human beings, is anti-Chicano and anti-male.

But let me tell you what being a Chicana means in Houston, Texas. It means learning how to best please the men in the Church and the men at home, not in that order. . . .

Source: First printed in *The Militant*, June 4, 1971. "Statement by Elma Barrea," Documents from the Women's Liberation Movement. An Online Archival Collection, Special Collections Library, Duke University, http://scriptorium.lib.duke.edu/wlm/chicana/.

I will take just one minute to read resolutions which came out of the Sex and the Chicana workshop: "Free, legal abortions and birth control for the Chicano community, controlled by Chicanas. As Chicanas we have the right to control our own bodies."

And then out of the workshop on Marriage: Chicana style: "We as *majeres de La Raza* recognize the Catholic Church as an oppressive institution and do hereby resolve to break away and not go to them to bless our union. So be it resolved that the national Chicana conference go on record as supporting free and legal abortions for all women who want or need them."

NATIONAL ORGANIZATION FOR WOMEN, *Lesbian Rights, NOW* (1971)

At its Sixth Annual Conference, held September 3–6, 1971, the National Organization for Women, under the leadership of Wilma Scott Heide, took a healing step when it passed the following historic resolution on lesbianism.

WHEREAS, the first wave of feminist anger in this Country recognized the fundamental issue of women's liberation as "the most sacred right of all—a woman's right to her own person." This is the right that NOW reaffirmed a century later when it took up the banner and dedicated itself to changing those conditions in society. . . . It has stopped short, however of clarifying its position on every woman's right to define—and express—her own sexuality, to choose her own lifestyle. Specifically, NOW has been silent on the issue of lesbianism. . . .

WHEREAS, the lesbian is doubly oppressed, both as a woman and as a homosexual, she must face the injustices and degradation common to all women, plus endure additional social, economic, legal, and psychological abuse. . . .

WHEREAS, this prejudice against the lesbian is manifested in the courts. . . . most divorced women are conceded the right to their children, a lesbian is automatically presumed unfit for motherhood, and can have her children taken from her. . . .

WHEREAS, these are but a few of the laws and practices in our society that reflect irrational assumptions about lesbians. . . . she [is] assumed to be unstable, sick or immoral . . . the lesbian is considered unnatural, incomplete, not quite a woman. . . .

WHEREAS, because she is so oppressed and so exploited, the lesbian has been referred to as "the rage of all women condensed to the point of explosion." This rage found a natural outlet in the women's liberation movement. . . . As a result of their

---

Source: Toni Carabillo, Judith Meuli, and June Bundy Csida, eds., *Feminist Chronicles, 1953–1993*, Los Angeles, CA: Women's Graphics, 1993, pp. 221–223.

activism in the movement, lesbians . . . reached a new consciousness, a new sense of their worth and dignity as women and human beings. . . . but instead of finding support from their sisters, lesbians discovered that NOW and other liberation groups reflected some of the same prejudices and policies of the sexist society they were striving to change. . . .

WHEREAS, lesbians were never excluded from NOW, but we have been evasive or apologetic about their presence within the organization. Afraid of alienating public support, we often treated lesbians as the step-sisters of the movement, allowed to work with us, but then expected to hide in the upstairs closet when company comes. Lesbians are now telling us that this attitude is no longer acceptable. Asking women to disguise their identities so they will not "embarrass" the group is an intolerable form of oppression, like asking black women to join us in white face . . . NOW must reassess the priorities that sacrifice principles to "image". . . .

WHEREAS, some members of NOW object that the lesbian question is too controversial to confront right now, that we will weaken the movement by alienating potential and current members. . . . That same argument . . . was raised . . . when NOW took a bold stand on the controversial abortion issue. The argument did not prove prophetic then, and we do not believe it is valid now. . . .

WHEREAS, another objection to the resolution contends that lesbian oppression is simply not "relevant" to the concerns of NOW. . . . If lesbians are women . . . the conclusion is inescapable: their oppression is not only relevant, it is an integral part of the women's liberation movement. . . .

WHEREAS, we are affected by society's prejudices against the lesbian . . . ; as feminists we are all subject to lesbian-baiting by opponents who use the tactic of labeling us . . . "lesbians," in order to divide and discredit the movement and bring women to heel. Even within NOW, this tactic is employed by some members who conjure up the sexist image of lesbians and shout "lavender menace" at anyone who opposes their views. NOW is inevitably weakened by these attempts to undermine the spirit and efforts of its members; we can no longer afford to ignore the problem. . . .

WHEREAS, the resolution does not mean that we are changing our emphasis and concentrating on specific lesbian issues. . . . We are giving notice that we recognize our sisterhood with all women and that we are fighting for every woman's "sacred right to her own person." As feminists we can do no less;

THEREFORE BE IT RESOLVED: That NOW recognizes the double oppression of women who are lesbians, and

BE IT FURTHER RESOLVED: That a woman's right to express her own person includes the right to define and express her own sexuality and to choose her own lifestyle, and

BE IT FURTHER RESOLVED: That NOW acknowledge the oppression of lesbians as a legitimate concern of feminism.

MARY ANN MANHART, *New York Radical Feminists Rape Conference, Workshop Summary* (1971)

Three months after the New York Radical Feminists' historic speak-out on rape, the group organized a conference on rape which became the blueprint for creating Rape Crisis Centers across the country.

COMMUNITY RESPONSIILITY AND SURVIVAL NOW: FINAL STATEMENT

The community of women must begin assuming responsibility for preventing and prosecuting acts of rape by the FORMATION OF A FEMINIST RAPE PROJECT . . .

1. Establish a central number which women would call in case of rape or attempted rape for information and moral support.
2. Establish a "protection squad" to accompany the victim to the police station—to see that she gets appropriate health and legal services. . . .
3. Organize transportation for women late at night by accompanying women to and from public transportation facilities.
4. Demand preventative and prosecuting actions from the community agencies which already exist. Force the police to be responsive to the problem of rape. . . . Community centers should offer free self-defense courses to women.
5. Educate the community. Hold seminars on rape which provide an opportunity for all members of the community to share experiences of rape. . . . Public hearings should help to raise consciousness of the whole population on the issue of rape.
6. Insist that schools provide psychological and physical self-defense education for all children. Women must begin taking responsibility at all times for the survival and well-being of other women.

NATIONAL ORGANIZATION FOR WOMEN, *Expanded Bill of Rights for the Twenty-first Century* (1989)

The backlash against feminism was in high gear during President Ronald Reagan's two terms in office—1980–1988—and the newly elected president, George Herbert Walker Bush—1988–1992—seemed to promise more of the same when the NOW leadership drafted its "platform" for the twenty-first century. How does this document compare to NOW's first declaration from 31 years ago?

Source: Noreen Connell and Cassandra Wilson, eds., *Rape: The First Sourcebook for Women*, New York: New American Library, 1974, p. 181.

Source: Toni Carabillo, Judith Meuli, and June Bundy Csida, eds., *Feminist Chronicles, 1953–1993*, Los Angeles, CA: Women's Graphics, 1993, p. 247.

Whereas, we are determined that an Equal Rights Amendment that bans sex discrimination in the United States Constitution is ratified; and

Whereas, the Supreme Court has begun to dismantle women's reproductive rights; and

Whereas, the Supreme Court has refused to grant the right to privacy on the basis of sexual preference; and

Whereas, the Supreme Court has dismantled affirmative action plans that fight institutional practices of race and sex discrimination . . .

Therefore be it resolved that it is time for an expanded Bill of Rights for the 21st Century which will ensure that all citizens of the United States enjoy basic, inalienable and indivisible human rights to which must be added:

1. the right to freedom from sex discrimination;
2. the right to freedom from race discrimination;
3. the right of all women to freedom from government interference in abortion, birth control and pregnancy and the right of indigent women to public funds for abortion, birth control and pregnancy services;
4. the right to freedom from discrimination on the basis of sexual orientation;
5. the right to freedom from discrimination based on religion, age, ongoing health condition, or a differently abled situation;
6. a right to a decent standard of living, including adequate food, housing, health care and education;
7. the right to clean air, clean water, safe toxic waste disposal and environmental protection; and
8. the right to be free from violence, including freedom from the threat of nuclear war.

22

Yelling Just as Loudly: Conservative Activism in the Sixties and Seventies

—GREGORY L. SCHNEIDER

Contemporary wisdom about the 1960s tends to categorize the protests and platforms of the decade as radical. The civil rights movement, the anti-war movement, the New Left, feminism, the counterculture—all revealed the fundamental discontent shared by thousands of Americans about Cold War culture, racism, and gender discrimination. Synonymous with our understanding of the decade is the view that young people and a growing majority of older ones as well were disenchanted enough to man the barricades and fight against America's political system.

Yet the total number of Americans who protested—in any form whatsoever—during the decade was remarkably small, even trivial, when compared to the number of people who went about their daily lives or who may have believed that while America had problems it was still a pretty good country. The individuals who Richard Nixon would label the "silent majority" in 1970 was the most prominent demographic group of the era—immortalized by the television character Archie

Bunker. Such people found more to admire in the conservatism of Green Bay Packer head coach Vince Lombardi than in the anti-war protests of Hollywood actress Jane Fonda.

For thousands of conservative Americans, the Sixties were not marked by participation in civil rights marches or by protests outside draft offices or the Pentagon; the heroes of the decade for these people were not Martin Luther King, Malcolm X, or John F. Kennedy. For a growing number of conservative Americans, the decade was marked by their participation in the Barry Goldwater presidential campaign, in their support for the war in Vietnam, and in their defense of traditional American religious values.

Conservatism had developed from a profound discontent with modern American life. In post–World War II America, the conservative movement which took shape was inspired by ideas. Classical liberals—those who believed in the primacy of the free market and individual rights—challenged modern liberalism with their ideas about reduced government spending and how capitalism and political freedom were intertwined. Economists F.A. Hayek, in *The Road to Serfdom* (1944), and Milton Friedman, in *Capitalism and Freedom* (1963), diagnosed the ills of government intervention and how growing government power threatened free markets and free minds.

Traditionalists also diagnosed the ills of modern American life, arguing that men had divorced themselves from religion, moral authority, and from the traditional political and constitutional heritage which had once governed American society. Writers like Richard Weaver and Russell Kirk argued for a return to an ordered society, one founded on the basis of respect for social authority and for God. Other traditionalists also argued on behalf of the veneration of America's Constitution.

By the mid-1950s, conservatism's growth was aided by Cold War hostility toward communism. Conservatives supported investigations into communism at home, with many young conservatives like William F. Buckley, Jr., and Irving Kristol (who would later be called the "Godfather of neoconservatism") endorsing the investigations of Joseph McCarthy (R-Wi.). But conservatives went further than most liberals at the time, demanding victory over communism in the Cold War. Grassroots anti-communists in the 1950s, many of them religious, mobilized in favor of the liberation of communist regimes and in support of efforts to overthrow communist governments and free the "captive nations" from communism.

The tremendous diversity and variety of conservative influence in American life operated as a subculture of the reigning Cold War consensus during the first decade of the post–World War II era. In 1955, Buckley mobilized these various strands of conservatism under the rubric of a weekly journal of opinion, *National Review*. Writing in the first issue that the journal's intention was "to stand athwart history, yelling stop," Buckley and his cohorts helped accelerate the "fusion" of conservative thinking—classical liberalism, traditionalism, and anti-communism—under the banner of a crisply written and well-edited weekly magazine.

The impact of Buckley's venture cannot be overstated. Frank Meyer, a former communist turned conservative, wrote that *National Review* was the conservative movement's "*Iskra*, its spark" referring to the Bolshevik publication. The editors (and readers) saw their mission in revolutionary terms, and while they never quite achieved Buckley's lofty goal of stopping history, they contributed immensely to the political and intellectual awakening crucial to the shaping of modern conservatism in America.

How? *National Review* did not have a large circulation and it was in perpetual financial trouble; within a few years was cut back to a biweekly. But it was read, increasingly by younger conservatives who idolized the young Buckley and who sought nothing less than the establishment of conservative views in the nation's politics. Young conservatives on campus had been organizing since the formation of the Intercollegiate Society of Individualists (ISI) by libertarian Frank Chodorov in 1953. ISI was founded "to uproot the collectivist seed which had been implanted in people's minds over the past generation" and distributed books, journals, and provided connections with other like-minded young people. It deliberately sought "to create a conservative leadership for America."

The person conservative young people most believed could bring about a renewal of conservative principles was Arizona Senator Barry Goldwater. Elected to the Senate in 1952, Goldwater was outspoken in his criticism of federal spending, supported a strong military, was anti-communist and fought to rein in the political power of labor unions. In 1958, following disastrous mid-term elections for Republicans, Goldwater was appointed to head up the Senatorial Campaign committee and gave hundreds of speeches to conservative audiences, writing a syndicated newspaper column in which he articulated his conservative views. A collection of his speeches were printed in a book, *Conscience of a Conservative* (1960), which within a few months had sold over two million copies and became a bible for young conservatives.

Young people in a variety of college conservative clubs and others affiliated with *National Review* established "Goldwater for Vice-President" clubs on campus, hoping to get the senator nominated as Richard Nixon's vice-presidential candidate at the Republican National Convention. It was not to be, however. Nixon chose liberal Republican Henry Cabot Lodge, Jr., as his vice-presidential candidate; when Goldwater spoke before the surly conservative crowd—who booed when Goldwater endorsed the ticket—he scolded them, enjoining them to "grow up conservatives! If we want to take back the historic home of conservatism [the GOP], then let's get to work." Young people proceeded to do just that.

Over the weekend of September 9–11, 1960, a group of young conservative activists, many of whom had participated in the futile effort just 10 days earlier to get Goldwater nominated as the vice-presidential candidate, met to form one of the more important youth groups of the 1960s. Young Americans for Freedom was the result, formed by 90 student members and several "older Americans for Freedom," including William F. Buckley, Jr., Frank Meyer, William Rusher, and Marvin Liebman. The Sharon Statement, a one-page statement named after the Sharon, Connecticut, the place where the meeting occurred, was agreed to, elucidating the basic principles of a growing conservative movement in America.

Drafted en route to the conference by *Indianapolis News* editor M. Stanton Evans—himself only 27 years old—the Sharon Statement emphasized a fusion of conservative beliefs and ideas. Among the statement's clearest principles were a belief "that foremost among the transcendent values is the individual's use of his God-given free will, whence derives his right to be free from the restrictions of arbitrary force." The decision to include "God" in the statement brought about the most controversy with a 44–40 vote agreeing to the inclusion. For free-market conservatives, there were principles which argued "that the market economy . . . is the single economic system compatible with the requirements of personal freedom and constitutional government." Finally, there was the strongly held belief "that the forces of international Communism are, at present, the single greatest threat to [American] liberties; [and] that the United States should stress victory over, rather than coexistence with, this menace."

Young Americans for Freedom experienced factional problems over the course of its history, but by 1962 YAF was the key grassroots organization behind the candidacy of Goldwater for president. A committee of GOP operatives and conservatives had proceeded to draft the unwilling senator to run for president in 1964, and YAF played a strong role in the process, hosting Goldwater in a Victory over Communism rally on March 7, 1962, in New York's Madison Square Garden which drew 18,000 people and drew front-page coverage in the *New York Times.*

Goldwater was finally persuaded to run by all the activities on his behalf. But after the death of Kennedy, he understood that he had little chance to win. Goldwater was popular with the grassroots in the GOP, especially in the West and South. He won the Republican nomination, defeating challenges from liberal Republicans Nelson Rockefeller and William Scranton. But he chose to isolate the liberal wing by giving a fiery acceptance speech, telling the assembled delegates "extremism in the form of liberty is no vice, moderation in the pursuit of justice is not virtue." "My God," one delegate exclaimed to a journalist, "they're going to let him run as Barry!"

He did run as Barry, refusing to play the game of modern electoral campaigning and glad handling. He told a crowd of senior citizens he favored privatizing Social Security; he told people in Tennessee he favored privatizing the Tennessee Valley Authority, the federal power plants; he bypassed waiting crowds to get to his limousine and generally was an indifferent campaigner, blunt, ornery, irascible, and stubborn. He faced even stiffer opposition in Lyndon Johnson, who had signed the Civil Rights Act into law that summer, begun the precipitous entry into Vietnam in August (which Goldwater voted for), and had the support of the majority of Americans in what some scholars are now labeling "the last liberal election." He destroyed Goldwater that fall, winning a huge electoral landslide and legitimizing his expansion of governmental programs and powers known as the Great Society.

But conservatism survived and even grew after Goldwater's defeat. Two years later, Ronald Reagan was elected Governor of California and Republicans made significant gains in Congress as the Democrats fractured over Vietnam abroad and race rioting at home. YAF members battled the New Left on campus, fought for a victory strategy in Vietnam, protested communism, and supported conservative politicians. YAF members would mimic the tactics of the Left. Where New Left groups would increasingly occupy and shut down campus, YAF members would occupy anti-war organization offices and hang South Vietnamese flags on the walls before leaving after a short time to signify their belief in private property rights. At the 1965 Indianapolis 500 auto race, YAF hired an airplane to fly over the track pulling a banner "The Vietcong Ride on Firestone" protesting the tiremaker's decision to build a synthetic rubber plant in communist Romania.

But YAF was splintered by the war as well. Increasingly libertarian students, many of whom opposed the war, opposed the draft of young men into the military and the legalization of drugs began to organize within YAF. At the University of Kansas, the president of YAF (a libertarian) was also president of the New Left group Students for a Democratic Society. Economist Murray Rothbard, historian Leonard Liggio, and Karl Hess, former speechwriter for Goldwater, began a publication *Left/Right* which sought an alliance between the two groups and attacked America for its imperialism in Vietnam.

At the 1969 YAF national convention in St. Louis, libertarians attempted to push through anti-draft platforms. One brave libertarian lit his draft card on fire before a group of conservative tackled him. A number of other libertarians left the convention, meeting Hess under the Gateway Arch to announce their opposition to YAF's platform to support the draft and the war in Vietnam. The split was more than symbolic. Libertarian students left YAF and began their own organization, Students for Individual Liberty (SIL). Within a few years, libertarians had founded their own political party, journals, and a think tank (The CATO Institute). It was clear that fusionist conservatism had its limits.

It split even further during the presidency of Richard Nixon. On many issues Nixon was conservative, but he angered conservatives when he traveled to communist China and began the process of normalizing relations with Mao Zedong. He also presided over an expansion of government and supported regulation of business. Nixon was not free market-oriented, endorsing wage and price controls to handle inflation and saying at one press conference, "we're all Keynesians now" much to the horror of free-market economists. In 1972, conservatives affiliated with *National Review* supported the candidacy of Rep. John Ashbrook in the New Hampshire primary to challenge Nixon; he failed to garner much support. Nixon was easily re-elected in 1972, before his own political shenanigans and dirty tricks caught up with his administration, forcing him to resign in August 1974.

Other issues mobilized conservatives in the 1970s. The Supreme Court had become active under the leadership of Chief Justice Earl Warren and conservatives had opposed this drift. But when it began ruling on issues once considered outside the realm of judicial interference, such as sexual relations, prayer in school, and abortion rights, conservatives began to mobilize. The 1973 *Roe vs. Wade* decision legalizing abortion helped propel Catholic traditionalists and evangelical Protestants into politics. So did the Equal Rights Amendment (ERA), supported by the GOP since the 1920s. When feminists reintroduced the ERA in Congress, it easily passed and within a few months was three states short of ratification. Then Phyllis Schlafly entered the debate.

Schlafly was a longtime anti-communist activist and conservative who wrote a best-selling book about Goldwater, *A Choice, Not an Echo,* which sold over three million copies. Schlafly was Catholic and deeply concerned about the Soviet military threat (she co-wrote three books on defense issues) and the cultural change which the counterculture produced in America. In 1972, she published an essay on the ERA, and encouraged by supporters, she started an organization, STOP-ERA to prevent the ratification of the amendment. In alliance with church-going traditionalist women, Schlafly, a very effective speaker and debater (antagonizing feminists, she would lead off most public appearances saying, "I want to thank my husband for allowing me to be here tonight") mobilized thousands of women and men to petition and protest against the ERA. It was defeated in 1981 when the state of Illinois refused to ratify the amendment.

The New Right of the 1970s mobilized around the social issues such as abortion. Linked to the 1960s Right and to those in conservative organizations like YAF, individuals like Paul Weyrich, Richard Viguerie, Howard Phillips, and Morton Blackwell, paved the way for conservative political success. They helped form think tanks, such as the Heritage Foundation, recruited conservatives to run for office, used specific issues to galvanize support (such as opposition to the Panama Canal Treaty giving the American-built canal back to Panama), and supported candidates like Ronald Reagan for the presidency.

They also established links between grassroots activists, Washington politicians, and churches throughout the country mobilized to fight the culture wars. Weyrich played a crucial role in getting Lynchburg, Virginia minister Jerry Falwell, who once criticized activist ministers like Martin Luther King, Jr., for paying more attention to politics than to prayer, to use his significant influence in evangelical and fundamentalist churches to fight on behalf of political issues such as abortion. In 1979, he helped form the Moral Majority which would become a significant force in the 1980 election and beyond. Other televangelists like Pat Robertson, son of a Virginia senator whose *700 Club* television show reached millions, also used his influence on behalf of conservative causes. By the end of the Reagan administration, Robertson would surpass Falwell in influence and ambition, running for the GOP nomination himself and mobilizing Christians to become more active in politics.

The end result of conservative organizing during the 1970s was the election of Ronald Reagan to the presidency in 1980. Conservatives united under the Reagan banner. Reagan benefited enormously from the decline of the Democratic Party and from the weaknesses of the presidency of Jimmy Carter. A poor economy, Soviet expansion in Afghanistan and Africa, the Iranian hostage crisis, and the general post-Vietnam "malaise" in the nation helped the patriotic, optimistic Reagan to tap into a disenchanted electorate hungry for change.

Yet equally important was the conservative movement in building up the strength and influence it had in American politics. Since the mid-1950s, conservatives had been building institutions, mobilizing like-minded individuals, and gaining political support for their ideas. Through a decade marked more for its radicalism, conservatives fought for their beliefs and while they did not win every battle, they wound up winning—however unlikely this would have seemed in 1968—the political war the Sixties helped produce.

WILLIAM F. BUCKLEY, JR. *National Review: Credenda and Statement of Principles* (1955)

The founding of the magazine *National Review* by William F. Buckley, Jr., helped develop the modern conservative movement. The fusion of diverse and often contradictory beliefs under the banner of a crisply edited and witty magazine contributed to the growth of conservative ideas.

. . . The launching of a conservative weekly journal of opinion in a country widely assumed to be a bastion of conservatism at first glance looks like a work of supererogation, rather like publishing a royalist weekly within the walls of Buckingham Palace. It is not that of course; if *National Review* is superfluous, it is so for very different reasons: It stands athwart history, yelling Stop, at a time when no one is inclined to do so, or to have much patience with those who so urge it.

National Review is out of place, in the sense that the United Nations and the League of Women Voters and the *New York Times* and Henry Steele Commager are *in* place. It is out of place because, in its maturity, literate America rejected conservatism in favor of radical social experimentation. Instead of covetously consolidating its premises, the United States seems tormented by its tradition of fixed postulates having to do with the meaning of existence, with the relationship of the state to the individual, of the individual to his neighbor, so clearly enunciated in the enabling documents of our Republic.

. . . One must recently have lived on or close to a college campus to have a vivid intimation of what has happened. It is there that we see how a number of energetic social innovators, plugging their grand designs, succeeded over the years in capturing the liberal intellectual imagination. And since ideas rule the world, the ideologues, having won over the intellectual class, simply walked in and started to run things.

Run just about *everything*. There never was an age of conformity quite like this one, or a camaraderie quite like the Liberals'. Drop a little itching powder in Jimmy Wechaler's bath and before he has scratched himself for the third time, Arthur Schlesinger will have denounced you in a dozen books and speeches, Archibald MacLeish will have written ten heroic cantos about our age of terror, *Harper's* will have published them, and everyone in sight will have been nominated for a Freedom Award. Conservatives in this country—at least those who have not made their peace with the New Deal, and there is serious question whether there are others—are non-licensed nonconformists; and this is dangerous business in a Liberal world, as every editor of this magazine can readily show by pointing to his scars. Radical conservatives in this country have an interesting time of it, for when

---

Source: Gregory Schneider, ed., *Conservatism in America since 1930*, New York: New York University Press, June 2003.

they are not being suppressed or mutilated by the Liberals, they are being ignored or humiliated by a great many of those of the well-fed Right . . .

There are, thank Heaven, the exceptions. There are those of generous impulse and a sincere desire to encourage a responsible dissent from the Liberal orthodoxy. . . .

We begin publishing, then, with a considerable stock of experience with the irresponsible Right, and a despair of the intransigence of the Liberals, who run this country; and all this in a world dominated by the jubilant single-mindedness of the practicing Communist, with his inside track to History. All this would not appear to augur well for *National Review.* Yet we start with a considerable—and considered—optimism.

After all, we crashed through. More than one hundred and twenty investors made this magazine possible, and over fifty men and women of small means, invested less than one thousand dollars apiece in it. Two men and one woman, all three with overwhelming personal and public commitments, worked round the clock to make publication possible. A score of professional writers pledged their devoted attention to its needs, and hundreds of thoughtful men and women gave evidence that the appearance of such a journal as we have in mind would profoundly affect their lives.

. . . We have nothing to offer but the best that is in us. That, a thousand Liberals who read this sentiment will say with relief, is clearly not enough! It isn't enough. But it is at this point that we steal the march. . . .

Among our convictions:

a. It is the job of centralized government (in peace-time) to protect its citizens' lives, liberty, and property. All other activities of government tend to diminish freedom and hamper progress. The growth of government—the dominant social feature of this century—must be fought relentlessly. . . .
b. The profound crisis of our era is, in essence, the conflict between the Social Engineers, who seek to adjust mankind to conform with scientific utopias, and the disciples of Truth, who defend the organic moral order. . . . On this point we are, without reservations, on the conservative side.
c. The century's most blatant force of satanic utopianism is communism. We consider "coexistence" with communism neither desirable not possible, nor honorable; we find ourselves irrevocably at war with communism and shall oppose any substitute for victory.
d. The largest cultural menace in America is the conformity of the intellectual cliques which, in education as well as the arts, are out to impose upon the nation their modish fads and fallacies, and have nearly succeeded in doing so. . . .
e. The most alarming single danger to the American political system lies in the fact that an identifiable team of Fabian operators is bent on controlling both our major political parties . . . . and we shall advocate the restoration of the two-party system at all costs.
f. The competitive price system is indispensable to liberty and material progress. It is threatened not only by the growth of Big Brother government, but by the pressure of monopolies—including union monopolies. . . . *National Review* will explore and oppose the inroads upon the market economy caused by monopolies in general, and politically oriented unionism in particular; and it will tell the violated businessman's side of the story.

g. No superstition has more effectively bewitched America's Liberal elite than the fashionable concepts of world government, the United Nations, internationalism, international atomic pools, etc. . . . It would make greater sense to grant independence to each of our 48 states than to surrender U.S. sovereignty to a world organization.

YOUNG AMERICANS FOR FREEDOM, *The Sharon Statement* (1960)

The Sharon Statement, adopted by the Young Americans for Freedom in Conference at Sharon, Connecticut, is the founding document of Young Americans for Freedom, the main conservative student group in America during the 1960s.

In this time of moral and political crisis, it is the responsibility of the youth of America to affirm certain eternal truths.

We, as young conservatives, believe;

That foremost among the transcendent values is the individual's use of his God-given free will, whence derives his right to be free from the restrictions of arbitrary force;

That liberty is indivisible, and that political freedom cannot long exist without economic freedom;

That the purposes of government are to protect these freedoms through the preservation of internal order, the provision of national defense, and the administration of justice;

That when government ventures beyond these rightful functions, it accumulates power which tends to diminish order and liberty;

That the Constitution of the United States is the best arrangement yet devised for empowering government to fulfill its proper role, while restraining it from the concentration and abuse of power;

That the genius of the Constitution—the division of powers—is summed up in the clause which reserves primacy to the several states, or to the people, in those spheres not specifically delegated to the Federal Government;

That the market economy, allocating resources by the free play of supply and demand, is the single economic system compatible with the requirements of personal freedom and constitutional government, and that it is at the same time the most productive supplier of human needs;

That when government interferes with the work of the market economy, it tends to reduce the moral and physical strength of the nation; that when it takes from one

---

Source: Gregory Schneider, ed., *Conservatism in America since 1930*, New York: New York University Press, June 2003.

man to bestow on another, it diminishes the incentive of the first, the integrity of the second, and the moral autonomy of both;

That we will be free only so long as the national sovereignty of the United States is secure; that history shows periods of freedom are rare, and can exist only when free citizens concertedly defend their rights against all enemies;

That the forces of international Communism are, at present, the greatest single threat to these liberties;

That the United States should stress victory over, rather than coexistence with, this menace; and

That American foreign policy must be judged by this criterion; does it serve the just interests of the United States?

YOUNG AMERICANS FOR FREEDOM, *New Left Violence* (1969)

New Left violence is a statement of condemnation by the Young Americans for Freedom dating from 1970. It chronicles young conservative views of the New Left on campus and discusses the violent history of the late New Left groups.

America is experiencing a nightmarish wave of New Left violence. The arsonist's firebomb and the assassin's bullet have become commonplace tools of radical 'protest' and the violence is taking its toll of human lives. Among the victims are Judge Harold Haley, Patrolman Larry Minard (of Omaha, Nebraska), Robert Fassnacht (graduate student at the University of Wisconsin) and a Boston policeman, Walter Schroeder. The accused murderers have a variety of New Left affiliations, including SDS, the Black Panthers, the Communist Party, the Weathermen, and other marxist-leninist organizations.

In the academic year 1969–1970, on various college campuses, there were 246 acts of arson, 14 bombed buildings, and the destruction of property valued at \$9.5 million. Add to this the fact that from July to October 1970 at least 26 policemen were killed by New Left guerrillas in unprovoked attacks. Recall Weatherwoman Bernadine Dohrn's promise of a new terrorist offensive that "Will spread from Santa Barbara to Boston. . . ."—the future seems to hold some frightening prospects.

By now most people are aware of the dangerous propensities of the New Left. But is it sufficient merely to condemn their acts of terror? Is the violence just a sign of their frustration (frustration at their inability to convince a significant number of Americans of the justice of their cause) or is it a physical manifestation of their philosophy.

The philosophy of the New Left, whether it is called socialism, Marxism, communism or fascism, is basically collectivist . . .

Source: The New Left Violence, Jameson Campaign Papers, Ottawa, Illinois.

If you want an idea of just how anti-individual freedom the New Left is, consider those countries which it lauds as ideal societies. These are invariably Cuba, North Vietnam, North Korea, Communist China, and the Soviet Union; bloody totalitarian dictatorships. . . .

The New Leftists show their contempt for individual freedom not only in their support of communist slave states, but in their actions in this country as well. They show their contempt for property rights by burning banks, by looting, by denying non-radical students the education they've paid for. They show their disdain for freedom of speech by shouting down opposition speakers, by driving military and industrial recruiters from the campus. . . . Only an individualist will consistently oppose violence and coercion, which are the inevitable result of collectivism. Reject the collectivism of the New Left and the Welfare State of Liberalism, for the individualism of Young Americans for Freedom.

RANDALL CORNELL TEAGUE, *Statement on the Draft* (1969)

Statement on the Draft is the testimony of Randall Cornell Teague before Congress giving YAF's view on a volunteer military.

Following is the transcript of remarks presented on September 29, 1969, to the President's Commission on an All Volunteer Armed Forces by Randal Cornell Teague, Executive Director of Young Americans for Freedom, Inc.:

YOUNG AMERICANS FOR FREEDOM (YAF) is in favor of the all-volunteer military as a replacement of conscription. Yet, unlike many of those who advocate a volunteer military, YAF is also in favor of an adequate military and defense system for the United States and for the free world . . .

What we are opposed to is the involuntary servitude known as conscription. Conscription is a system which deprives the individual—the cornerstone of liberty and, therefore, of free government—of his freedom of choice, and it puts him squarely into a system of involuntary servitude.

. . . YAF's activities in support of the volunteer military has become one of our six major programs. These programs are known, collectively, as Young America's Freedom Offensive. Specifically, the Voluntary Military Legislative Action Program is designed to provide the advocate of a volunteer military system—as a replacement for conscription—with the necessary information and materials with which to launch and carry through with successful state and local efforts to educate draft age and older Americans, and their Representatives in Congress, on the case for a voluntary military system.

Source: The Statement on the Draft, *New Guard*, copyright YAF.

Towards this end, YAF has instituted the following activities, to date:

— Distribution of the Voluntary Military Legislative Action Kit to youth leaders and to Members of Congress.
— The use of YAF's volunteer military issues papers and wall posters to generate interest on campuses.
— Participation in teach-ins and seminars on the draft, to express our viewpoint.
— Circulation of petitions to be sent to Members of Congress and the appropriate committees.
— Having major speakers appear on the high school and college campuses in support of the volunteer military.
— Full-page advertisements on YAF's volunteer military posture in college and high school newspapers.
— Several statewide conferences on the volunteer military.
— Appearances on local television and radio programs in general support of an all-volunteer military.
— Getting college, civic, business, political, labor, religious, and educational organizations to pass resolutions in support of the concept.

Our activities in this area are continually expanding.

PHYLLIS SCHLAFLY, *What's Wrong with Equal Rights for Women?* (1972)

What's Wrong with Equal Rights for Women was the first salvo fired by Phyllis Schlafly against the feminist demand for the ERA. This led to the formation of STOP-ERA which successfully lobbied against the ERA in the 1970s.

Of all the classes of people who ever lived, the American woman is the most privileged. We have the most rights and rewards, and the fewest duties. Our unique status is the result of a fortunate combination of circumstances.

We have the immense good fortune to live in a civilization that respects the family as the basic unit of society. This respect is part and parcel of our laws and customs. It is based on the fact of life—which no legislation or agitation can erase—that women have babies and men don't.

If you don't like this fundamental difference, you will have to take up your complaint with God because He created us this way. The fact that women, not men,

Source: Phyllis Schlafly, *Feminist Fantasies,* Spence Publishing, 2003.

have babies is not the fault of selfish and domineering men, or the establishment, or any clique of conspirators who want to oppress women. It's simply the way God made us.

Our Judeo-Christian civilization has developed the law and custom that, since women bear the physical consequences of the sex act, men must be required to pay in other ways. These laws and customs decree that a man must carry his share by physical protection and financial support of his children and of the woman who bears his children, and also by a code of behavior that benefits and protects both the woman and the children.

This is accomplished by the institution of the family. Our respect for the family as the basic unit of society, which is ingrained in the laws and customs of our Judeo-Christian civilization, is the greatest single achievement in the history of women's rights. It assures a woman the most precious and important right of all—the right to keep her own baby and to be supported and protected in the enjoyment of watching her baby grow and develop.

The institution of the family is advantageous for women for many reasons. After all, what do we want out of life? To love and be loved? Mankind has not discovered a better nest for a lifetime of reciprocal love. A sense of achievement? A man may search thirty to forty years for accomplishment in his profession. A woman can enjoy real achievement when she is young by having a baby. She can have the satisfaction of doing a job well—and being recognized for it.

Do we want financial security? We are fortunate to have the great legacy of Moses, the Ten Commandments, especially "Honor thy father and thy mother that thy days may be long upon the land." Children are a woman's best social security—her best guarantee of social benefits such as old age pension, unemployment compensation, worker's compensation, and sick leave. The family gives a woman the physical, financial, and emotional security of the home for all her life.

The second reason why American women are a privileged group is that we are the beneficiaries of a tradition of special respect for women that dates from the Christian Age of Chivalry. The honor and respect paid to Mary, the Mother of Christ, resulted in all women, in effect, being put on a pedestal. . . . We were lucky enough to inherit the traditions of the Age of Chivalry in America, a man's first significant purchase (after a car) is a diamond for his bride, and the largest financial investment of his life is a home for her to live in. American husbands work hours of overtime to keep their wives in fashion, and to pay premiums on their life insurance policies to provide for their widow's comfort (benefits in which the husband can never share). . . .

In Illinois, as a result of agitation by "equal rights" fanatics, the real-estate dower laws were repealed as of January 1, 1972. This means that in Illinois a husband can now sell the family home, spend the money on his girlfriend or gamble it away, and his faithful wife of thirty years cannot stop him. "Equal rights" fanatics have also deprived women in Illinois and in some other states of most of their basic common-law rights to recover damages for breach of promise to marry, seduction, criminal conversation, and alienation of affections. . . .

The great heroes of women's liberation are not the straggly haired women on television talk shows and picket lines, but Thomas Edison, who brought the miracle of electricity to our homes to give light and to run all those labor-saving devices—the equivalent, perhaps, of a half-dozen household servants. Or Elias Howe who gave us the sewing machine that resulted in such an abundance of readymade clothing. Or Clarence Birdseye, who invented the process for freezing foods. Or Henry Ford, who mass produced the automobile so it is within the price range of almost every American.

. . . Household duties have been reduced to only a few hours a day, leaving the American woman with plenty of time to moonlight. She can take a full- or part-time paying job, or she can indulge to her heart's content in a tremendous selection of interesting educational or cultural or homemaking or volunteer activities. It's time to set the record straight. The claim that American women are downtrodden and unfairly treated is the fraud of the century. The truth is that American women never had it so good. Why should we lower ourselves to "equal rights" when we already have the status of special privilege?

JERRY FALWELL AND THE MORAL MAJORITY, *The Moral Majority and Its Goals* (1979)

The Moral Majority and Its Goals contains the basic beliefs and goals of the Moral Majority founded in 1979 by fundamentalist minister Jerry Falwell.

Alarmed by what they considered to be the spiritual and social decay of the nation, the Reverend Jerry Falwell and others organized the Moral Majority. Its membership quickly ballooned, the result of a deep-seated belief that moral decline was both widespread and pernicious. More than 20 years later, most of the issues that the Moral Majority confronted remain controversial and unresolved.

Organizing the Moral Majority

Facing the desperate need in the impending crisis of the hour, several concerned pastors began to urge me to put together a political organization that could provide a vehicle to address these crucial issues. . . . Together we formulated the Moral Majority, Inc. Today Moral Majority, Inc., is made up of millions of Americans, including 72,000 ministers, priests, and rabbis, who are deeply concerned about the moral decline of our nation, the traditional family, and the moral values on which our nation was built. We are Catholics, Jews, Protestants, Mormons, Fundamentalists—blacks and whites—farmers, housewives, businessmen, and

Source: The Moral Majority, Robert Muccigrosso, *Basic History of American Conservatism*, Florida: Krieger Publishers, 2001. Also: *The Fundamentalist Phenomenon: The Resurgence of Conservative Christianity*, ed. Jerry Falwell with Ed Dolson and Ed Hendson, New York: Doubleday, 1981, pp. 188–190. Reprinted with the kind permission of the author.

businesswomen. We are Americans from all walks of life united by one central concern: to serve as a special-interest group providing a voice for a return to moral sanity in these United States of America. Moral Majority is a political organization and is not based on theological considerations. . . . We are opposed to abortion, pornography, the drug epidemic, the breakdown of the traditional family, the establishment of homosexuality as an accepted alternate life-style, and other moral cancers that are causing our society to rot from within Here is how Moral Majority stands on today's vital issues:

1. *We believe in the separation of Church and State.* Moral Majority, Inc., is a political organization providing a platform for religious and nonreligious Americans who share moral values to address their concerns in these areas. Members of Moral Majority, Inc., have no common theological premise. We are Americans who are proud to be conservative in our approach to moral, social, and political concerns.
2. *We are pro-life.* We believe that life begins at fertilization. We strongly oppose the massive "biological holocaust" that is resulting in the abortion of one and a half million babies each year in America. We believe that unborn babies have the right to life as much as babies that have been born. We are providing a voice and a defense for the human and civil rights of millions of unborn babies.
3. *We are pro-traditional family.* We believe that the only acceptable family form begins with a legal marriage of a man and a woman. We feel that homosexual marriages and common-law marriages should not be accepted as traditional families. We oppose legislation that favors these kinds of "diverse family forms," thereby penalizing the traditional family. We do not oppose civil rights for homosexuals. We do oppose "special rights" for homosexuals who have chosen a perverted life-style rather than a traditional life-style.
4. *We oppose the illegal drug traffic in America.* The youth in America are presently in the midst of a drug epidemic. Through education, legislation, and other means we want to do our part to save our young people from death on the installment plan through illegal drug addiction.
5. *We oppose pornography.* While we do not advocate censorship, we do believe that education and legislation can help stem the tide of pornography and obscenity that is poisoning the American spirit today. Economic boycotts are a proper way in America's free-enterprise system to help persuade the media to move back to a sensible and reasonable moral stand. We most certainly believe in the First Amendment for everyone. We are not willing to sit back, however, while many television programs create cesspools of obscenity and vulgarity in our nation's living rooms.
6. *We support the state of Israel and Jewish people everywhere.* It is impossible to separate the state of Israel from the Jewish family internationally. Many Moral Majority members, because of their theological convictions, are committed to the Jewish people. Others stand upon the human and civil rights of all persons as a premise for support of the state of Israel. Support of Israel is one of the essential commitments of Moral Majority. No anti-Semitic influence is allowed in Moral Majority, Inc.

7. *We believe that a strong national defense is the best deterrent to war.* We believe that liberty is the basic moral issue of all moral issues. The only way America can remain free is to remain strong. Therefore we support the efforts of our present administration to regain our position of military preparedness—with a sincere hope that we will never need to use any of our weapons against any people anywhere.
8. *We support equal rights for women.* We agree with President Reagan's commitment to help every governor and every state legislature to move quickly to ensure that during the 1980s every American woman will earn as much money and enjoy the same opportunities for advancement as her male counterpart in the same vocation.
9. *We believe ERA is the wrong vehicle to obtain equal rights for women.* We feel that the ambiguous and simplistic language of the Amendment could lead to court interpretations that might put women in combat, sanction homosexual marriage, and financially penalize widows and deserted wives.
10. *We encourage our Moral Majority state organizations to be autonomous and indigenous.* Moral Majority state organizations may, from time to time, hold positions that are not held by the Moral Majority, Inc., national organization.

CONTRIBUTORS

Kathleen C. Berkeley is Associate Dean in the College of Arts and Sciences and Professor of History at UNC Wilmington. Her research and teaching interests focus on issues of race, class, gender, and sexuality in nineteenth- and twentieth-century America. She is the author of several articles and two books, *The Women's Liberation Movement in America* (1999), which won a Choice award and *"Like a Plague of Locusts": From an Antebellum Town to a New South City, Memphis, Tennessee, 1850–1880.* A founding member of the Women's Studies Minor and the Women's Resource Center, she has twice served as interim director of the Women's Resources Center. Berkeley has also served on the board of the Domestic Violence Shelter and Services of the Lower Cape Fear and is currently serving on the board of the North Carolina Humanities Council.

Jane Dailey is Associate Professor of History at the University of Chicago. She is a historian of the nineteenth- and twentieth-century United States, with an emphasis on the American South. Dailey's first book, *Before Jim Crow: The Politics of Race in Postemancipation Virginia* (2000), analyzed the conditions that facilitated and, ultimately, undid interracial politics in the postwar South. An edited collection, *Jumpin' Jim Crow: Southern Politics from Civil War to Civil Rights* (2000), continued the theme of African American resistance to white domination from Reconstruction through the 1950s. Her current project is a book on race, sex, and the civil rights movement from emancipation to the present.

Matt Garcia is Associate Professor of American Civilization, Ethnic Studies, and History at Brown University. His book, *A World of Its Own: Race, Labor and Citrus in the Making of Greater Los Angeles, 1900–1970* (2001) was named co-winner for the best book in oral history by the Oral History Association in 2003. His current book project, *Nature's Candy: Labor, Protest and Grapes in the California-Mexican Borderlands,* explores grape cultivation and the formation of the Farmworkers Movement during the second half of the twentieth century.

Kenneth J. Heineman is Professor and Chair of the Department of History, Angelo State University and the author of four books. These include *Campus Wars: The Peace Movement at American State Universities in the Vietnam Era, God Is a Conservative: Religion, Politics, and Morality in Contemporary America, A Catholic*

New Deal: Religion and Reform in Depression Pittsburgh, and *Put Your Bodies Upon The Wheels: Student Revolt in the 1960s.* In 2004, Heineman received the Ohio University Regional Higher Education Outstanding Professor Award and was honored by the Ohio House of Representatives for his contributions to teaching, community service, and scholarship. In addition, he served as an evaluator for the U.S. Department of Education's Teaching American History Grant program.

Troy Johnson is Professor of American Indian Studies and U.S. History at California State University, Long Beach. He is the author, editor, or associate editor of 15 books and numerous scholarly journal articles. His publications include *Distinguished Native American Spiritual Practitioners and Healers, The Occupation of Alcatraz Island, Indian Self-determination and the Rise of Indian Activism*, and *American Indian Activism, Alcatraz to the Longest* Walk. His areas of expertise also include American Indian activism, Federal Indian Law, Indian Child Welfare, and Indian Youth Suicide. Dr. Johnson's historical documentary of the American Indian Occupation of Alcatraz Island 1969–1971 was awarded first place honors at the 26th American Indian Film Festival and was screened at the Sundance Film Festival in January 2001.

Felicia Kornbluh is the Director of the Women's and Gender Studies Program and Associate Professor of History at the University of Vermont. She is the author of *The Battle for Welfare Rights: Politics and Poverty in Modern America* (2007). She teaches history at Duke University, with an emphasis on the history of the 1960s and the 1980s, public policy history, women's history, and the history of social welfare. She has written for many publications, including *The Nation*, *Feminist Studies*, *The Women's Review of Books*, *Los Angeles Times* op-ed page, and *Journal of American History.* She co-founded Historians for Social Justice and is a longtime member of the feminist advocacy group the Women's Committee of 100. Kornbluh holds a Ph.D. in history from Princeton University and a B.A. from Harvard-Radcliffe.

Paul K. Longmore is Professor of History at San Francisco State University, specializes in Early American history and the history of people with disabilities. He is the author of *The Invention of George Washington* (1988; 1998) and *Why I Burned My Book and Other Essays on Disability* (2003). With Lauri Umansky, he co-edited *The New Disability History: American Perspectives* (2001), an anthology of essays, and is co-editing a book series, *The History of Disability.*

Daryl J. Maeda is Assistant Professor of Ethnic Studies at the University of Colorado at Boulder. He is currently completing a book, *Chains of Babylon: The Rise of Asian America* (forthcoming) that examines the formation of Asian American racial identity from the 1960s to the 1970s. His next project comparatively examines the emergence of radical social movements by people of color in the United States during the 1960s and 1970s.

Joseph A. McCartin is Associate Professor of History at Georgetown University. He is the author of *Labor's Great War: The Struggle for Industrial Democracy and the Origins of Modern American Labor Relations, 1912–1921* (1997). McCartin also edited a new edition of Melvyn Dubofsky's *We Shall Be All: A History of the*

Industrial Workers of the World, and co-edited *American Labor: A Documentary History* (2004) with Melvyn Dubofsky. In 2006, McCartin co-edited *Americanism: New Perspectives on the History of an Ideal* with Michael Kazin (2006).

Heather J. McCarty is an Associate Professor of History at Ohlone College, and specializes in twentieth century United States history with an emphasis on issues of race, class, and gender. She is the co-founder and co-director of the Center for Civic and Community Engagement. Her current book project, *From Con Boss to Gang Lord: Prisoner Social Relations in California Prisons*, explores the intersection of race, state, and punishment from 1944 to 1984.

Angela G. Mertig has a Ph.D. in Sociology (1995) and is currently Associate Professor of Sociology in the Department of Sociology and Anthropology at Middle Tennessee State University in Murfreesboro, Tennessee. She specializes in studying the environmental movement and public opinion, attitudes and behavior regarding the natural environment, wildlife, land use, and related issues. Mertig's scholarly publications can be found in numerous journals including *Applied Environmental Education and Communication, Population and Environment*, and *Social Science Quarterly.*

Rusty Monhollon is Associate Professor of History and Director for the Masters of Arts in Humanities program at Hood College in Frederick, Maryland, where he teaches courses in U.S., African American, and women's history. His book *"This is America?" The Sixties in Lawrence, Kansas* (2002), received the Edward H. Tihen Publication Award from the Kansas State Historical Association.

Susan J. Pearson is Assistant Professor of History at Northwestern University. She is currently completing a book, entitled *Rights of the Defenseless: Animals, Children, and Sentimental Liberalism in Nineteenth-Century America*, which examines the links between animal and child-protection organizations. She has also published articles about changes in the concept of cruelty and the problem of writing animals into history.

Wendell Pritchett is Professor of Law at the University of Pennsylvania, where he teaches property, land use and urban policy. His new book, *Robert Clifton Weaver and the American City: The Life and Times of an Urban Reformer* (University of Chicago Press, 2008) examines the life of the first African-American cabinet secretary and the first head of the Department of Housing and Urban Development. His first book, *Brownsville, Brooklyn: Jews, Blacks and the Changing Face of the Ghetto* (University of Chicago Press 2002), explores race relations and public policy in 20th century Brooklyn.

James Ralph is Professor of History at Middlebury College. Ralph's research interests include postwar America, race relations in modern America, the American civil rights movement, and modern urban America. He is the author of *Northern Protest: Martin Luther King, Jr., Chicago, and the Civil Rights Movement*. He is currently at work on a study of the pursuit of racial equality in Peoria, Illinois.

Craig A. Rimmerman is Professor of Public Policy Studies and Political Science and currently holds the Joseph P. DiGangi Endowed Chair in the Social Sciences at Hobart and William Smith Colleges. Rimmerman is the author, editor, and co-editor of a number of books, including *The Politics of Gay Rights* (co-edited with Kenneth Wald and Clyde Wilcox, 2000), *From Identity to Politics: The Lesbian and Gay Movements in the United States* (2002), and *The New Citizenship: Unconventional Politics, Activism and Service* (3rd edition, 2005). He is also a former American Political Science Association Congressional Fellow. Rimmerman is currently working on a book that examines the contemporary lesbian and gay movements' political organizing strategy in light of three key policy areas: HIV/AIDS, military integration, and same-sex marriage.

Jürgen Ruckaberle is an international student from Germany with a Staatsexamen degree from the University of Tübingen and an M.A. in History from the University of Oregon. He is currently working on a dissertation at the University of Oregon that explores the political mobilization of consumers; charting the achievements, limits, and legacies of the consumer activism in the 1960s and 1970s and shedding light on consumer activists and their response to other forms of activism in this period.

Gregory L. Schneider is Associate Professor of History at Emporia State University in Kansas. He is the author of *Cadres for Conservatism: Young Americans for Freedom and the Rise of the Contemporary Right* (1999) and editor of *Conservatism in America Since 1930: A Reader* (2003) and *Equality, Decadence and Modernity: The Collected Essays of Stephen J. Tonsor* (2005).

Heather Ann Thompson is Associate Professor of African American Studies and History at Temple University. Her first book, *Whose Detroit? Politics, Labor, and Race in a Modern American City* (2001), explored the social and political activism that played out in the streets and workplaces of the Motor City during the tumultuous 1960s and 1970s. Currently she is completing a history of the Attica prison uprising of 1971 and its legacy for Pantheon books.

William L. Van Deburg is Evjue-Bascom Professor of Afro-American Studies at the University of Wisconsin-Madison. His publications on Black Power era cultural history include *New Day in Babylon* (1992), *Black Camelot* (1997), and *Hoodlums* (2004), as well as two collections of documents, *Modern Black Nationalism* (1997) and *African-American Nationalism* (2005).

Carmen Teresa Whalen is Professor of History and Chair of the Latina/o Studies Program at Williams College. She is the author of *From Puerto Rico to Philadelphia: Puerto Rican Workers and Postwar Economies* and of *El Viaje: Puerto Ricans of Philadelphia*, a photographic history. Concerned with Puerto Rican communities throughout the United States, she is also co-editor and contributor to *The Puerto Rican Diaspora: Historical Perspectives*. Her current research explores Puerto Rican women, the International Ladies' Garment Workers' Union, and New York City's garment industry.

Lawrence S. Wittner is Professor of History at the State University of New York/Albany, has written or edited 10 books and authored over a hundred articles, mostly on peace and foreign policy issues. They include the award-winning scholarly trilogy, *The Struggle Against the Bomb—One World or None*, 1993, *Resisting the Bomb*, 1997, and *Toward Nuclear Abolition*, 2003—and *Peace Action: Past, Present, and Future* (2007).